SAH
CITY GUIDE
BUS

BUILDINGS OF

Savannah

Bonaventure Cemetery (17.1).

BUILDINGS OF Savannah

ROBIN B. WILLIAMS

with David Gobel, Patrick Haughey, Daves Rossell, and Karl Schuler

UNIVERSITY OF VIRGINIA PRESS

Charlottesville | London

University of Virginia Press

Printed in the United States of America on acid-free paper

First published 2016

9 8 7 6 5 4 3 2

Library of Congress Cataloging-in-Publication Data
is available from the Library of Congress

The Society of Architectural Historians gratefully acknowledges the support of the following, whose generosity helped bring *Buildings of Savannah* to publication:

Founders' Fund of the Buildings of the United States
National Park Service, Heritage Documentation Programs, HABS/HAER/HALS Division
National Endowment for the Humanities, an independent federal agency
National Endowment for the Arts, Art Works
Richard C. Kessler
Charles C. Taylor and Samir Nikocevic
Vantosh Realty, LLC
Poverty Row Entertainment
Morrison and Fenella Heckscher in memory of Dolf and Bev Placzek
Georgia Humanities Council
Savannah College of Art and Design (SCAD)

Initial and ongoing support for the Buildings of the United States series has come from:

National Endowment for the Humanities, an independent federal agency
Graham Foundation for Advanced Studies in the Fine Arts
Pew Charitable Trusts
Ford Foundation
Samuel I. Newhouse Foundation
Samuel H. Kress Foundation
Donald I. Perry Fund
Society of Architectural Historians
Southeast Chapter, Society of Architectural Historians

Contents

How to Use This Book

This book is divided into three main sections—ten downtown tours best done on foot, four tours of the historic suburbs close to downtown that are most efficiently accessed by car, and six tours striking out across the greater Savannah area following paths radiating from downtown in different directions that are best driven. The building entries within each tour are arranged in the order they are encountered as one moves along.

The downtown tours are organized to reflect the chronological and spatial evolution of the historic city. Six of the downtown tours address the areas defined by the Savannah plan, which is divided into urban modules called "wards," each centered on a square. In addition to the original six wards, the first chapter's tours reflect the sequence of expansions of the Savannah plan, and focus on areas that flank the Savannah plan area to the north (Riverfront), west (Central of Georgia Complex), east (Beach Institute) and south (Forsyth Park and the Victorian District).

Each entry is identified by a sequential tour number and the name of the property (or by generic type if no formal name exists), with historic or alternate names in parentheses. On the next line appear the primary date(s) of construction and the name of the architect or designer (if known; if the work has undergone a subsequent, substantial addition or alteration by another architect or designer, that name appears as well), followed by the address and other location information.

Given the more than 1,500 historic buildings in downtown alone and thousands more in the surrounding areas, this book is far from comprehensive, offering instead as broad and inclusive a representative sampling of the city's architectural and urban traditions as possible. Only those buildings, structures, and landscapes extant at the time of writing are listed, but a visitor should be prepared to find that a few of the works addressed may no longer exist or may have been substantially modified. We trust that our readers will always respect the property rights and privacy of others as they view the buildings.

Foreword

The primary objective of the Buildings of the United States (BUS) series, and this inaugural City Guide, is to identify and celebrate the rich cultural, economic, and geographic diversity of the United States of America as it is reflected in the architecture of each state. The series was founded by the Society of Architectural Historians (SAH), a nonprofit organization dedicated to the study, interpretation, and preservation of the built environment throughout the world.

The BUS series will eventually comprise more than sixty volumes documenting the built environment of every state and many of their cities. The idea for such a series was in the minds of the founders of the SAH in the early 1940s, but it was not brought to fruition until Nikolaus Pevsner—the eminent British architectural historian who had conceived and carried out the Buildings of England series, published from 1951—challenged the SAH in 1976 to do for the United States what he had done for his country.

The authors of each BUS volume and city guide are trained architectural historians who are thoroughly informed in the local aspects of their subjects. Although the great national and international architects of American buildings receive proper attention, outstanding local architects, as well as the buildings of skilled but often anonymous carpenter-builders, are also brought prominently into the picture.

The BUS series and city guides, as well as this specific volume, have received generous and ongoing support from the donors listed on the copyright page, as well as the many individual members of the SAH who have made unrestricted contributions to the series.

We thank the authors, the University of Virginia Press, the SAH Board, the members of the BUS Editorial Advisory Committee listed at the back of the volume, Alison K. Hoagland, Beth Lattimore Reiter, and Aaron Rose. We are also grateful to Morrison and Fenella Heckscher, whose gift in memory of Dolf and Bev Placzek honors one of the founding editors-in-chief of the BUS series.

Karen Kingsley / Editor in Chief / Buildings of the United States

Acknowledgments

This book would not have been possible without the vision and support of the Society of Architectural Historians and the University of Virginia Press in their collaborative decision to make Savannah the inaugural volume of a new series of city guides associated with the Building of United States series. In particular, Karen Kingsley and Mark Mones have provided clear guidance and timely feedback at every stage, while welcoming the new opportunities presented by a volume focused on a single city. Likewise, the completion of the book over the past four years relied on a team effort of the five authors, divvying up research and writing responsibilities that capitalized on our collective knowledge of Savannah acquired over the past two decades through a variety of initiatives, including the Virtual Historic Savannah Project, directed by Robin Williams from 1997 to 2006, and the guide prepared for the 2007 Vernacular Architecture Forum annual meeting, *Savannah and the Lowcountry: A Guidebook*, edited by Daves Rossell and Marisa Gomez. Our efforts in turn were greatly aided by the contributions of many SCAD students, principally from the Architectural History department, as research assistants or through dedicated class assignments. We're grateful for the help we received from Kacie Alaga, Jessica Archer, Ian Braithwaite, Elizabeth Clappin, Tatum Clinton-Selin, Lindsay Cross, Jennifer Cutrona, Michela Davola, Christen DeNicholas, Stephanie Heher, Kimberly Herman, Penny Clarke Johnson, Olivier Maene, Lauren McCardle, Erin McMahon, Milagros Mujica, Meghan Nagle, Emily Polgardi, Pratik Satani, Glen Umberger, and Katherine Williams.

Creating the most current and comprehensive guide to the city's built environment benefited tremendously from the contributions of information, insight, and perspective of many individuals in Savannah and beyond. A special thanks goes to archivist Luciana Spracher, along with Virginia Blake and Lisa Cisco, who helped unlock the treasures within the City of Savannah's Research Library and Municipal Archives; to Ellen Harris at the Metropolitan Planning Commission and her intern Ellie Isaacs, who provided extensive information about buildings throughout the county and their various changes through time; and the excellent staffs at the Georgia Historical Society and the Kaye Kole Genealogy and Local History Room at the Bull Street Library. Other members of the city's heritage community generously shared their knowledge, including Donna Adamson, Gillian M. Brown, Farris Cadle, Daniel Carey, Robert Ciucevich, Jamie Credle, Dr. Stan Deaton, Stewart Dohrman, Barbara Fertig, Hugh Golson, Vaughnette Goode-Walker, Becki Harkness, Dr. Christopher Hendricks, Karen Jenkins, Patricia Jenkins, Tom Kohler, Sherryl Lang, Connie Pinkerton, Beth Reiter, Deborah Rouse, Tania Sammons, Lynette Stoudt, and Charles E. Varner. Valuable information also came from colleagues beyond Savannah: the late Cullen Chambers at the Tybee Island Historical Society; Gretchen Brock, Steven Moffson, and Lynn Speno at the Georgia State Historic Preservation Office; Willie Graham, Jeffrey Klee, and Carl Lounsbury at the Colonial Williamsburg Foundation; Bailey Ball at the National Building Museum; Dennis De Witt at the Metropolitan Waterworks Museum in Boston; and Professor Richard Longstreth at George Washington University. The editorial insight of Kimberly Morrill and Gregory Williams was greatly appreciated.

A diverse range of professionals within the planning and building trades in Savannah also generously shared their knowledge, including architects Gerry Cowart, John Deering, Jerry Lominack, Forrest Lott, Eric Meyerhoff, Pat Shay, Daniel Snyder, Christian Sottile, and Rick Wissmach; preservation contractors David Bloomquist, Omar El-Khalidi, Mark Fitzpatrick, Meagan Hodge, and Ramsey Khalidi; preservationists Rebecca Fenwick and David Kelley; developer Michael Brown; Robert Hedengren and Mia Phan at SCAD's Design Group; Housing Authority of Savannah Executive Director Earline Davis; and Gordon Denney, Director of the City of Savannah's Park and Tree Department.

The images that grace the pages of this volume involved contributions of many sorts. New photographs were taken mainly by Daves Rossell and Robin Williams, with additional images by Patrick Haughey. Permission to shoot images on private property was kindly granted by the Barrow family at Wormsloe and by Bret Bell. John and Virginia Duncan, Jerry Lominack, and Tanya Bailey all generously lent historic images from their personal collections, while Jeffrey Klee and Christian Sottile shared more recent photographs. Other historic images could not have been secured without the assistance of David Anderson, Luciana Spracher, Lynette Stoudt, and Allen Tuten.

In addition to the organizations and individuals noted in the list of funders on page iv, we gratefully acknowledge the contributions made by Seacrest Partners, Sottile and Sottile, AIA Savannah, the Historic Savannah Foundation, the Savannah Victorian Society, the Southeast Chapter of the Society of Architectural Historians, Cowart Group Architects, Dawson Architects, Lominack Kolman Smith Architects, and The Grey Restaurant LLC, and by Nonnie Balcer and Gavin Macrae-Gibson, Richard Beattie and Ted Gale, Deborah and Roy Williams, Hugh S. Golson, and an anonymous donor.

BUILDINGS OF

Savannah

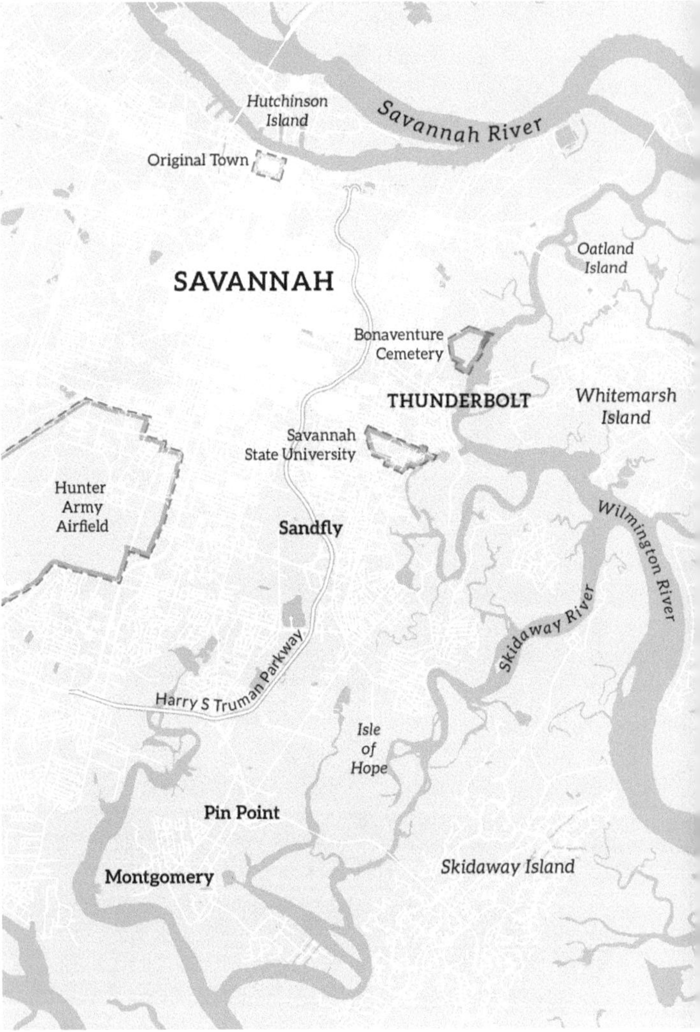
Hutchinson Island
Savannah River
Original Town
Oatland Island
SAVANNAH
Bonaventure Cemetery
THUNDERBOLT
Whitemarsh Island
Savannah State University
Hunter Army Airfield
Wilmington River
Sandfly
Skidaway River
Harry S Truman Parkway
Isle of Hope
Pin Point
Montgomery
Skidaway Island

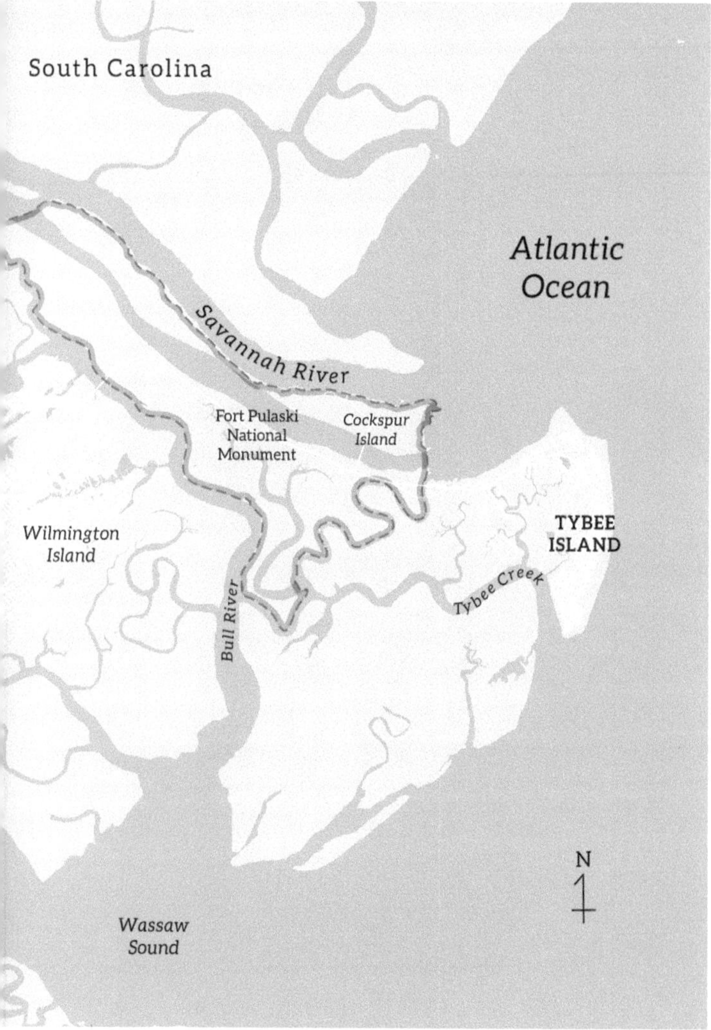
South Carolina
Atlantic Ocean
Savannah River
Fort Pulaski National Monument
Cockspur Island
TYBEE ISLAND
Wilmington Island
Bull River
Tybee Creek
Wassaw Sound
N

Introduction

Few cities in America enjoy so distinctive an urban identity as Savannah, with its squares and broad streets, its trees and bordering marshes, and its remarkable state of preservation. Yet it is also a place marked by paradox. Founded in 1733 as an agrarian colony of equals, the city prospered greatly from industry, trade, and slavery. Its urban plan attracts worldwide attention, yet few of its buildings are famous or appear in histories of American architecture. Historically a relatively small city (with a population in 2015 of about 150,000), Savannah has nonetheless played a significant role on the national stage in terms of the religious, military, agricultural, transportation, and industrial history of the country. Most recently the city has served as a model of urban design for both American and foreign planners. This volume attempts to paint a more comprehensive picture of Savannah's urban, architectural, and landscape history than previous studies have done, for to understand Savannah, one must look at its built environment holistically.

Ideals and Realities in Savannah's Urban Planning History

Before the site for the city had even been chosen, Savannah and the Georgia colony for which it would initially serve as capital already possessed a remarkable social significance. The Trustees for the Establishment of the Colony of Georgia in America was formed around 1730 by a London-based group of philanthropists who sought to create a charitable colony in the New World. James Oglethorpe, a British parliamentarian with a military background, was one of the leaders of this group. Combining Christian charity and Enlightenment idealism, its members sought a solution to the appalling abuses in debtor prisons and the religious persecution of Protestants by Catholics in continental Europe. The Georgia Trustees envisioned a place of equality, where charity settlers would receive fifty acres (forty-five acres of farm land, a garden lot near the town, and a 60 × 90–foot town lot). Non-charity settlers were invited to pay their own way and could acquire plantations of up to five hundred acres. Certain prohibitions reflected the founders' idealism

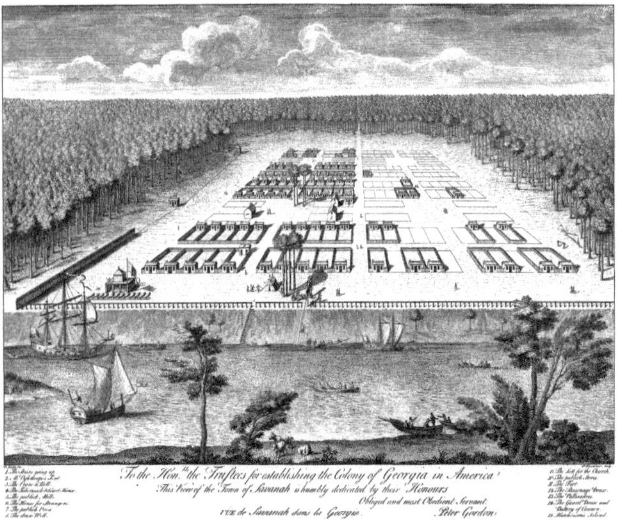

Peter Gordon's view of Savannah (1734).

and prejudices—no slavery; no rum, brandies, or strong liquors; no lawyers; and no Catholics. The colony, named in honor of George II, also offered strategic military benefits as a buffer protecting the prosperous Carolina colonies from the Spanish in Florida. The Trustees received their royal charter to establish the colony in July 1732.

Upon his arrival in February 1733, Oglethorpe selected a site on the Savannah River, seventeen miles from the coast and atop a bluff forty feet above the surrounding lowcountry marshes, a location that had important consequences for the town's long-term success as a port. At first, the river, one of the longest navigable waterways on the Eastern Seaboard, provided access deep into the state. More recently Savannah's westernmost position on the coast has led to its becoming the nation's fourth-busiest container port, despite being the world's shallowest deepwater harbor. As the city grew, the surrounding landscape of marshes and tidal waterways constrained movement and expansion, with more affluent communities and subsequently the airports built on the highest ground. Initially, some peripheral settlements were accessible only by boat. As railways and

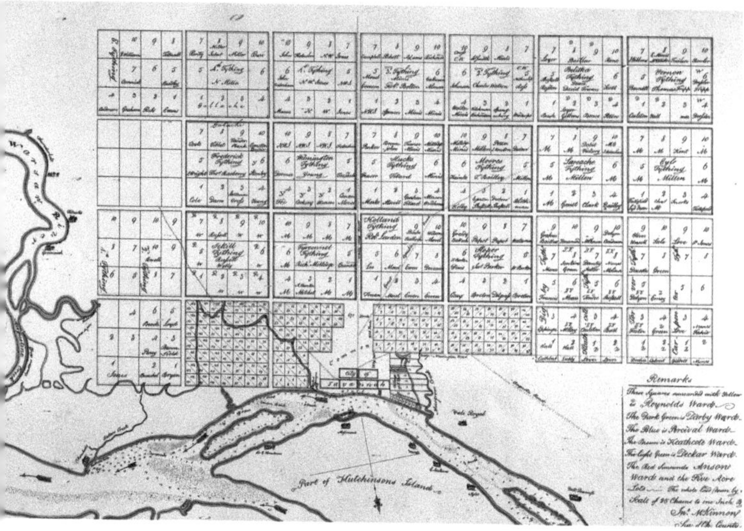

Thomas McCall's plan of Savannah (1798), redrawn by John McKinnon, showing Oglethorpe's regional plan of farm lots, garden lots (smaller grid), commons, and town.

roads were established, a radial configuration developed, and even today some communities can be reached by only one or two roadways. The arrangement of the chapters in this volume reflects the constraints imposed by the lowcountry geography.

When he established Savannah in 1733, Oglethorpe aimed to create a physical map for the Trustees' egalitarian vision. He laid out a regional plan, known as the "Oglethorpe plan" (described in detail by Thomas Wilson in his eponymic book), with the town surrounded on east, west, and south sides by common land and on the north by the Savannah River. Beyond the Common to the east and south lay a zone of five-acre triangular garden lots (with land to the west reserved for the local Yamacraw Indians, led by Tomochichi, a strategic supporter of the nascent colony) and beyond these, extending several miles into the broader landscape, was a grid of forty-five-acre farm lots. Beyond the farm lots tracts of undeveloped land divided into one-mile squares yielded a regional plan of about sixty square miles. That larger grid informed the location of the major streets as suburbs developed in the nineteenth and twentieth centuries. Both in the "historic district" and beyond, the Trustees' plan

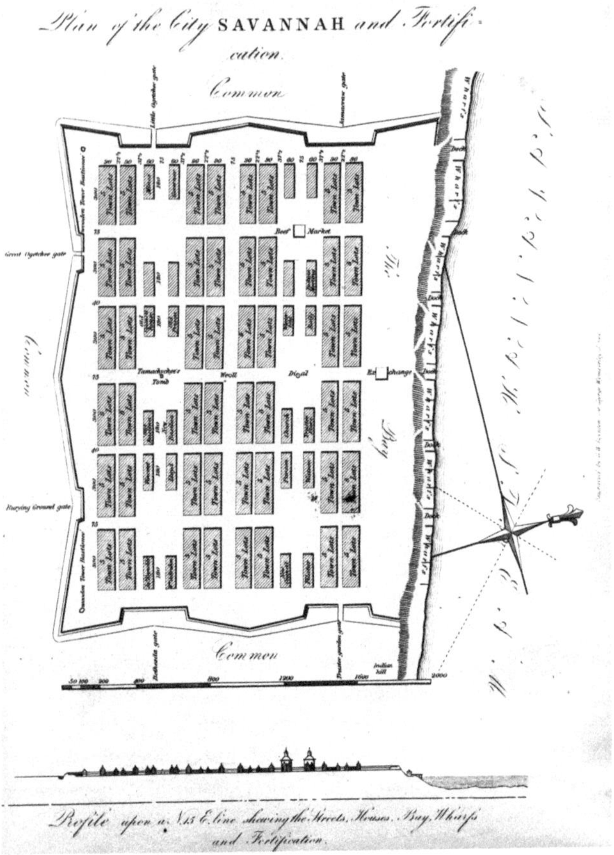

William Gerard De Brahm's map of Savannah (1757), from his History of the Province of Georgia: With Maps of Original Surveys *(1849).*

structured and informed urbanism and architecture in Savannah and the region in a fashion unique to American urban history.

Many historians have speculated about the sources of Savannah's urban plan, suggesting ancient and Renaissance architectural treatises, a seventeenth-century representation of Beijing, the grid plan of Turin, Masonic interpretations of biblical cities, sixteenth- through early-eighteenth-century military architecture treatises, and the residential developments centered on squares in London in the seventeenth and early eighteenth centuries. No evidence has been found that points to any specific source, but it is hard to imagine the Trustees were not influenced by the residential squares of London's fashionable West End. Indeed, one of the original squares in Savannah was named after St. James Square, which was home to at least two of the Trustees. Likewise, the colony's strategic role and Oglethorpe's own training make military precedents a likely inspiration.

The "Savannah plan," as we shall call the urban plan to distinguish it from the regional Oglethorpe plan, was laid out using a neighborhood unit, or ward, as its module. The module was repeated to form a six-ward town (four wards laid out in 1733 and two more a year later), arranged in two rows of three. Each ward has a square at its center, flanked to the east and west by "Trust lots" reserved for public buildings and allocated as needed by the Trustees, and along the north and south sides of the square stretching across the width of the ward are pairs of "tything" blocks, each comprising ten town lots arranged in two rows of five divided by a service lane. The urban use of the word "tything" is peculiar to Savannah (at least in the United States), deriving from an Old English term for a group of ten householders. Two networks of streets divide the various blocks: a primary set of broad civic streets intersecting on axis with and flanking each square, as well as wide streets running east–west between the wards; and a set of narrower secondary utilitarian or service streets running north– south between each ward and the lanes dividing the tything blocks. These features of the Savannah plan influenced the development of distinctive local housing forms—the elevated townhouse with its signature raised stoop, its rear carriage house fronting the lane, and the trust lot mansion.

This seemingly rigid set of parts actually proved to be remarkably flexible. The first act of preservation in the city's long historic embrace of that concept was the city council proposal of 1790 to retain Oglethorpe's planning module as the basis for the town's first expansion approved and implemented a year later, but adapted (by reducing the new wards' east–west dimensions) to fit the available land in the Common. Citizens, visitors, and civic officials alike had recognized early on the unique merits of the Savannah plan and replicated it for six expansions, yielding a total of twenty-four wards by the 1850s. This combination of piecemeal growth which nonetheless conformed to the original planned vision is unique in the history of the country's cities and contrasts with the normal scenario where a grand plan is laid out (as in Philadelphia in 1682) and gradually filled in without adherence to the original precepts. Besides adjusting the dimensions and proportions of the wards and the squares within them, planners added a new feature to Savannah's downtown plan—the broad avenue with a generous green median (akin to a linear square)—that would be replicated elsewhere in the city. The most enduring part of the plan was its most humble aspect—lanes (never called alleys here), which continued to serve as the necessary utilitarian corridors in all urban developments in the city until the 1940s.

Despite this fidelity to the original plan, the growth of

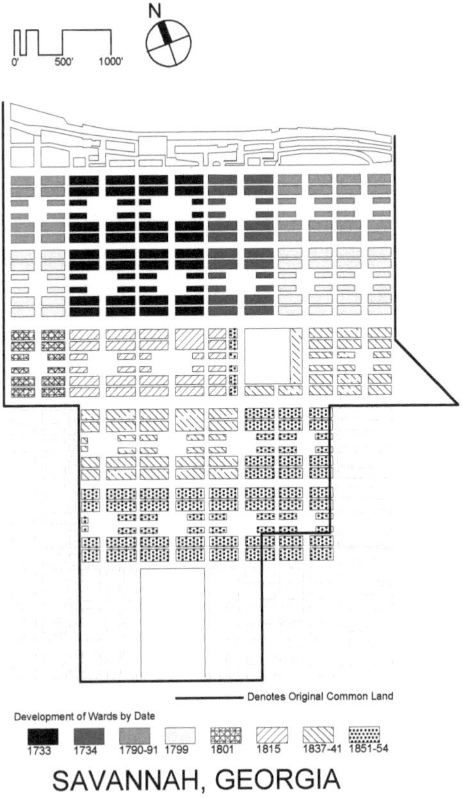

Diagram showing the evolution of the Savannah plan from 1733 to 1854.

Savannah was nonetheless challenged throughout its existence by disease, fires, and hurricanes (though the last proved less a problem than in some other Southern cities). Yellow fever epidemics afflicted the city's residents on four occasions—in 1804, 1820, 1854, and 1876. The city experienced seven major fires, one each in 1796, in 1820 (when almost half the city was destroyed), in 1865, in 1876, and in 1883, and two in 1889. An 1804 hurricane laid waste to all of the warehouses below the bluff, while the strongest hurricane to hit Savannah, in 1893, devastated the city's trees. Such disasters prompted the city to change its building codes, improve its sanitation services, and plant its present canopy of resilient live oaks.

Savannah's Defining Urban and Architectural Characteristics

A spirit of commemoration permeates the city, particularly in the downtown area. Beyond the conventional use of street names to honor people, institutions, and values, the Savannah plan included wards and squares (and in the first four wards even tythings) whose names offered additional commemorative opportunities. As early as 1739, monuments became a defining feature within the squares along Bull Street, in Forsyth Park, and on the waterfront, with the erection of a large fieldstone pyramid over the tomb (**2.31**) of Yamacraw Indian chief Tomochichi in the center of Percival (now Wright) Square—possibly the first public monument in America. Curiously there is no pattern to the naming of wards and squares: some honor the same subject while others offer three commemorations in one space, such as the Greene Monument (**2.2**) in Johnson Square (**2.1**) in Derby Ward.

Green space has been an essential part of Savannah's urban identity since its founding. The Trustees' plan was fundamentally, if not radically, agrarian and anti-urban. The population of Savannah would have been limited to 240 families (perhaps 1,200 persons), surrounded by commons, gardens, and farms, as well as the experimental Trustees' Garden. But even inside the town, the squares were conceived as both utilitarian spaces to quarter soldiers and livestock in the event of a siege and as places of public recreation open to all. Upon the city's incorporation in 1789, the municipal government passed ordinances, beginning in 1793, to promote and regulate the planting of trees as ornaments as well as for their ecological benefits on each side of the city's streets and in the squares, at a time when other cities sought to banish them as fire hazards. By 1796, the City passed an ordinance protecting trees, which in 1810 were placed under the special protection of the city council. The city's twenty-four squares, its waterfront Strand, its tree-lined boulevards of South Broad Street (now Oglethorpe Avenue) and Liberty Street, as well as the establishment of Forsyth Park (**10.1**) as one of the earliest municipal parks in the nation, inspired people in the nineteenth century to call Savannah "Forest City." As traveler Charles Mackay commented in his *Life and Liberty in America: or, Sketches of a Tour in the United States and Canada, in 1857–8* (New York, 1859), "Of all the cities in America, none impresses itself more vividly upon the imagination and the memory than this little green bowery city of the South." The city's commitment to green space provided an ideal setting for pioneering landscape architect John Nolen of Cambridge, Massachusetts, to undertake one of his first professional commissions, designing Daffin Park (**14.8**) in 1907.

With Georgia established as a strategic buffer between South Carolina and Spanish Florida, the colony's founding by Oglethorpe instilled a military consciousness into the city's DNA. Its ability to withstand a siege was aptly demonstrated in October 1779, when a French and American attack, in one of the bloodiest battles of the American Revolution, failed to dislodge the British who controlled the town. Along the Savannah River a series of forts chronicles the history of American fortifications from the mid-eighteenth to the early twentieth century in a more concentrated area than any other place in the nation. At the end of his devastating March to the Sea across Georgia in 1864, General William Tecumseh Sherman spared the city and offered it as a Christmas gift to President Lincoln. Monuments to military figures and organizations are prevalent throughout Savannah, and militia companies and their armories defined the social order of the city, including those of the Chatham Artillery, one of the oldest military organizations in the United States and in whose headquarters the U.S. Eighth Air Force was born.

Georgia was founded with no dominant faith; its charter allowed the free exercise of religion (except Catholicism at first), welcoming some of the earliest congregations in America persecuted for their beliefs in their native lands. Guided by the powerful evangelical idealism of some of the Trustees, Christian charity repeatedly shaped Savannah's development. The colony witnessed the founding of America's first Sunday school and an orphanage for boys south of the city called Bethesda, among the country's oldest charitable organizations. The 1804 establishment of a seaman's hospital, one of the oldest hospitals in the country and first in Georgia, led to the creation of the Savannah Poor House and Hospital (see **10.19**) in 1808. Its building from 1818 still stands; its alteration in 1877 accommodated what may have been the first "Nightingale wards" in the country. Chartered in 1832, the Georgia Infirmary (**12.6**), the oldest known black hospital founded by whites in the United States, included the nation's first nursing school for African American students, operating from 1904 to 1937. A strong tradition of female philanthropy was led by Mary Telfair, who bequeathed her wealth in 1883 to create the Telfair Academy of Arts and Sciences (**2.38**), the first public art museum in the South, and the Telfair Hospital for Females (**10.16**) a year later, the first of its kind in Georgia. Such actions inspired another wealthy Savannah woman, Juliette Gordon Low, to establish the Girl Scouts of the United States of America (see **2.25**) in Savannah in 1912.

Although Savannah was founded as the center of an intended agrarian colony, industry and trade early on defined the city's growth. Slavery and the invention of the cotton gin by Eli Whitney at nearby Mulberry Grove Plantation revolutionized agriculture in the South, fueling the city's prosperity and transforming its built environment, as well as facilitating the globalization of the textile industry. Hermitage Plantation (c. 1820, Henry McAlpin; demolished 1930s) just west of Savannah became the city's first true industrial complex, using slave labor and early railroad technology to mass produce "Savannah Grey" bricks. In fact, slave and free black craftsmen contributed much to the city's construction. Savannah played an important role in trade between mercantilist empires, shipping a succession of export products: rice and indigo in the eighteenth century, followed by the dominance of cotton in the nineteenth (when Savannah's exchange regulated its price for a time), and shifting around 1900 as the city became the world's leading exporter of naval stores (wood-based products for ships). In the 1930s, Savannah native and leading American chemist Charles Herty discovered that fast-growing Southern pine could be used to make pulp for fine quality paper as well as cardboard and coarse

View of African American workers in sewer line trench (c. 1870).

paper products. This dramatically reshaped the southern landscape to produce sufficient trees for a vast Southern pine and paper industry and prompted the Pennsylvania-based Union Bag and Paper Company in the 1930s to erect one of the world's largest pulp and paper mills in Savannah. A major employer that helped the city through the Great Depression, the mill and the water pollution it produced prompted Ralph Nader's critical 1971 assessment *The Water Lords*. That mill, now controlled by International Paper, which has considerably improved its pollution controls, continues to be a major presence within Savannah's rapidly expanding port complex. During World War II, the city was a manufacturing center for Liberty ships. Today, Savannah is home to a number of leading global manufacturers drawn to one of the world's fastest growing ports.

Progress, Preservation, and Beyond

Savannah has witnessed generations of its citizens welcoming new ideas and technologies. The wealth generated by the invention of the cotton gin facilitated early markers of progress. In 1816, shipping merchant Richard Richardson gave the young British architect William Jay his first American commission, now the Owens-Thomas House (**2.19**), into which Jay incorporated advanced British plumbing technology and structural cast iron, both among the earliest American use of these elements. The Savannah shipping firm of Scarbrough and Isaacs commissioned the SS *Savannah* (see **5.6**), which in 1819 was the first steamship to cross the Atlantic Ocean. Savannah businessmen embraced nascent railroad technology with gusto, establishing the Central of Georgia Railroad in 1833 and completing its first line to Macon by 1843. By the 1850s the company's complex (**7.1**)—still standing on the western edge of downtown—was an innovative combination of corporate and design operations, passenger and freight depots, and repair facilities all set on one large site (now its own National Historic Landmark district). Savannah also embraced other emerging technologies—horse-drawn streetcars in 1869, asphalt paving in 1881, electricity in 1882, skyscraper construction in 1895, and powered flight in 1911. The city's enthusiasm for "autoing" saw it host the nation's first stock car and American Grand Prix races in 1908, establishing what came to be called the Great Savannah Races, and spawning the development of automobile suburbs Ardsley Park (**14.1**) and Chatham Crescent (**14.2**) in 1910.

Efforts to preserve the city's character date back to the 1790s, when the first expansion of the colonial city replicated the original ward module devised by Oglethorpe, establishing a pattern repeated by subsequent generations of civic officials. General Sherman's decision to occupy but not destroy Savannah in December 1864 stands as a significant moment of preservation in its history (and contrasts the devastation the war brought to nearby Atlanta, Charleston, and Columbia, South Carolina). Stewardship of the city's history was dramatically enhanced by the founding of the Georgia Historical Society in 1839, nurturing generations of historians and amateur architectural historians to document the city's heritage. Among the most active was Thomas Gamble, who moved to Savannah in 1888 and became a newspaper reporter, eventually holding various positions in city government before serving several terms as mayor, beginning in 1933. In 1921, he mobilized the city's first preservation group, the Society for the Preservation of Parks, in an effort to stop U.S. 17 from cutting through the squares on Montgomery Street. That proposal prompted an ongoing battle until the automobilists prevailed in 1935, the same year the short-lived Savannah Commission for the Preservation of Landmarks was established. During the 1930s, Works Progress Administration (WPA) programs in the city focused on various projects that further documented the past and the present, including the Historic American Buildings Survey and a Cadastral Survey (preserved at the Chatham County Superior Court Records Room) which documented every property in the city and laid the groundwork for the efforts of building preservationists after World War II.

During the 1950s through the 1970s, American cities grew at an unprecedented rate, with suburbs sprawling across the countryside and historic downtowns replaced by large-scale buildings and parking lots, all in the name of progress. Savannahians shared in the heady enthusiasm for modernization, extending the city's boundaries far to the south. Unlike most other cities, however, here the interstate highway system played little role in this growth. In downtown, meanwhile, the demolition of architectural landmarks—the Wetter House in 1950, the City Market building in 1954, Union Station in 1963, the Hotel Desoto in 1966, and the block of warehouses beside City Hall in 1969—stirred the forces of civic pride. Established in 1955, the Historic Savannah Foundation (HSF), under the leadership of Leopold Adler II, successfully saved hundreds of buildings, mostly houses, using an innovative "revolving fund" to purchase threatened properties and then sell them to buyers committed to their preservation, a strategy that would become a national

Historic photograph (1906) of Union Station (demolished 1963).

ABOVE *Historic postcard (c. 1890) of the City Market (1872; demolished 1954).* BELOW *Historic photograph (c. 1910) of Hotel Desoto (1890; demolished 1966).*

model. The HSF continues to advocate for the protection of the city's heritage. Private preservationists, notably Jim Williams and Mills B. Lane Jr., saved numerous houses during the 1970s, a tradition carried on by Lane's son, Mills B. Lane IV, who used his philanthropic Beehive Foundation to support numerous restoration and urban renewal projects. Meanwhile, Walter Hartridge Jr., president of the Georgia Historical Society from 1952 to 1961, rescued and preserved records documenting the city's heritage.

Most unusual within the broader panorama of the historic preservation movement nationwide was the establishment of the Savannah College of Art and Design (SCAD) in 1978, repurposing the old Savannah Volunteer Guards Armory (**8.10**). Since that time, the college has found new uses for more than sixty historic buildings scattered throughout the city. As of 2015, Savannah boasts one of the country's largest National Historic Landmark districts, twelve National Register districts, and three districts with design review procedures integral to the development process. As is evident in its varied buildings, landscapes, monuments, squares, and parks, Savannah remains a living city, balancing new and modern designs with the ongoing preservation and adaptive reuse of the past.

Downtown

Until the 1850s, what is now considered downtown Savannah constituted the entire city. Although the growth of suburban neighborhoods since that time has attracted most of the city's residents, the downtown area is remarkable for its continued rich and heterogeneous character, retaining residential enclaves, a healthy variety and distribution of commercial enterprises, more than twenty houses of worship spread evenly across the district representing at least nine distinct faiths, and numerous public buildings serving as the civic focus for the southeast Georgia region. During the 1960s and 1970s, as residents, businesses, and a few congregations followed the national pattern of moving to the suburbs, parts of downtown were abandoned and numerous buildings were lost to demolition (sometimes for their cherished Savannah Grey bricks). Throughout the postwar years, however, public and private investment in downtown—sometimes as heavy-handed urban renewal, more often as sensitive historic preservation—sustained its continued survival, allowing it to avoid the fate of other cities and towns whose downtowns all but died. Despite the influx of millions of tourists annually and the proliferation of museums, downtown Savannah retains the vibrancy of a living community.

The organization of this guidebook follows the chronological growth of Savannah from the city's founding in 1733 through the successive expansions of the Savannah plan between 1791 and 1855, along with the development of the flanking areas of the Beach Institute on the east and the Central of Georgia Railroad complex to the west. Although all parts of Savannah comprise wards, nowhere is this concept more significant than in downtown, where they are direct expressions of James Oglethorpe's visionary plan. The tours in this and the two subsequent chapters highlight a representative variety of buildings, monuments, structures, and landscapes.

Savannah Riverfront

Savannah's historic riverfront straddles a forty-foot bluff creating a unique ensemble of buildings, cobbled ramps, stone retaining walls, terraced lanes, and more than forty iron and

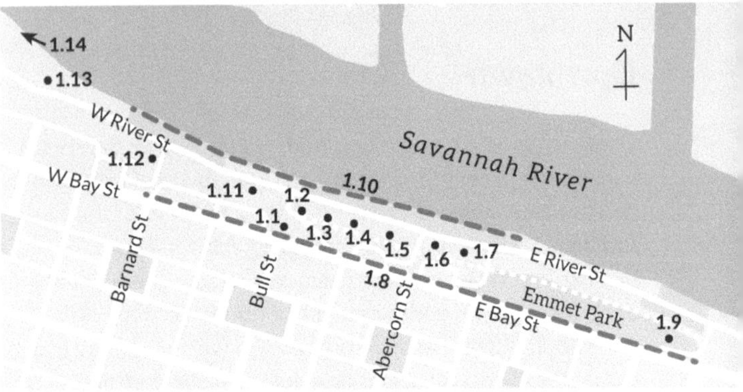

wooden bridges. The row of historic warehouses, stretching for almost a mile, constitutes one of the best-preserved nineteenth-century waterfronts in the country, interrupted for only one block by the modernist Savannah Hyatt Regency Hotel (**1.11**). Development began below the bluff, with warehouses appearing by 1744 and the first wharf in 1759. The first warehouse to rise above the top of the bluff, Commerce Row, was built in 1789. An 1804 hurricane destroyed nearly all of the warehouses, leading to a city ordinance that banned the use of exterior wood construction for these structures and resulted in a majority using stone or brick for walls, with wooden mill construction for interior supports and floors. Most of the extant warehouses were erected in the prosperous 1850s.

In contrast to the orthogonal nature of the Savannah plan, the wharf lots developed in an arc paralleling the river. River Street was created in 1834 and preserves the city's longest stretch of granite "Belgian blocks," a common pavement by the late 1800s, so named because originally they were quarried in the Low Countries and squared to fit between the ribs of sailing ships as ballast. The south side of the warehouses became known as Factors' Walk, denoting the cotton planters' agents (or factors), whose offices occupied the upper floors of the warehouses. With one formal facade looking south to the city (but with subterranean lanes for the passage of cotton wagons) and a towering work facade facing north toward the Savannah River, no spot better depicts the diverse business duties of the port. During the second half of the nineteenth century, warehouse construction extended along the river beyond the edges of downtown.

The retaining walls and ramps of Savannah's waterfront are a vivid reflection of the relative imbalance in the city's trade. Departing ships carried the lowcountry's abundant rice, cotton, or naval stores, but they arrived comparatively empty, save for ballast stones. The earliest reference to a stone retaining wall north of Bay Street dates to 1820, but the majority of the random ashlar walls appear to have been constructed between 1854 and 1858 by Michael Cash, an Irish contractor and masterful stonemason. During the Civil War, however, they were partially dismantled by the occupying Union forces and deposited in the river to make it impassable to Confederate ships. As documented by various stone plaques embedded in the walls, they were reconstructed by Cash in 1866. The many cast- and wrought-iron bridges linking the upper stories of the warehouses to the top of the bluff, mostly dating from the late 1800s, exhibit varied structural methods, including bow-string, box, and arched trusses.

1.1 City Hall

1904–1905, Hyman W. Witcover. Bay St. at Bull St.

In 1904, the city council made the controversial decision to demolish the venerable City Exchange (1799–1801, Adrien Boucher), whose 1802 bell survives in a reconstructed belfry on Bay Street east of Drayton, to make room for the new city hall as a symbol of modern Savannah. Like its predecessor, City Hall is the linchpin that connects Savannah to its waterfront. In a city of multiple squares with numerous prominent building sites, it enjoys a singular prominence, aligning with Bull Street to the south (though slightly off axis) and directly fronting both Bay Street and the river. The building reflects the planning principles of the City Beautiful movement, and resembles the domed central Administration Building from the highly influential World's Columbian Exposition of 1893 in Chicago, employing the same Beaux-Arts features, including the clear cubic massing, deeply channeled ground floor masonry, deep entrance arches, and conspicuous statuary. The original design for the city hall called for extravagant sculptural quadrigas (chariots drawn by four horses abreast) at the corners, but these were never realized. A gift from local philanthropist Mills B. Lane IV's Beehive Founda-

tion allowed the original copper dome to be gilded in 1987, and it was regilded in 2008.

The spacious yet surprisingly compact foyer boasts an impressive three-story atrium topped by an artificially lit stained glass dome. Lining the edges of each level are prominent electric, glass globe fixtures symbolizing the modernity of this then-new source of illumination. Beyond the foyer, the stair hall wraps around another modern symbol—the elevator, which originally had an open-cage front (still visible on the sides and rear) allowing a view of its dynamic movement. The council chamber fills the western portion of the second floor and is peculiar in its elongated rectangular proportions. A semicircular railing divides the council area from the surrounding public space. The desks originally paralleled the rail facing the centrally placed mayor, but were moved to face the public when Savannah switched its civic governance to a council–city manager system in 1954.

1.2 Thomas Gamble Building (Kelly's Block)

1876–1877, W. G. Butler, engineer. 2–10 E. Bay St.

The only warehouse on Savannah's waterfront to rise three stories above Bay Street, this building is also the most elaborately decorated, with cast-iron shopfronts, window hood molds, bracketed cornice, and corner quoining. Kelly's Block was commissioned by New York businessman Eugene Kelly to replace the near-identical warehouse he erected in 1869–1870, which was designed by Muller and Bruyn and destroyed in a fire in 1876, but omits the original curving mansard roof. Acquired in 1945 by the City as an annex for City Hall and promptly renamed after Thomas Gamble, mayor of Savannah from 1933–1937 and 1939–1945, the building contains municipal offices and a public library branch in these upper stories. Two of the longest metal bridges among the many in this area connect the building to the top of the bluff and provide a view of the starkly utilitarian stories below. Facing the Gamble Building on the south side of the ramp are four one-story Embankment Stores (1840–1842), rectangular brick enclosures with segmental barrel vaults and round-arched entrances. Possibly the first masonry stabilization of the bluff face, they were designed by Charles B. Cluskey as storage chambers for cotton awaiting shipment. He had a twenty-year lease for their use, but sold it after only one year. Recent archaeological excavations have disproved claims that the sites housed slaves.

1.3 John Stoddard's Upper Range Warehouses

1858–1859, John S. Norris; 1876–1877 partial reconstruction, C. S. Gay, contractor. 12–42 E. Bay St.

This dramatic row of warehouses, erected for local industrialist and plantation owner John Stoddard, breaks up its long mass with arched end wings and a central gabled section. The rhythmic pattern of round arches and simple brick cornice are reminiscent of Rundbogenstil. A plaque on the north elevation stating "John D. Mongin's Wharf, 1824" (evidently from an earlier building) honors Stoddard's wife's grandfather, who erected earlier warehouses on this site. The row sustained fire damage in 1876. Inside the Vic's on the River restaurant at 26 E. Bay is a wall mural depicting a map of Sherman's March to the Sea, drawn by Union soldiers billeted in the building and uncovered in 1901.

1.4 Solomon's Masonic Lodge No. One (Savannah Cotton Exchange)

1886–1887, William G. Preston; 1975 alterations, Thomas E. Stanley and Associates. 100 E. Bay St.

The Savannah Cotton Exchange was established in 1872 by a group of local cotton financiers, and in 1886 they received

permission from the City to erect a building over the Drayton Street ramp on the condition the ramp remain passable. Its location at the head of Drayton Street closes a rare long vista in Savannah. A competition awarded the commission to Boston architect Preston, who went on to create several of Savannah's most iconic buildings. His Queen Anne design is characterized by its stout classical proportions, bold reddish color brick and terra-cotta details, a steep triangular gable, and a copper-clad ventilator crowning the roof. Bas-relief representations of the world at the building's outer edges declare the scope of the city's cotton trade. The building's most remarkable achievement, however, is not readily apparent: it stands on cast-iron columns to allow Drayton Street to pass beneath it, making it a rare public building erected completely over a street.

The decline of the cotton trade in Georgia due to the boll weevil infestation brought an end to the building's use as a mercantile exchange in 1920 and led to its conversion to a Masonic lodge beginning in 1975, when their sign was added and the interior entrance altered. The trading hall within remains largely intact, including the impressive stained glass window featuring the word "Cotton," but with modern seating installed by the Freemasons. The terra-cotta Winged Lion Fountain (1889) in front of the building, also designed by Preston, symbolizes power and authority and may also reference the winged Lion of St. Mark, the symbol of Venice, one of history's great trading centers. The original fountain was destroyed by a car in 2008; the 2009 reproduction is a faithful copy by restoration artist Randy Nelson. The surrounding cast-iron fence is a section of railings cast by the Wood and Perot foundry in Philadelphia for the proposed state capitol building in Milledgeville, Georgia, but which was never completed once the capital was moved to Atlanta. The railings found their way to Savannah in 1857, where they adorned the magnificent Wetter House on West Broad Street (demolished 1950) until they arrived here in 1958. The medallions depict notable statesmen and literary figures.

1.5 Warehouses

1857, attributed to Sholl and Fay. 102–130 E. Bay St.

These two rows of warehouses illustrate two strategies for dressing up the commercial fronts facing the city—cast iron (102–110) and granite (112–130)—and reflect the prosperity of the late 1850s. Fronting the buildings is one of the most impressive and densely packed sets of pedestrian bridges over the terraced lanes below. The bridges spanning Abercorn Ramp at the building's east end are the longest and most dramatically sited on Savannah's waterfront. The bridge crossing from Bay Street formerly spanned Drayton ramp on the site of the Cotton Exchange.

1.6 Warehouses (Archibald Smith's Factor's Building)

1823. 202–206 E. Bay St.

Unique in its stepped end gables, this cotton warehouse showcases steeply pitched roofs that signal its early date. The row nicely illustrates a remarkable characteristic of the warehouses in this area: that all four principal stories can be accessed at grade, either directly as with the lower two stories, or via bridges. The prominent "X"s are the flanges of earthquake bolts tying the building together. The metal roof was replaced with copper in 2002.

1.7 John Stoddard's Lower Range Warehouses

1858–1859. 208–230 E. Bay St.

Complementing his Upper Range warehouses (**1.3**) upstream, Stoddard erected this lower (downstream) row. It likewise vividly reflects the dual nature of Savannah's warehouses, with the high-style facade of fine red brick and handsome arches facing the city to the south decorating the building only above the level of Bay Street, while in plain view the stories below have starkly utilitarian walls of ballast stone and rough brick. The central pedimented section is slightly recessed, disguising the subtle bend of the south elevation that responds to the curving river bank.

1.8 The Strand

1733. W. and E. Bay St. from Barnard St. to East Broad St.

This swath of green space paralleling the waterfront, called variously "The Bay" and "The Strand" especially prior to 1900, has never been built on, remarkable in a city already endowed with ample open space. The City planted two rows of chinaberry trees along the north side of Bay Street as early as 1790, placing Savannah among the first American cities to plant street trees in a formal pattern for the purposes of recreation. The small portion of the Strand between Abercorn and Lincoln streets was renamed Salzburger Park in 1996, the same year that the Salzburger Monument of Reconciliation (1994, Anton Thuswaldner, sculptor) was dedicated—a gift to the Georgia Salzburger Society from the people of Salzburg, Austria. The section from Lincoln Street east to East Broad was renamed in 1900 after Irish patriot Robert Emmet and contains numerous monuments, including the Irish Monument (1983, Milton J. Little and William Fogarty, designers; Cathal Cregg, sculptor), the Chatham Artillery Monument (1986, Milton J. Little), Georgia Hussars Memorial (1960), Dr. Noble Wimberly Jones Memorial (2004, Kevin Conlon) and the Vietnam Veterans Memorial (1991, design by Matthew Dixon; implemented by Gilpin and Bazemore, Architects and Planners).

1.9 Old Harbor Light (Beacon Rear Range Light)

1858; 2000–2001 restoration. Emmet Park near East Broad St.

Constructed in 1858 in response to growing port activity, the Beacon Range Light (later nostalgically named the Old Harbor Light) served as the rear range light aligned with a front range light on Fig Island to the east, allowing ships to navigate past the sunken wreckage of warships scuttled by the British during the American Revolution. Its ornamental character, fluted with numerous acanthus leaves—unusual for a range light, reflects the formality of the Strand as a public space, effectively analogous to the city's squares. The twenty-five-foot-tall cast-iron structure was fitted with a sixth-order catadioptric (compound lens) apparatus emitting a constant red light. Nearby is one of the best views of the Savannah River. The ornate cast-iron fence along the edge of the ramp to the south came from the Wetter House following its demolition in 1950.

1.10 John P. Rousakis Riverfront Plaza

1975–1977, Gunn and Meyerhoff. River St. between Jefferson and Price sts.

As the city's port facilities relocated farther upstream in the 1940s to service increased traffic, the historic waterfront was abandoned. Five-time Savannah mayor John Rousakis led opposition to proposals to replace warehouses with parking structures and instead used funding from the federal Urban Renewal program, the newly created Community Development Block Grant program, and the Environmental Protection Agency to transform the riverfront wharfs north of River Street into a popular destination for tourists and locals. Named in honor of the mayor, Rousakis Plaza features open stretches of red brick

Savannah's Modern Port

One of the most significant features of Savannah's built environment is its port, a vast network of international trade and commerce, intermodal transport, and regional production. By 2007 it had become the fourth largest container port in the nation (behind Long Beach, Los Angeles, and New York) and the only one in the country that exports nearly as much cargo as it imports. The port's growth has come with important consequences for the natural and built environments. The ongoing push for deeper water to accommodate larger ships prompted dredging campaigns beginning in 1873, progressively taking the river to its current forty-seven-foot depth, with an additional five feet of dredging planned to be completed in 2022 to accommodate the "post-Panamax" cargo ships (those that do not fit in the older Panama Canal). By the 1950s, the port had completely migrated beyond the original boundaries of Savannah's historic riverfront, which was largely abandoned, thereby facilitating its preservation and adaptive reuse of its warehouses since newer facilities were being built elsewhere. Port expansion upriver, however, came at a price for other significant historical sites, notably the complete destruction of the Irene Mounds, a rare coastal Georgia example of Native American mounds from the Middle and Late Mississippian periods (1100–1600 CE). Prior to this expansion, the mounds were thoroughly excavated in 1937–1940 by archeologists as part of a WPA project, the most complete excavation of a mound site in Georgia. In 1945, the Georgia General Assembly

---

paving alternating with more intimate areas defined by changes of grade, low walls for seating, and planters for trees and bushes. More than ten years in the making, the African American Monument (2002) by sculptor Dorothy Spradley to the north of City Hall was the first monument in the city's history to commemorate African Americans. The World War II Memorial (2010), by local architect Eric Meyerhoff, commemorates veterans with two hemispheres representing the two major theaters of conflict during the war (Europe and Africa; Asia and the

Aerial view of Savannah port facilities

created the Georgia Ports Authority to oversee the development of the ports at Savannah and Brunswick to promote international trade, industrial development, and agricultural and natural resources, while protecting the environment. The 1954 construction of the steel-trussed Talmadge Memorial Bridge (1.15), with its 135-foot clearance above the river, prominently symbolized the port's growing importance. In the 1980s, the rapid growth of twenty-foot equivalent unit (TEU) containers as the primary means of moving goods around the world prompted the expensive but necessary switch of Savannah's port to container shipping, which brought in ever-larger ships and necessitated the taller bridge completed in 1991.

Pacific), with the gap between providing a space for the names of Savannah's war dead.

1.11 Savannah Hyatt Regency Hotel

1979–1981, M. Garland Reynolds and Associates; atrium, Ferry-Hayes Designer. 2 W. Bay St.

Erected on the site of the only warehouses to bridge River Street, this hotel, developed by Merritt W. Dixon III, followed their precedent, but greatly increased the scale. Initially planned in 1969 to rise fifteen stories following the demolition of the warehouses, the hotel met strenuous opposition from local preservationists. A brokered compromise led to the involvement of Philadelphia city planner Edmund Bacon, who recommended lowering its height to match that of City Hall below its dome. The hotel's bland exterior belies a dramatic full-height lobby atrium with prominent glass-fronted elevators that connect this building to its famous corporate brethren in Atlanta designed by John Portman, who popularized these now-pervasive features in the world of hotel architecture. The Bohemian Hotel (2009, Design Reese Architects and Associates) to the west at 102 W. Bay Street displays considerably more urban sensitivity. Erected by hotelier Richard Kessler, the hotel features a blend of historicist and modernist design on a long-vacant site. The rooftop terrace, the first on Savannah's riverfront, has redefined how people experience the area with its panoramic views.

1.12 William Taylor Stores

c. 1817; later additions. 202–206 W. Bay St.

Among the most picturesque buildings in the city, these warehouses built for cotton merchant William Taylor are unique in Savannah in being constructed mostly with rubble masonry of ballast stones. Their steep roofs reflect the form of the city's early warehouses. The older, eastern portion of the building encroaches on the Barnard Street "Public Dock," as noted in a 1817 map at the Chatham County Land Records office (Book 2G, p. 299). The adjacent warehouses (1852–1854, Sholl and Fay) across the ramp at 112–130 W. Bay Street display fine craftsmanship and high-quality materials (cast iron and imported hard-pressed red brick) facing the city which dramatically contrast the taller utilitarian elevation facing the river. The building's adaptive reuse as the Cotton Sail Hotel (2013–2014, Dawson Architects) included a boldly modernistic rooftop addition inspired by industrial architecture and reflects the rapid influence of the Bohemian Hotel (see **1.11**). The warehouse (1910) to the west at 214 W. Bay Street was the last erected on the historic Savannah waterfront.

1.13 Savannah Power Company Riverside Station

1912, Stone and Webster Engineering Co.; 1926, 1949–1952 expansions; 2011 partial demolition. W. River St. at Montgomery St.

The Savannah Power Company brought this station online beginning in 1912 and it was fully operational by 1913, greatly expanding the power generating capacity of their earlier plant on Indian Street (now the Savannah College of Art and Design's [SCAD] Hamilton Hall), and making it Savannah's principal source of power until the mid-1950s. The large-scale arched windows and detailed brickwork reflect how people in the early twentieth century viewed this piece of municipal infrastructure as a civic landmark. Stone and Webster's distinctive triangular logo ornaments the western gable end. The River Street facility was designed in 1912 to allow for eastern additions and was expanded multiple times. Originally built to burn coal, it was converted in 1920 to oil and later to natural gas and had a capacity of one hundred megawatts. The turbine engine room features prominent iron flat-trusses spanning the interior and large skylights. The station, which closed in 2005, will be the centerpiece of a multibuilding hotel and retail complex developed by Richard Kessler.

1.14 Talmadge Memorial Bridge

1991, T. Y. Lin International/DRC Consultants. U.S. 17 spanning the Savannah River

Honoring four-time Georgia governor Eugene Talmadge, the original steel-trussed bridge of 1953–1954 was built to connect what is now U.S. 17 from Florida to South Carolina through Savannah. It had a clearance of 135 feet to allow for the growth of shipping, and was replaced when the port expanded to accommodate larger ships. The old supports are still visible on both sides of the river, concrete monuments to what was once considered a triumph of engineering and Georgia's finest bridge. Completed in 1991, the new bridge is a cable-stay concrete suspension bridge with 417-foot-tall towers (offset above the roadbed to allow the cables to pass through the tower shafts) anchoring the 1,140-foot-long span with a clearance of 185 feet above the river that allows larger container ships to reach the expanded modern Port of Georgia upriver. While the bridge is the most prominent monument on the river, its name is a subject of ongoing debate, as Talmadge was an ardent segregationist during an era of the racially divided South.

The Original Town

This area is the oldest planned part of the city. The colonial town established by James Oglethorpe comprised six virtually identical wards, with Johnson Square in Derby Ward being slightly larger than the other five squares. He laid out four wards in 1733 (Derby, Decker, Percival, and Heathcote) and the other two (Reynolds and Anson) soon after for a total of 240 town (tything) lots and 24 public building trust lots. Throughout the history of Savannah, this area has remained the heart of the city. Commercial development initially focused on Bay Street and around Ellis Square, site of the city's market since at least 1757 (as documented on the De Brahm map; see page 8), and then gradually spread to Broughton Street. Despite the formation of Savannah's first fire company in 1759, the area has

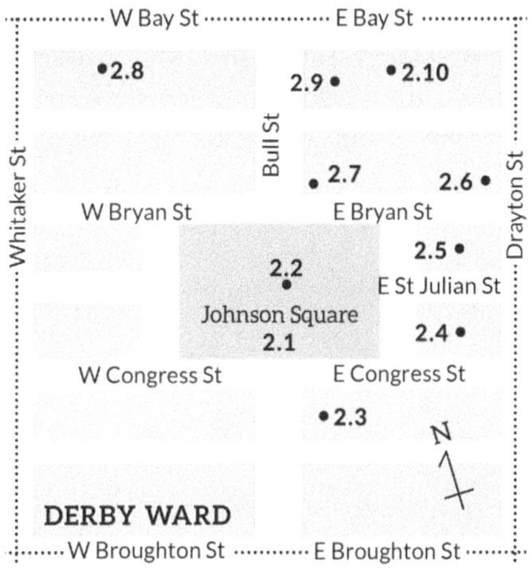

been devastated by fire five times—in 1796, 1820, 1865, 1883, and 1889 (destroying 229, 463, 100, 300, and 50 buildings, respectively)—as well as enduring a six-day bombardment from October 3–8, 1779, during the Revolutionary War.

DERBY WARD

Derby Ward honors the Right Honorable James, Tenth Earl of Derby, one of the Georgia Trustees. Here James Oglethorpe pitched his tent upon arrival in Georgia, and from here the development of Savannah began.

2.1 Johnson Square

1733; 1967 relandscaped, Sasaki, Dawson, DeMay Associates

The largest of Savannah's squares (along with Chippewa), Johnson Square has enjoyed a first-among-equals status as the focus of civic life since the town's founding. The square commemorates South Carolina governor Robert Johnson, who assisted Oglethorpe with the founding of the Georgia colony. Here Oglethorpe erected a sundial, recalled by the modern version (1932–1933, Henrik Wallin) installed by the Society of Colonial Wars in the State of Georgia. By the early twentieth century, the square was sometimes referred to as "Bank Square." It was one of seven squares to host an "engine house" for firefighting equipment (from at least 1820 until the 1850s at this location). Like other Savannah squares, Johnson Square has been relandscaped on several occasions, with different kinds of trees, enclosing fences, and varying amounts of grass and bushes. In 1967 local banker Mills B. Lane Jr. sponsored the current landscaping of the square, including a pair of paved plazas with circular pools, fountains, and underwater night illumination.

2.2 Nathanael Greene Monument (Monument to Casimir Pulaski and Nathanael Greene)

1825–1830, William Strickland; Amos Scudder, contractor; 1886 bronze plaques. Johnson Square

The highly celebrated tour of the United States by French general the Marquis de Lafayette in 1824–1825 inspired the creation of monuments throughout the country to memorialize the Revolutionary War. Savannah mayor William Daniell appointed a committee for a monument—to be paid for by a lottery—to both Pulaski and Greene, who served as generals in the Continental Army. Lafayette laid the cornerstone for this monument on March 31, 1825, which, when completed, commemorated both men until 1855, when a separate monument was inaugurated for Pulaski (**8.41**) in Monterey Square. Designed by Philadelphia architect Strickland, the fifty-foot-tall marble monument is among the earliest large-scale public memorials in the country. The bronze plaques dedicating it to Greene were added in 1886 on the centenary of his death, with Jefferson Davis participating in the ceremony. In 1902 the remains of Greene were interred below the monument, along with those of his son, George Washington Greene.

2.3 Commercial Building (Hotel Savannah)

1912, William L. Stoddart; 1919 rear addition; 1992 exterior restoration, Kolman and Smith, Architects. 32 Bull St.

Stoddart designed the two-hundred-room Hotel Savannah (later the Manger Hotel) in the Renaissance Revival style typical of urban hotels in which he specialized. The ten-story high-rise conforms to the Sullivan tripartite division of early skyscrapers with a two-story base, plain buff brick middle section, and ornate top area that is distinguished by the unusual use of colorful glazed terra-cotta. Only the rear portion of a planned one-hundred-room expansion, visible in historic postcards of the hotel, was carried out. The 1992 restoration involved stabilizing and replacing crumbling exterior elements.

2.4 Christ Church Episcopal

1838, James Hamilton Couper; 1869 portico stairs and apse modified; 1897 interior rebuilt, William G. Preston. 28 Bull St.

Christ Church Episcopal, originally Anglican, was the first church of the Georgia colony, having been assigned this site by Oglethorpe in 1734, though without a building of its own until 1750. (This first church was designed by William Stephens, perhaps with the assistance of a local builder named Joubert. Colonial records also mention a design having been prepared by Henry Flitcroft in England, but this has been lost.) Planned by plantation owner and amateur architect Couper, the current building is the fourth church on this site. Filling the entire trust lot, Christ Church follows the form of a Roman temple and as such originally had a single set of stairs rising directly from the sidewalk to the portico, altered to their present form in 1869 when an original round apse was replaced by the current square one. The interior, rebuilt after a fire in 1897 to the designs of Preston, features colossal Corinthian pilasters, galleries, and a stained glass Ascension window by Redding and Baird of Boston in the apse.

2.5 Bank of America (Citizens and Southern National Bank)

1907–1908, Mowbray and Uffinger. 22 Bull St.

The Citizens and Southern National (C&S) Bank was formed by the 1906 acquisition of Southern Bank of Georgia by its rival, the Citizens Bank of Savannah, a move spearheaded by Citizens' president Mills B. Lane Sr. The building represents the bank's grander stature and aura of stability and tradition through the use of a classical style. It forms a handsome complement to Christ Church (**2.4**), yet sits low to the ground to facilitate easy access. Luxurious character and refined details outside and in bespeak the style of its New York City architects and include colossal freestanding Ionic columns (complete with entasis) made of white Georgia marble.

2.6 Propes Hall, SCAD (Citizens Bank of Savannah)

1895, Gott ried L. Norrman. 15 Drayton St.

Savannah's first true skyscraper, this six-story building was surprisingly early in utilizing the key components of contemporary high-rises in larger American cities—internal steel frame, fireproof terra cotta walls and floors, and an elevator. It follows the conventional tripartite composition, but with an eclectic combination of a rusticated ground floor reminiscent of Richardsonian Romanesque buildings of the 1880s and baroque details of Beaux-Arts classicism above. SCAD acquired the building in 1992.

2.7 Commercial Building (Savannah Bank and Trust Company)

1911, Mowbray and Uffinger; 1973–1975 addition, Pietro Belluschi, consultant to Thomas E. Stanley and Associates. 2 E. Bryan St.

The Savannah Bank and Trust Company was established in 1869 in the wake of several post–Civil War bank failures. Its headquarters, at fifteen stories, remains Savannah's tallest downtown skyscraper, yet it occupies a single 60 × 90–foot lot. The architects dramatized the conventional tripartite composition with a three-story white marble base and an unadorned middle section and ornate top floors, both upper sections clad in glazed white terra-cotta. In 1950, the bank acquired the Citizens Bank and Trust Company, making it one of the leading financial institutions in Savannah. Prominent modernist architect Belluschi assisted with the design of the limestone addition, which reflects the sleek minimalism of the 1970s. The adjacent Federal-style house at 24–26 E. Bryan Street (1824, attributed to Amos Scudder) is the sole reminder of the residential character of this square through the mid-nineteenth century.

2.8 Moon River Brewing Company (City Hotel)

1819–1821. 21 W. Bay St.

Housing the city's first hotel, this building was constructed for Charleston native Eleazer Early, who leased the first floor for use as a restaurant, a branch of the Bank of the United States, and the city's first post office (Early served as postmaster). The simple four-story, seven-bay-wide structure stands above a full basement, which is typical of buildings on Bay Street. Its original interior (well preserved on the second floor) boasted ample circulation, large rooms, and rich decoration, making it one of the finest hostelries in the Southeast during the first half of the nineteenth century. Among its guests the hotel counted William Henry Harrison, the Marquis de Lafayette, John James Audubon, and the first three commodores of the U.S. Navy. Typical of older commercial buildings, it has seen a wide variety of subsequent uses and tenants, including lumber and coal storage, a printing company, and currently a brewery. This block contains one of the best-preserved ensembles of early-nineteenth-century buildings in downtown, with numbers 5–11 dating to c. 1820 and the sizable corner building at number 1 dating to 1819 (enlarged in 1847). The adjacent beer garden, designed by Kevin Rose at Lominack Kolman Smith Architects, was added in 2013.

2.9 United States Custom House

1848–1852, John S. Norris. 1 E. Bay St.

The custom house is one of the most significant buildings in Savannah, set on one of its most historically notable sites. Here Oglethorpe occupied a house, and at the rear of the site John Wesley, later the cofounder of Methodism, preached his first sermon in America. The grand edifice reflects the importance of Savannah's port by the mid-nineteenth century and the growing assertion of federal power. New York architect Norris gave the building an appropriately stern character in a severe Greek Revival style virtually devoid of ornament and clad the exterior with gray granite from Quincy, Massachusetts. A steep staircase

leads to the imposing and remarkable portico of six monolithic columns, true feats of engineering that accurately follow the unusual form of the baseless Corinthian order used at the Tower of the Winds in ancient Athens. (The historic marker's reference to tobacco leaves in the capitals is erroneous.) Still-functional iron shutters and heavy iron doors provided palpable security and—along with the accordion-pleated, self-spanning wrought-iron roof (one of the earliest in the county)—protection against fire. Inside, the lobby leads to an impressive grand stair with paired curving cantilevered flights above the landing and a half dome above. In the basement an impressive column supports the thick granite floor slabs of the lobby above. Originally also housing a U.S. post office and federal courthouse, this remains the oldest functioning federal building in the state of Georgia, and still serves as the city's custom house.

2.10 Commercial Building (Central Railroad and Bank Building)

1853; 1999–2001 interior renovation and restoration, Dawson Wissmach Architects. 7–13 E. Bay St.

This representative 1850s commercial building with a cast-iron shopfront served as the military headquarters of General J. W. Geary, post commandant during the Union occupation of Savannah from December 1864 to December 1865. The obliquely angled glass-fronted rooftop skylight dates to 1931, when the building's second floor was converted into a federal government cotton classification and grading office, its true-north-facing skylight admitting light without shadows. The neighboring buildings, originally houses (c. 1822), at

15–23 E. Bay Street retain the scale of early-nineteenth-century Savannah and its waterfront architecture.

REYNOLDS WARD

Originally named Lower New Ward when laid out in 1734, the ward and its square commemorate Captain John Reynolds, first colonial governor of Georgia, 1754–1757.

2.11 Savannah Area Chamber of Commerce (Hibernia Bank of Savannah)

1915, Mowbray and Uffinger. 101 E. Bay St.

This former bank building evokes the distinctive Propylaeum of the Athenian Acropolis with its muscular Doric columns, complete with entasis, and wide central intercolumniation framing the entrance. Its airy, full-height interior features elegant classical Greek details. An impressive vault space looms at the rear, fronted by a section of floor that moves up and down at the push of a lever to allow the vault door to swing open. The Savannah Area Chamber of Commerce, which was established in 1806 and is the seventh-oldest such organization in the country, relocated to this building in 1998. A forty-four-panel mural depicting the history of the city, painted by local artist Augusta Oelschig in 1972–1975 for the Home Federal Savings and Loan Association Bank on Telfair Square, was moved here in 2000 and occupies the first-floor corridor of the adjacent building at 105–107 E. Bay.

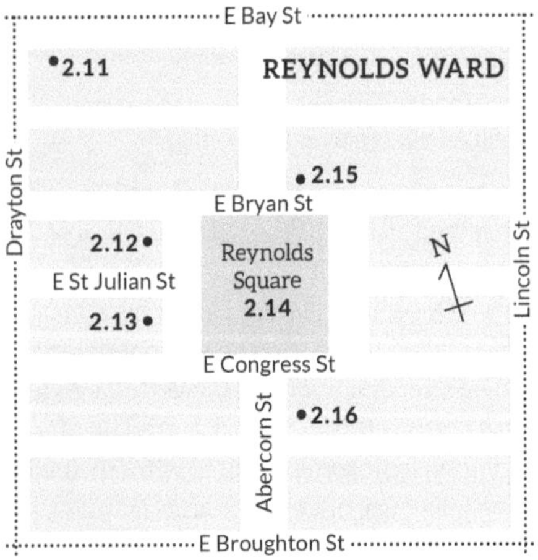

2.12 Olde Pink House Restaurant and Planters Tavern (James Habersham Jr. House)

1789; 1812 north wing; 1820 portico; 1929, 1970 renovations; 2006–2007 rear addition, Mark P. Finlay Architects. 23 Abercorn St.

The oldest surviving house to occupy a trust lot, this "public" building was the residence of James Habersham Jr., a member of a prominent colonial-era family. The symmetrical side-gabled composition features a central-hall single-pile plan, corner quoining, and a Palladian window over the entrance. The heavily restored interior retains its original fireplaces and mantels, as well as two large kitchen fireplaces in the basement. In 1812 the house was converted for use by Planters Bank, which added the north wing and, soon after, the Doric portico. The window lintels were added c. 1870. Alida Harper saved the building from demolition and opened the Georgia Tea Room and an antiques store in the house in 1929, which operated until 1970, when it acquired its current name. Some debate surrounds the source of the distinctive pink color—whether pigment from the red bricks beneath bled through the stucco, or if this is the faded remains of "Spanish brown" tinting applied to the surface.

2.13 Morris Multimedia (Oliver Sturges House)

1813; 1835 third floor; 1973 restoration. 27 Abercorn St.

This stunning example of a Federal town house (originally joined by a twin to the south) was erected for Savannah merchant Oliver Sturges, a two-fifths investor in the SS *Savannah*, the first steamship to cross the Atlantic. Planning for the

voyage took place in this house. The nine-over-nine double-hung windows reflect the small pane size typical of that time. Less typical is the extra-wide entrance bay and side elevation perforated with a gracefully proportioned set of windows that flank the paired chimneys. The unusual rear elevation features a handsome arched doorway and polygonal second-floor west wall. The neighboring Planters Inn (1916; 1931 expansion; 102–118 E. Congress Street) was initially constructed on the east end of the trust lot fronting the square as the Hotel Collins (renamed the John Wesley Hotel in 1924). It was seamlessly extended to the west end of the trust lot using the same design, resulting in a building unique in Savannah, occupying only half of the width of a trust lot but its full depth. After closing in 1982, the hotel reopened as the Planters Inn in 1987 after a renovation by J. T. Turner Construction.

2.14 Reynolds Square

1734; 1969 relandscaped, Marshall Daugherty

Two of the most important public buildings of the colony, the Filature and the New Council House, were erected on the northeast and southeast trust lots, respectively, overlooking Reynolds Square. Constructed in 1751, the Filature reflected the goal of establishing a silk industry in the Georgia colony. It burned in 1758, but was promptly rebuilt (1758–1759) by Peter Tondee and Benjamin Goldwire and continued in operation until 1771. The building hosted city council meetings from 1790 until the council moved to the City Exchange in 1812, as well as public gatherings (including a ball for George Washington's visit), schools, a theater and concert hall, barracks and a hospital, and boarding houses. It was destroyed by fire in 1839. The

New Council House, originally constructed as a second filature, was just a shell in 1754–1755 when Noble Jones completed it to replace an earlier Council House located on the southwest trust lot overlooking Percival (Wright) Square, which had collapsed while the council was in session in November 1754. In 1776, the Declaration of Independence was read for the first time in Georgia at a meeting of the Colonial Assembly inside the New Council House, followed by a second reading out front in Reynolds Square, and two more readings elsewhere in the city. From 1877 until 1946 a streetcar line ran through the square in line with Abercorn Street. The rather staid John Wesley Monument and surrounding landscaping (1969, Marshall Daugherty, sculptor) honors the founder of Methodism, who came to Savannah as the Trustee-appointed minister to Georgia (1736–1737). His parsonage was on the southwest trust lot overlooking this square.

2.15 Christ Church Parish House (Lee Roy Myers Cigar Company)

1911, Henrik Wallin; 1955 addition. 18 Abercorn St.

Wallin's fanciful Mediterranean-style cigar factory, maker of Regalos Cigars, originally featured a balconied belvedere crowning the corner tower, removed sometime after 1960. The building reflects the shift of this area by the early twentieth century from residential to port-related activities. Christ Church acquired the building in 1954, adding the Bland Tucker Building to the north a year later. A weather vane from the twelfth-century All Saints Church in Cranham, Essex, England (where Oglethorpe and his wife, Elizabeth, are buried in the chancel), was installed atop the roof in 1967.

2.16 Lucas Theatre for the Arts

1921, Claude K. Howell; 1986–2000 restoration, Lott and Barber. 32 Abercorn St.

One of forty theaters in the South owned by Savannah-born theater developer Arthur Lucas (who partnered here with Paramount Pictures) and the only one bearing his name, the Lucas accommodated both silent films and Keith Circuit vaudeville. Richmond architect Howell used Spanish Baroque Revival for the exterior and designed an equally lavish Adamesque interior. The unusual broad and shallow proportions of the interior

provide a striking sense of intimacy. As of 1924 the theater's German-made air conditioner was "the first of its kind below the Mason-Dixon Line," according to a 1981 article in the *Savannah Morning News*. Racial segregation forced African Americans to enter through a side exterior stairway and sit in the upper balcony. The theater closed in 1976 and later saved from demolition in 1986 by a nonprofit organization, the Lucas Theatre for the Arts, which undertook a $13 million restoration. It reopened in 2000, but without its original Wurlitzer pipe organ (reputed to be in storage in Atlanta).

ANSON WARD

Known as Upper New Ward when laid out in 1734, Anson Ward honors Lord George Anson, the Admiral of the Fleet in

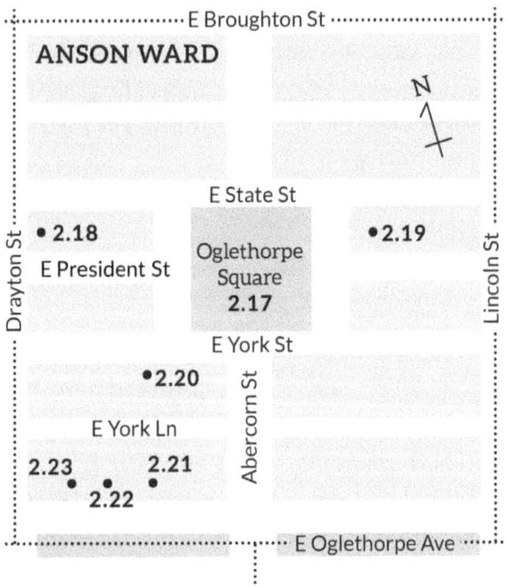

the English navy assigned to protect the Carolina and Georgia coasts in the 1720s and 1730s. The southern half of Anson Ward preserves the greatest concentration of historic houses within the original six wards of Savannah. These include many fine examples of detached, paired, and groups of Savannah's elevated town houses with their distinctive raised stoops and stairs.

2.17 Oglethorpe Square

1734

Oglethorpe Square (originally Upper New Square) commemorates Savannah's founder. From 1874 until at least 1897, a decorative stone mound occupied its southeast corner and was crowned by a cast-iron vase. Unique among the mounds erected in the city's squares during the 1870s, this was privately built (despite being in a public space) by Captain Henry J. Dickerson, who lived across York Street from this site. Streetcar tracks crossed the square from 1877 until 1946 in line with Abercorn Street. The modest columnar monument (1933, Henrik Wallin and Max Kleinstuber) honors the Moravian colonists of 1735–1740, who maintained a mission to Native Americans in the area.

2.18 Lott and Barber (Standard Oil Station)

1924; 1985 restoration and renovation, Lominack Associates, PC; 2005 restoration, Lott and Barber. 110 E. President St.

Originally this building housed a gas station and offices erected for one of the subsidiary and successor companies continuing in the name of Standard Oil (one inscription is still visible on the north elevation) after that company's dissolution in 1911. Dressed in Renaissance Revival garb, the modern fireproof

Savannah's Elevated Town Houses

The Savannah elevated town house, a form unique to the city with over 400 extant examples downtown, likely owes its genesis to the Savannah plan. During the early 1800s, as the city's economy rapidly expanded, progressively grander architectural expressions of success and social standing appeared throughout Savannah. For the elite, freestanding mansions on trust lots, with broad dimensions, a front garden, and elegant portico, symbolized status. For less wealthy Savannahians, the Georgian three-bay row house, popular in northern cities since 1790, slowly gained appeal, either with the main entrance almost at grade or accessed by a short staircase perpendicular to the sidewalk, as seen in the early 1820s houses (**6.19**) at 101–105 East Oglethorpe Avenue. But a desire for greater architectural prominence, and possibly to facilitate social and ethnic sorting, had led by the 1830s to a Savannah variant on the conventional Georgian row house involving a raised basement with its own at-grade entrance, the main living floor and its entrance elevated a full story above grade (called the first floor like a European piano nobile), accessed by an external staircase (normally paralleling the facade) to a raised stoop. Beyond the obvious status implications of elevated living space, having entrances on two levels allowed servants or slaves direct access to the utilitarian basement level, while leaving the elevated first floor the preserve of the owners. To achieve greater height within the confines of shallow tything

---

structure was the grandest service station in downtown Savannah. It diverged from the others by incorporating the drive-through area into the body of the building rather than setting it under an attached canopy. Glazed terra-cotta blocks mimic rusticated masonry with an elegantly bracketed cornice and metal sash windows set in delicate spiral colonette decoration. The 1985 renovation included excavating the underground gas tanks beneath the porte-cochere, revealing the subterranean brick walls and stairs of an earlier building, and leaving the

Elevated town houses of Gordon Block (8.45), prior to restoration

lots, the front wall of a town house typically meets the street line, forcing the external stairs and stoops onto the sidewalk, an encroachment on the public realm allowed by the City. Forming the focal point of Savannah elevated houses, the staircases may be solitary, grouped, or in rows usually descending in the same direction to rhythmic effect. Staircases also vary in shape (straight, curving, or doglegged), in their materials, in the degree of openness, and in whether the stoop is covered. The result is seemingly countless variations on this elevated theme. Behind such houses was typically a shallow two-story side-gabled carriage house fronting the rear lane, accommodating horses below and servants or slaves above.

---

space as a sunken court, which was covered over to restore its drive-through use for a bank in 2005.

2.19 Owens-Thomas House (Richard Richardson House)

1816–1819, William Jay; 1830s rear addition; 2004–2009 and 2014 interior restorations. 124 Abercorn St.

One of Savannah's most significant buildings, this house reflects the rapid expansion of the city's fortunes during the early nineteenth century. Wealthy banker and shipping merchant

Richardson commissioned young English immigrant architect William Jay to design the mansion and accompanying carriage house at the rear. The design reflects a creative adaptation of the neoclassical forms of British architects Sir John Soane and John Nash, which is often called the Regency style. Sited prominently on a trust lot, the central-hall-plan house sits back from the street in a gesture of wealth and status, allowing the elegant and gently bowing one-story portico and reflecting curving staircases to form a sculptural composition that contrasts with the flat simplicity of the rest of the facade. Jay made extensive use of English building materials and technology, including the remarkable one-story cast-iron portico extending from the south elevation that is one of the first uses of structural cast iron in America, as well as gravity-fed plumbing, supplied by cisterns in the attic and basement, which included flush toilets—among the earliest in the country. For the main structure he used the regional building tradition of walls constructed of tabby (a mixture of lime, sand, water, and crushed oyster shells) on the basement and first floors and coquina (a sedimentary rock comprising shells) on the second floor. Inside, elegant neoclassical details are complemented by experimental indirect lighting in the dining room and a dramatic central staircase that includes a bridge on the second floor. The carriage house is the best-preserved slave quarters in Savannah and retains extensive traces of rare "haint blue" paint on its ceilings, a color believed to ward away evil spirits in African traditions. The original work yard was redesigned as a parterre garden "in the Regency Manner (1820 A.D.)" by Savannah landscape architect Clermont Lee in 1954, when the main floor of the house opened as a museum; Lee revised the garden plan in 1959. The house is believed to have had such a garden on a residential lot across State Street to the north. Public access to other parts of the house came later, beginning with the basement in 1958, then the upstairs in 1977, the carriage house in 1998, and the butler's pantry in 2014.

2.20 Bradley Hall, SCAD (U.S. Marine Hospital)

1906, James Knox Taylor, Supervising Architect of the U.S. Treasury; 1923 expansion; 2007 restoration and renovation, Hansen Architects. 115 E. York St.

Originally a maritime veterans' hospital, the Mediterranean Revival building was designed by the office of the Architect of the Treasury Department. Its location, centered on the three-hundred-foot-long tything block, allowed ample open space to front the opened galleries of the end pavilions, with the principal entrance facing York Street and Oglethorpe Square (**2.17**). The large and rather utilitarian 1923 addition to the east with its regular pattern of windows contrasts the more dynamic fenestration of the original building. It has been used by SCAD since 2007. The southeast tything block across Abercorn contains notable examples of Savannah elevated town houses, including the Marshall Row (1855–1856, 230–244 E. Oglethorpe Avenue), developed by Mary Marshall, and a stunning pair unusual for their Queen Anne style at 124–126 E. Oglethorpe.

2.21 Camphor Cottage

c. 1760–1767; 1871 raised with ground-floor addition; 1907 remodeled with balcony added. 122 E. Oglethorpe Ave.

Possibly the oldest intact building in the city, this house began its life as a modest two-room residence one-and-a-half stories tall, typical of eighteenth-century Savannah. Its broad clapboard planks, informal fenestration, and small window panes attest to its early date, while the extension of the side-gabled roof at a gentler pitch above an attached rear shed followed the New England saltbox form. In 1871 the house was raised and a brick ground floor erected beneath to emulate an elevated town house, giving the building its distinctive dual character.

2.22 Law Office (House)

1872; 1963 remodeled, Gunn and Meyerhoff. 114 E. Oglethorpe Ave.

This narrow house originally mirrored its Italianate neighbor at number 112 to the west, but in 1963 was radically transformed for use as a law office by architects Gunn and Meyerhoff into an essay in minimalist forms of the International Style—white walls, cantilevered horizontal plane over the glazed entrance, groups of elongated single-pane windows evoking ribbon windows, and vertical copper ribs linking the stories together.

2.23 Lachlan McIntosh House

c. 1765–1782, John Eppinger, builder; 1876 third story; 1973 restoration. 110 E. Oglethorpe Ave.

Despite being one of the oldest and most venerable houses in Savannah, the home of Revolutionary War patriot General McIntosh lacks the prominence of other landmark buildings. Local builder Eppinger purchased the property in 1764 and may have erected the house, perhaps as a tavern, as early as 1765. The original two-story, side-gabled Georgian central-hall house is barely legible beneath the second-floor iron balcony and dis-

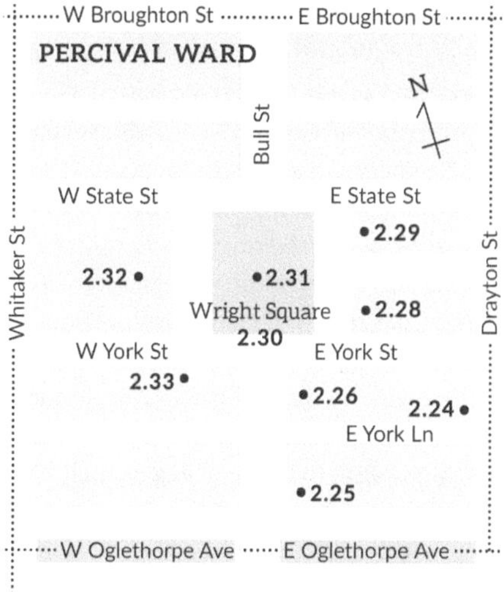

proportionately tall third-floor addition. The first constitutional session of the Georgia General Assembly met here in 1783, and George Washington visited in 1791.

PERCIVAL WARD

Originally both the ward and the square honored the president of the Trustees, the Right Honourable John Lord Viscount Percival. The ward was one of the first four laid out by Oglethorpe in 1733.

2.24 Cowart Insurance Group (Morris and Morris Law Firm)

1965. 139 Drayton St.

Attached to the rear of a nineteenth-century town house, this stark, white, windowless office building hovers on hefty H-beam pilotis infilled with Savannah Grey brick lattice. Typical of modernization efforts occurring across the city and especially in the vicinity along Drayton Street, few Savannah buildings are so gratifyingly bold as this. A recessed bay cuts into the sharply geometric mass and connects ground-level parking with second-story offices. Steel rods echoing the H-beams act as banisters supporting exposed concrete tread steps. Every interior space is artificially lit and originally featured a different finish of plywood from historic local manufacturer Dixie Plywood and Lumber Company, and many interior appointments remain untouched. The law firm Cowan Zeigler Downing and McAleer commissioned the sprawling one-story modernist building (1965) adjacent to the south at 24 E. Oglethorpe. These buildings, along with the remodeling of 114 E. Oglethorpe (**2.22**) reflect the progressive image of the city's law firms during the 1960s.

2.25 Juliette Gordon Low Birthplace (James Moore Wayne House)

1820, attributed to William Jay; 1886 additions, Detlef Lienau; 1993 restoration, Kolman and Smith, Architects; 2012–2014 restoration, Lott and Barber with Robert Silman Associates. 10 E. Oglethorpe Ave.

Attributed to Jay due to its striking similarity to the other four houses (**2.19, 2.38, 5.6,** and the Bulloch House, demolished 1916) he erected in Savannah, this residence commissioned by Savannah mayor Wayne (later a U.S. Supreme Court associate justice appointed by President Andrew Jackson) represents a bold departure from the local tradition of mansions facing a square by addressing, instead, the newly defined boulevard of

South Broad Street. The design, originally two stories over a raised basement, reflects the abstract classicism of the period, where sculptural massing (such as the robust porch and the two apsidal projections at the rear) replaced detailed ornament. In 1886, the Gordon family, who had acquired the house from Wayne in 1831, commissioned New York City architect Lienau to add the third floor and the elaborate verandah on the east side. The house is renowned as the birthplace of Juliette Gordon Low, who in 1912 founded the Girl Scouts of the United States of America, which opened the house as a Girl Scout National Center in 1956. In that year, Savannah landscape architect Clermont Lee designed the house's formal garden "in the style of 1860–1880" (as noted on her drawing); she revised her design in 1978. The 1993 restoration, carried out by Sterling Builders and Restoration, included a major structural upgrade to the interior staircase, which was reinforced with steel to support the thousands of annual visitors. The extensive recent restoration, carried out by J. T. Turner Construction, included replacing the non-porous cement stucco (which had replaced the original lime-based stucco in 1964), worn brownstone details, and metal brackets and soffit in the 1886 cornice.

2.26 John Schwarz Building

1890, Alfred S. Eichberg; 1909–1913 remodeled. 136–140 Bull St.

Commissioned by Savannah mayor Schwarz, this handsome commercial building helped push the city's commercial district southward. Eichberg made use of various design strategies typical of later nineteenth-century commercial buildings to both break up and unify the large building mass, such as having different window shapes on each floor that were nonetheless tied together by sets of piers. The subtly projecting rounded turretlike corner, originally capped by a tall dome, acknowledges the importance of the corner site fronting both Bull Street and Wright Square. The building's ornate cornice and dome were removed before 1955.

2.27 Savannah Blueprint Company

1959, Helfrich and Grantham. 11 E. York St.

Although modest in size, this well-proportioned and well-preserved commercial building illustrates the innovative use of signage with stylized raised white letters set against blue metal panels as dominant design features within the International Style. To the right of the door, rough-faced beige and pink stone fronts a single pier. The play of solids versus voids and contrasting textures are typical of this firm's work. The store's continued operation attests to the diverse economy of downtown Savannah.

2.28 Chatham County Courthouse Annex (Chatham County Courthouse)

1889, William G. Preston; 1954–1990 interior renovations. 124 Bull St.

The third county courthouse on the site, replacing a Greek Revival county courthouse designed by Providence architects Russell Warren and James C. Bucklin in 1832, this is Preston's boldest Savannah building. Drawing on elements of Richardsonian Romanesque (particularly the large entrance arch) and using the varied massing of Queen Anne and foliate ornament typical of the 1880s, it reflects the eclectic nature of design of the time. Yet the use of yellow brick instead of the more common red and the avoidance of polychromatic effects marked a striking departure from prevailing trends. The corner tower best exhibits Preston's creativity and confidence. Its corner placement eschews the formal symmetry one would expect of a courthouse and makes instead an urbanistic gesture to the center of the ward, while its tapered form, deeply penetrating roofs, and stylized clock anticipate design trends of a decade later in Europe, especially the Vienna Secession and Art Nouveau. The installation of a large air conditioner compressor has marred the tower.

2.29 Lutheran Church of the Ascension

1844, J. F. Posey; 1875 redesigned, George B. Clarke. 120 Bull St.

The Lutheran church and the neighboring courthouse (**2.28**) form one of the most engaging architectural pairings of trust-lot buildings and the diversity of architectural possibilities such prominent sites inspire. Initially established in 1741 at Ebenezer twenty-five miles northwest of Savannah, the congregation relocated to Savannah by 1771. In 1844 they erected a Greek Revival church on this site, whose walls were retained in a redesign of the building by Clarke (an amateur architect who worked for a local bindery company), modeled after a design for a "Village Church" in the "Romanesque style" in Samuel Sloane's *The Model Architect* (1852, volume 1, design XIX).

2.30 Wright Square

1733

Originally named Percival Square when laid out with the ward in 1733, Wright Square was renamed by 1762 after Sir James Wright, the third and last royal governor of Georgia (1760–1782). The space was colloquially known as "Courthouse Square" in recognition of the presence of a county courthouse on the southeast trust lot since 1735. From 1882 to the end of that decade, a metal moonlight tower (one of six erected in Savannah) of arc lights stood south of the Gordon Monument (**2.31**) and rose to a height of approximately 130 feet. Essentially a stopgap measure to get urban areas illuminated as cheaply and quickly as possible, the tall yet flimsy towers only lasted a few years here (one was knocked over by a cow), where the dense tree canopy rendered them less successful than in cities like Austin, Texas, where seventeen of thirty-one survive.

2.31 William Washington Gordon Monument

1882–1883, Van Brunt and Howe; Walter F. Peach, builder. Wright Square

The Central Railroad and Banking Company of Georgia commissioned Boston architects Van Brunt and Howe to design this imposing monument to honor their founder and first president, William Washington Gordon. In 1739 Oglethorpe erected an earlier stone monument on this site (possibly the first public monument in America) over the tomb of Tomochichi, but it had

disappeared by the late eighteenth century. Photos of a decorative earthen mound installed here by the City in 1872 (one of at least four placed in Savannah squares) and removed for the 1882 tribute gave rise to the local myth that the Gordon Monument "desecrated" the chief's tomb. Van Brunt and Howe's design incorporates a limestone base with relief panels supporting four polished red granite columns and crowned by four angelic cherubs supporting a globe. The nearby Tomochichi Monument (1899) resulted from rekindled interest in the local Indian chief, or Mico, in the late nineteenth century, paralleling improved attitudes towards Native Americans nationally. The Society of the Colonial Dames of America in Georgia (led by their first president, Gordon's daughter-in-law, Eleanor Kinzie Gordon), who secured the large granite boulder from the Stone Mountain Company in Atlanta for one dollar, commissioned this monument.

2.32 Tomochichi Federal Building and U.S. Courthouse (U.S. Post Office and Courthouse)

1894–1899, Jeremiah O'Rourke and William M. Aiken, Supervising Architects of the U.S. Treasury; 1930–1932 expanded, James A. Wetmore; 2014–2015 restoration. 125 Bull St.

One of the grandest and most extravagant buildings in Savannah, this prominent federal building illustrates the constraints

imposed by the Savannah plan, which designated trust lots as sites for public buildings. True to form, the original building, designed at first by O'Rourke in 1894 and completed by Aiken, who took over as Supervising Architect in 1895, occupied the southwest trust lot facing north onto President Street. The Renaissance Revival design exuded prosperity and cultural confidence with its luxurious white Georgia marble cladding, subtly rusticated base of alternating broad and narrow courses of masonry, elaborately and deeply framed arched windows, richly decorated frieze of colored marble, and red terra-cotta tile roof. Even the curbstones are marble. In 1932 the federal government dramatically expanded the building across President Street and onto the northwest trust lot, with an addition seamlessly tripling its size and reorienting its now paired entrances to the square, while leaving the 150-foot-tall Venetian Renaissance–styled tower, formerly centered over the entrance, to rise incongruously from the roof. A portion of the original north facade can still be viewed from the rear above the loading dock. In the 1980s a new courtroom was added on the second floor, and in 1992–1993 the building's interior was partially restored. The post office relocated to a building on Telfair Square in 1999, though the entrance hall preserves the historic post boxes. The Department of Homeland Security installed protective bollards and a swath of greenery in front of the building in 2002 (Eberly and Associates), as well as bombproof windows on the ground floor. The building acquired its current name in 2005.

2.33 **Lindsay and Morgan Building**

1921; 2005–2007 renovation and restoration, Gunn Meyerhoff Shay Architects. 9 W. York St.

Erected on the site of a colonial burying ground, this commercial building is unusual in Savannah in exhibiting the influence of the Chicago School, with its clear articulation of the structural frame clad in brick and large windows filling most of the areas in between. It preserves prismatic glass along the top of the first-floor windows and in the sidewalk. Decorative patterning with lighter brick at the top and extension of the piers above the roofline would become typical of Art Deco later in the 1920s. The building's most remarkable feature is its projecting display pavilion supported on large brackets but appearing to hover above the door. The building was converted by Bloomquist Construction into lofts as part of restoration and renovation work completed in 2007, with individual tenant build-outs finished in 2011.

HEATHCOTE WARD

Named in honor of George Heathcote, one of the Georgia Trustees, Heathcote Ward defined the southwest corner of the colonial town when laid out in 1733 as one of the first four wards.

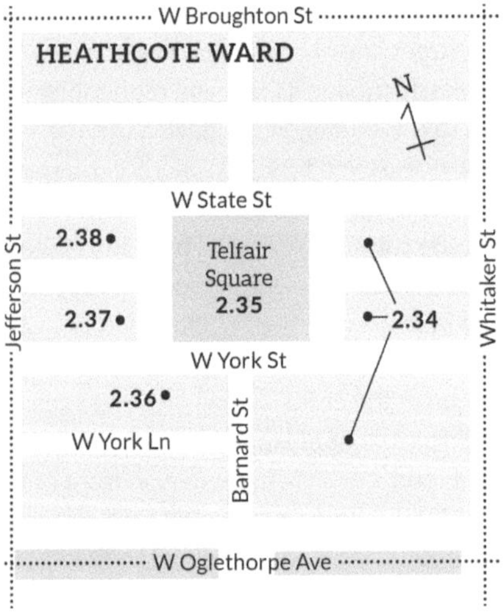

2.34 Juliette Gordon Low Federal Buildings

1980–1982, Stevens and Wilkinson. 100 W. Oglethorpe Ave. and 120 and 124 Barnard St.

This group of three Postmodern federal buildings, unified by their cladding of smooth dark-gray first-floor masonry with deeply cut channels and glazed six-inch tiles above, reveals the limits of 1980s contextualism. The two smaller edifices respect the tradition of trust-lot buildings through their scale, orientation toward the square, and use of abstracted porticos to signify their civic purpose. The main building, however, occupies an entire ten-lot tything, obliterating the lane. Its shifting wall planes—intended to recall the rhythmic pattern of row houses—fail to mask its low-budget enormity. Atlanta-based Stevens and Wilkinson's original design was dramatically altered due to budget constraints.

2.35 Telfair Square

1733; 1962 relandscaped, after a design by G. Bignault and Sons, landscape architects

Originally named St. James after a square of the same name in the City of Westminster in London, Telfair Square was unique in commemorating a place rather than a person. On the northwest trust lot stood Government House, home of the royal governor James Wright (1760–1782). In 1883, the square was renamed for the prominent local Telfair family, who lived on the northwest trust lot from the early nineteenth century until 1875, and by the early twentieth century it was frequently called Telfair Place. The family patriarch, Scottish-born Edward Telfair, was a successful colonial merchant, Revolutionary War patriot, signer of the Articles of Confederation, and Georgia governor (1786–1787 and 1789–1793). Telfair and his wife, Sarah Gibbons Telfair, had seven children, including Thomas Telfair, who served in the U.S. Congress (1813–1817). Youngest son Alexander Telfair became head of the family following the deaths of his three older brothers. Mary Telfair, the last of the Telfairs, died in 1875. From 1877 to 1946 streetcar tracks crossed the square in line with Barnard Street. It was relandscaped by the Garden Club of Savannah in 1962 following a 1935 design by the city's landscape architect, Paris-born Georges Bignault, who had been sent by the French government in 1908 to study the cultivation of Sea Island cotton in Beaufort, South Carolina, but chose to settle in Savannah after visiting the city later that year. During the 1930s, his firm authored plans for the beautification of most of Savannah's squares, but it is unclear how many were implemented.

2.36 **Jepson Center for the Arts**
2005–2006, Moshe Safdie and Associates with Hansen Architects. 207 W. York St.

Downtown Savannah's boldest twenty-first-century building, the Jepson Center follows the trend begun in the late twentieth century for major art museums to serve as a symbol of a city's cultural vitality. The building occupies roughly half of a tything block, but does so in a unique way by bridging a lane, a requirement to preserve the city's urban plan imposed on designer Moshe Safdie by the local design review board. Similarly, the rectangular concrete frames that define the north and south facades resulted from local opposition to the original design for simple glass expanses. The relatively simple exterior gives way to an interior of dynamic curving geometry, both clad in light-colored Portuguese limestone, and an impressive grand stair that rises two stories and cleverly disguises the bridge over the lane. Supported by a large donation from local philanthropists Alice A. and Robert S. Jepson Jr., the Jepson Center serves the Telfair Museums as its principal galleries for modern art and a children's gallery, as well as housing administrative offices, café, and gift shop.

2.37 Trinity United Methodist Church (Trinity Methodist Church)

1848–1850, John B. Hogg; 1969 and 1991–1993 interior restorations; 2005 exterior restoration, Lominack Kolman Smith Architects. 127 Barnard St.

The city's first Methodist congregation, established in 1807, occupied the Wesley Chapel—originally on northeast corner of Lincoln and South Broad streets (the latter now Oglethorpe Avenue), since demolished—from 1812 to 1850 prior to moving here. Filling the east half of a trust lot (which formerly served as the private garden of the Telfair family), this restrained Greek Revival church maximizes its small site with its recessed portico of two colossal Corinthian columns in antis. It boasts the oldest preserved church interior in the city, which barely escaped the great fire of 1889 and was somewhat damaged by a 1991 fire that destroyed the McIntire Building (1927) attached at the rear. The simple interior includes flanking galleries and an impressive organ case imitating the entrance portico.

2.38 Telfair Academy of Arts and Sciences (Telfair Mansion)

1818–1819, William Jay; 1883–1886 addition and modifications, Detlef Lienau, with Augustus Schwaab; 1989 interior restoration; 2016 exterior restoration. 121 Barnard St.

The site of the colonial governor's house, the Telfair family home was the most restrained design of the four mansions in Savannah designed by Jay. Alexander Telfair commissioned the house to accommodate himself, his wife, his mother, and his three unmarried sisters. The simple exterior, dominated by a one-story Corinthian portico and the thermal window above,

offers little hint of the dramatic interior spaces of various geometric shapes and a double-height central hall.

Mary Telfair bequeathed the house and its contents to the Georgia Historical Society for the establishment of an art museum, founded in 1883 and opened in 1886, making it one of the oldest in the country and the first in the South. German-born Lienau transformed the house into a museum, adding a parapet to the exterior to accommodate the inscription, which reads "Telfair Academy of Arts & Sciences," flanked by relief portraits of Aristotle and Alexander von Humboldt (removed after 1975) and, to the rear, a semidetached Beaux-Arts classical pavilion lavishly decorated with colossal pilasters and a highly sculpted cornice that contrast the simplicity of the original house. Construction was supervised by fellow German immigrant and local designer Augustus Schwaab. Lienau altered Jay's design most significantly in the central hall, removing decorative pendentives and replacing the original double flight of stairs with his marble stairs located farther from the entrance. The rear wing includes a large sculpture gallery, which retains now-rare full-scale plaster copies of famous ancient sculptures, and the "rotunda" above, a grand square room with a tall coved ceiling. As part of the transformation, the museum's first director, Carl Brandt, commissioned Viennese sculptor Viktor Tilgner to carve the five statues that front the building (installed 1884). In the 1940s numerous neoclassical architectural fragments, including mantles and interior wood doorframes, from the Mackay House (125 E. Congress St., c. 1757; demolished c. 1940) were incorporated into the rear portion of the building, originally used for classrooms and now housing offices. The building was restored to its orignal yellow in 2016.

DECKER WARD

One of the first four wards laid out by Oglethorpe in 1733, Decker Ward honors Sir Matthew Decker, one of the colonial Trustees.

2.39 Ellis Square

1733; 2008–2010 redesigned, EDAW AECOM, with Lominack Kolman Smith Architects

Originally called Decker Square, Ellis Square was renamed sometime between 1757 and 1770 to honor Sir Henry Ellis, the second colonial governor of Georgia (1757–1760). From the mid-eighteenth century until 1954, a series of progressively grander market buildings occupied this square. To help revitalize the area and attract more shoppers, the City permitted the last market (1870–1872, Muller and Schwaab; see page 17) to be razed in 1954 and replaced a year later with the two-level Park and Shop Garage. By the late twentieth century, public discontent with the loss of the market and distaste for the parking facility prompted the City in 2002 to solicit public input for revamping the space after the deck's fifty-year lease expired (demolished 2005). The project involved a bold public-private development partnership, with preliminary studies and public forums conducted by Sottile and Sottile and Cooper Carry, leading to the clear preference for an active-use modern square, rather than a re-creation of the lost market building.

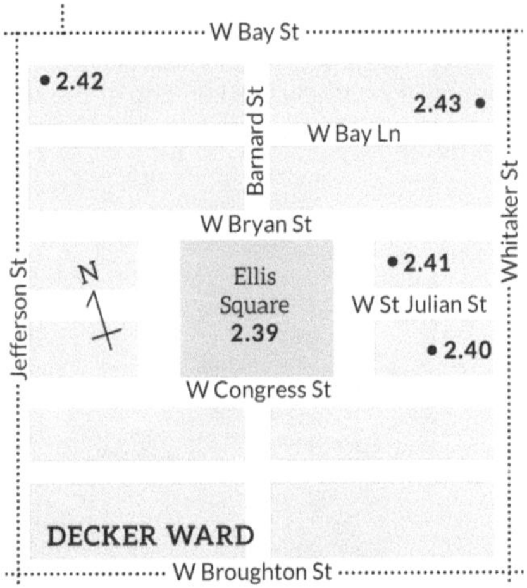

Prior to constructing the new square, the site and neighboring vacant parcels were excavated to a minimum depth of forty-five feet to form an enormous underground parking garage able to accommodate more than one thousand cars (2005–2008), a design-build project by Batson Cook Developers. On top of the garage, the urban fabric of streets, square, and two buildings was reconstructed. The 2008–2010 landscape design of the new public space reinterprets the traditional form of Savannah's historic squares, notably through the brick paths that align with the sidewalks of adjacent streets and the use of live oaks, with features new to a Savannah square—an oval design, changes of grade, splash fountains, and movable tables and chairs. The diagonal eastern edge of the fountains aligns with true north. The corner pavilion, the Ellis Square Hospitality Center (2009–2010, Lominack Kolman Smith Architects), the city's first LEED-certified project, adds a retro-modern element into the square. The life-size Johnny Mercer Monument (2009, Susie Chisholm, sculptor) honors the Savannah native who became one of the most successful songwriters of the twentieth century.

2.40 Commercial Buildings (Thomas Gibbons Block)

1820. 102–116 W. Congress St.

One of the few surviving trust-lot blocks of nineteenth-century commercial buildings, this row of eight attached properties was given a grander appearance through the embellishment of colossal fluted brownstone pilasters with wooden Corinthian capitals. The adjacent row of commercial buildings at 121–127 W. State Street retains the most elaborate and refined cast-iron shopfronts in the city. Number 127 (1873) is particularly exuberant.

2.41 Cay Building

2011–2012, Smallwoods, Reynolds, Stewart, Stewart, with Sottile and Sottile. 22 Barnard St.

Among the several recent buildings in Savannah employing a traditional vocabulary, the five-story Cay Building exudes the greatest degree of conviction. Carried out by New South Construction Company, this neo-Palladian palazzo, which resembles early-twentieth-century commercial blocks, is characterized by high-quality materials, including limestone and bronze, and fine detailing, such as the street names carved into the corner blocks, sculpted keystones, and boldly projecting cornice. The building, along with the adjacent and more modernist Andaz Hotel (originally Avia Hotel, 2005–2009, Krehbiel Architecture and J. Webb Design and Associates), stands atop Ellis Square's (**2.39**) vast underground parking garage, and helps restore the urban enclosure around the square.

2.42 Hotel Indigo Savannah Historic District (Guckenheimer and Company Wholesale Store)

1888, Fay and Eichberg; 1981 expanded; 2005–2006 restoration, Gunn Meyerhoff Shay Architects; 2015–2016 renovation, Greenline Architecture. 225 W. Bay St.

This twenty-first-century adaptive reuse of a nineteenth-century wholesale store, combined with a hotel built in 1981, illustrates two significant phases of commercial architecture in this part of Savannah. The Guckenheimer Wholesale Store was a monument to the rags-to-riches success of retailer Simon Guckenheimer. Its hulking mass of red brick and white limestone once dwarfed the other commercial buildings on Bay Street. Steady decline in commercial activity in the City Market area in the mid-twentieth century was countered by a growth in tourism, as evidenced by the adjacent four-story hotel.

2.43 Commercial Building (Savannah Morning News Building)

1875, Miller B. Grant; c. 1885 addition of four bays and two stories. 5 Whitaker St.

At the time of its construction in 1875 this Italianate building alone served the needs of the *Savannah Morning News*. Stylistic enrichments—notably ground-floor detached marble columns, segmental and flat cast-iron lintels, elaborate cornice bracketing, and corner quoining—broadcast the company's success. Around 1885, the four-bay-wide edifice was doubled to eight and two floors were added, with the sixth story in the form of a fashionable mansard roof, increasing the building's height to 62 feet (raised further by a now-lost two-story tower) and making this the tallest commercial structure in the city at the time. The *News* expanded its facilities within this block in 1926 and 1958, but finally left the site for a new suburban home in 2004. The News Place redevelopment (2005–2008, Dawson Wissmach

Architects and Design Reese Architects) by Batson Cook Developers incorporated two historic facades at 121–123 W. Bay Street (1852) and 111 W. Bay (1926), which are ornamented with spandrel panels depicting local flora (pine bough and palm frond) and a torch, symbol of enlightenment and truth, a concept often adopted by newspapers in the early twentieth century.

Broughton Street

Since the founding of Savannah in 1733, Broughton Street has served as the principal commercial corridor of the downtown area, a remarkable fact given how frequently commercial districts migrate in cities. Of the original three major east–west streets defining the edges of the two rows of wards of the colonial town (Bay, Broughton, and South Broad), it alone had buildings fronting both sides. The street was named in honor of South Carolina governor Thomas Broughton. Although downtown Savannah is laid out in wards centered on squares, Broughton Street exhibits the way certain streets form linear corridors between the wards. It played a prominent role in the American Revolution as the site of the city's first Liberty Pole, erected in front of Tondee's Tavern on the northwest corner with Whitaker Street.

By the mid-nineteenth century, the blocks west of Lincoln Street and especially the blocks closest to the market in Ellis Square were predominantly commercial, while the blocks east remained largely residential. In 1882 Broughton Street became the city's first street to be electrified. After World War II, many owners sought to modernize their shops by covering their historic facades with simple, often blank, modernist fronts, allowing signage to become the focal point of the design. Those same years witnessed a trend of retailers shifting their establishments to locations farther south in the city, beginning in 1946 with Sears and Roebuck (**10.13**) on Henry Street. The 1969 opening of Oglethorpe Mall, five miles south of downtown, attracted businesses away from Broughton Street, which gradually declined. By the early 1970s, the section of Broughton east of Lincoln was dominated by auto dealerships (some of which remain), repair shops, and parking lots.

The revitalization of downtown Savannah since beginning in the 1980s prompted several building owners to restore the

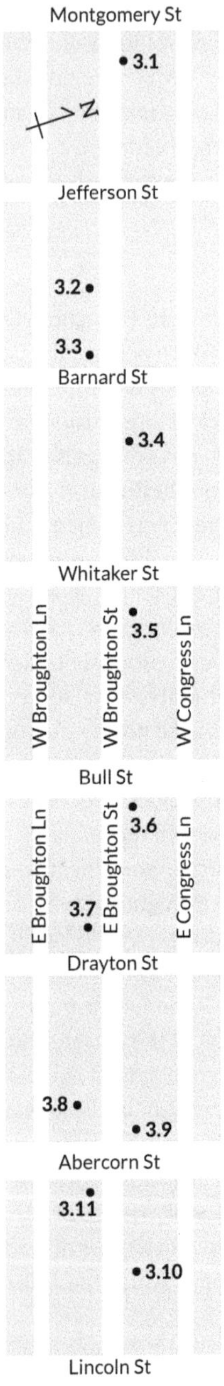
Montgomery St
3.1
N
Jefferson St
3.2
3.3
Barnard St
3.4
Whitaker St
W Broughton Ln
W Broughton St
3.5
W Congress Ln
Bull St
E Broughton Ln
E Broughton St
3.6
3.7
E Congress Ln
Drayton St
3.8
3.9
Abercorn St
3.11
3.10
Lincoln St

historic store fronts, especially in the western blocks of the street, a process that is ongoing. One consequence of the revitalization has been the displacement of small-scale local retail establishments by national franchises. Taken as a group, the commercial buildings along Broughton Street, ranging from the mid-nineteenth to the mid-twentieth centuries, remain one of the most intact main street corridors in Georgia.

3.1 Commercial Building (Houses)

Before 1853; c. 1913 altered; 2006 restored.
322 W. Broughton St.

Composed of a pair of conventional Savannah elevated side-hall town houses and rear carriage houses, this building reflects the area's transformation into a commercial zone and the remarkable adaptability of traditional residential forms. Around 1913 the yard space between the main houses and carriage houses was filled and the raised basement and elevated parlor level above it were converted into a dramatically tall commercial space with a mezzanine wrapping around the perimeter of the interior (reflected in the smaller row of windows above the main display windows). The upper-story windows retain their residential spacing and proportions. RK Construction and Development restored the building in 2006.

3.2 Urban Outfitters (Commercial Building)

1903; 1939, c. 1960 alterations; 2007–2008 restoration, Hansen Architects. 217–221 W. Broughton St.

The rough-faced granite facade is unique among commercial buildings on Broughton Street and highly unusual in Savannah, as is the bridge over the lane in the rear, apparently an original feature of the building (though later expanded in size) that provided direct access to a separate warehouse to the south. When Sears took over the building in 1939, they updated the ground floor with black Vitrolite glass, which is evoked by the current material. In 1946, Belk department store acquired the building and c. 1960 reclad it and its older eastern neighbor with an elaborate windowless facade that differed from others on Broughton Street in having blind-arched windows, a large projecting arch over the main entrance, and a false mansard roof covering the top story. The 2007–2008 restoration conducted by RK Construction and Development removed this facade addition. The nearby commercial building (1898) at 301 W. Broughton Street similarly had a later facade removed, but the restoration (2002–2003, Lominack Kolman Smith Architects) re-created original cornices in a modernistic manner using aluminum.

3.3 **Weed Building**

1900; 2003 restoration. 201–203 W. Broughton St.

This compact commercial block, occupying a 60 × 90–foot building lot, flexes its architectural muscles with robust vertical piers defining the bays, white marble skewback blocks at the corners of the window arches that contrast with the red brick walls, and a playful cornice of segmental arches and stylized corbels that feels almost Postmodern in spirit. The central arch facing Broughton comprises individual white marble voussoirs, each block with a letter to spell out "Weed Building." For most of the twentieth century, Silver's, a five-and-dime subsidiary of McCrory Stores, occupied the building. The lane elevation retains most of its original iron shutters, and there is an old Savannah Grey brick tunnel/well in the basement.

3.4 **Gap (S. H. Kress and Company)**

1923, E. J. T. Hoffman; 1938 expansion, Edward F. Sibbert; 1947 and 1959 show windows replaced; 2000–2001 renovation, Dawson Wissmach Architects. 114–124 W. Broughton St.

One of the five-and-dime chains, S. H. Kress and Company established their first store in Savannah in 1913 in an existing building on this site (demolished 1922). Kress stores were recognized for their architectural character and their Savannah store is no exception, with its abstracted classical facades enlivened by inset panels of terra-cotta and limestone, as well as decorative brickwork. A 1938 expansion to the east, altering the adjoining Blumberg Building, seamlessly doubled the store's size (noticeable only by the central pair pilaster strips on the upper stories) and adding the metal canopy. McCrory Stores purchased the location in 1980, closing this Kress store in 1997. In 2001 the upper stories were converted to residential use.

3.5 Paris Market (Lyons Block)

1878, Miller B. Grant; 2004 restoration, Dawson Wissmach Architects. 36 W. Broughton St.

Originally spanning two building lots as a harmonious sixteen-bay ensemble, only the western half retains the elegant Italianate design, thanks in part to an award-winning restoration in 2004, which involved removing a modernist facade to reveal the original cast-iron cornice, window lintels and sills, and first-floor columns (the last along Whitaker Street). Fronting Broughton Street, the missing columns were re-creating in wood. Only the building name plaque and the vestiges of quoining on number 26 hint at the former larger row. Across the street, the 2002–2003 restoration of 5–15 W. Broughton (1868) revealed this exuberant group of commercial buildings and necessitated reconstruction of the tall gable and flanking Baroque parapet.

3.6 Levy Jewelers (Lerner Shops)

1947, William P. Bergen; 2012 renovation, Hansen Architects. 2 E. Broughton St.

Designed for the New York–based Lerner Shops apparel store chain, this International Style building (incorporating the east

party wall of the previous building on the site) illustrates post-war retail philosophy with an all-glass ground floor to display merchandise, sheltering cantilevered canopy, and windowless upper stories to maximize display space. Variously spaced horizontal channels and (originally) the store name in large cursive script enlivened the large white stucco expanse. This Lerner Shops location closed in 1989. Restored by J. T. Turner Construction, the building now serves as the flagship store for venerable local retailer Levy Jewelers, established in 1900.

3.7 Globe Shoe Company

1929, Levy and Clarke; 1950s 2nd-floor facade altered.
17 E. Broughton St.

This is Savannah's Art Deco jewel, reflecting the exuberant stylishness of 1920s commercial architecture. Locally based Globe

Shoe Company (established 1892) is the city's oldest retailer continuously operating on Broughton Street and the principal occupant of this store throughout its history. The design employs an eclectic range of Art Deco motifs that include Cubist angling of the display windows, Native American sunburst motifs on the entrance ceiling and along the top of the second story, stylized floral motifs in etched windows flanking the doors, and abstract classical pilasters framing the entire facade. The angled display-window glass originally rose into the second floor to form a square arch that framed a mural above the surviving ceiling of stylized people against a backdrop of angled spotlights; this was replaced by the modernist opaque glass and Streamline Moderne aluminum lettering on the second floor. Much of the original interior decor remains intact, including on the second floor, which originally also served as retail space.

3.8 The Marshall House

1850; 1857 iron portico; 1880 expanded; 1998–1999 restored, Hansen Architects. 123 E. Broughton St.

Savannah businesswoman Mary Marshall opened this hotel in 1851. A rare survivor among nineteenth-century hotels, the Marshall House (later the Geiger Hotel and the Gilbert Hotel) occupies conventional Georgian brick town houses with the ground floor framed by granite piers. The hotel expanded in 1880, absorbing the neighboring Florida Hotel. Closed in 1956 due to noncompliance with state fire codes, the building subsequently accommodated a wide variety of businesses. Shopfront modernization removed the two-story cast-iron verandah and covered the whole facade with blank stucco. The restoration of the building to its original appearance and function in 1998–1999 included the reconstruction of the verandah.

3.9 Broughton Municipal Building (First Federal Savings and Loan Association Bank)

1960–1961, Levy and Kiley. 132 E. Broughton St.

Built on the site of the former Odeon Theatre, this six-story bank, with its abstract interplay of polished gray granite walls, white concrete projecting frames, first-floor canopy, and blue, gray, and white tile piers, brought a daring modern accent to Broughton Street. Originally the building had movable vertical louvers within the large concrete frames that shaded the upper

stories, an early use of green design through passive solar control, but these were later removed. Acquired in 1991 by the City of Savannah to house municipal services (and ensure the building's survival), the two-story banking hall with a surrounding mezzanine and basement vault (visible inside the front window) remains little changed. Levy and Kiley also designed the Woolworth's store (1954; 127–133 E. Broughton Street) across the street, showing a simpler, more conventional International Style modernism. Although the original canopy has been removed, the corner entrance retains the store's name in the terrazzo pavement. These buildings, along with the remodeling of Levy's Department Store at 201 E. Broughton (**3.11**), represent a distinctive ensemble of modernist commercial architecture all by the same firm.

3.10 Trustees Theater, SCAD (Weis Theater)

1946, Tucker and Howell; 1989–1998 restoration; 2013 renovation. 216 E. Broughton St.

This is one of several theaters built by the Weis family of Savannah. The mid-block location and positioning of the auditorium parallel to Broughton Street behind a row of storefronts reflect the dexterous situating of theaters within commercial blocks. The sculptural neon-lit marquee (containing three-quarters of a mile of cathode tubing) and sign are typical of Art Moderne, and the streamlined rounded wall returns and the recessed lighting reflect the later phase of Art Deco. The small lobby spaces belie the large auditorium, which seats more than 1,100.

This was the first theater in Savannah designed with modern air-conditioning, considered an engineering marvel for the time, as was the state-of-the-art sound and projection equipment. The theater closed in 1980, was purchased by SCAD in 1989, and reopened in 1998. In 2013, the college installed new seats and modified some interior details; the historic seats found new life in the Savannah Theater (**6.14**) and the Tybee Post Theater (**15.6.3**).

3.11 Jen Library, SCAD (Levy's Department Store)

1925; 1953–1954 expanded and remodeled, Levy and Kiley; 1996–1999 remodeled. 201 E. Broughton St.

In 1925 local retailer Levy's Department Store constructed a traditional brick building on the western two-fifths of this site. The pioneering department store ownership group, Allied Stores, acquired Levy's in 1947 and in 1953 embarked on a dramatic remodeling of the existing building and a reinforced-concrete expansion on the rest of the block (with the two structural systems visible through ceiling grills). Levy and Kiley's design reflects 1950s modernism, with the cantilevered canopy, projecting blade sign, and predominantly blank windowless upper stories that took advantage of artificial lighting and air-conditioning inside. Opening in 1954, the new store featured a "motorstair," possibly the city's first escalator. Levy's operated here until it was merged in 1985 with Maas Brothers (also owned by Allied), which operated the store under the latter name until 1987, when it closed. SCAD acquired the building in 1996 and after extensive interior renovations and minor exterior modifications (mainly covering the original green tiles at the corners and adding the metal shades) opened it in 1999 as its main library, renamed in honor of college supporters Lancy and Jim Jen.

East Side Expansion Wards and Trustees' Garden

In 1791 the newly formed municipal government began expanding Savannah's colonial town plan by adding two new wards—Warren and Washington—to the east of the northernmost row of wards, following the pattern established by Oglethorpe in 1733. A second expansion occurred in 1799, adding Columbia and Greene wards. Constrained by the size of the East Common and the establishment of a one-hundred-foot-wide broad street (c. 1770) at its edge, these four easternmost wards are necessarily narrower in their east–west dimension, with tythings comprising four rather than five lots across and smaller squares, yet all streets maintain the widths of streets in the original town wards. Consequently, these wards and their squares are more intimate in scale than the original six. Because of their more peripheral location and because they escaped the devastating fire of 1796, some of the city's oldest buildings are found in these wards. They also have a greater percentage of wood-frame structures and are more residential in character than the more central wards. These neighborhoods saw extensive and enthusiastic renovation and preservation efforts in the 1960s, leading to some rather imaginative results and several

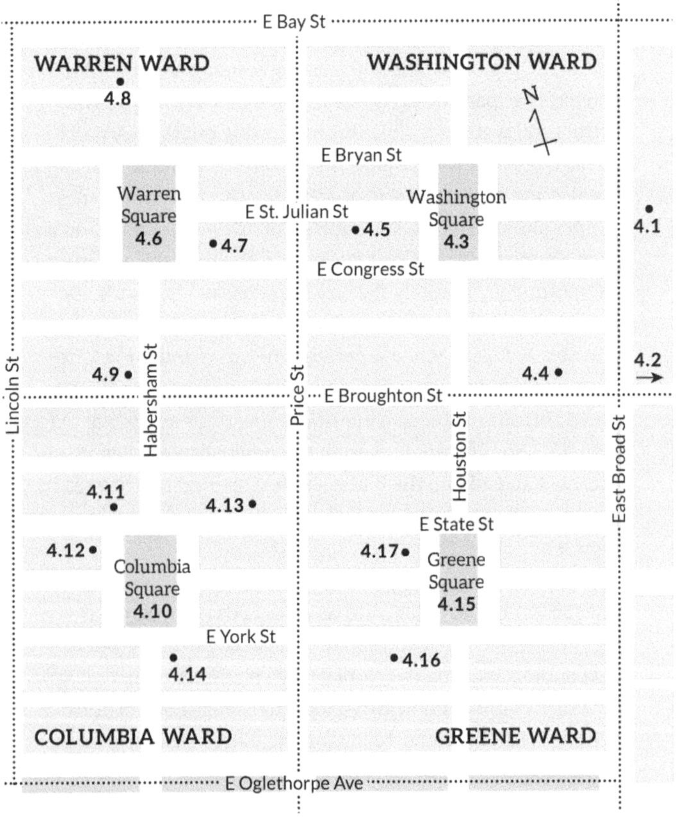

cases of buildings being moved here from other locations in the historic district.

TRUSTEES' GARDEN

The ten-acre garden created by the Georgia Trustees for "Incouraging and Improving Botany and Agriculture" was described by Francis Moore in 1735 as "cleared and brought into such Order that there is already a fine Nursery of Oranges, Olives, white Mulberries, Figs, Peaches and many curious Herbs. Within the Garden there is an artificial Hill, said by the Indians to be raised over the Body of one of their ancient Emperors." Marvelous and promising from its inception, the Trustees' Garden was, nevertheless, a failed experiment, the victim of unanticipated temperature fluctuations, poor soil, mismanagement, and a change in priorities. Governor John Reynolds acquired the property for his own use in 1755. A fort was constructed at the edge of the bluff by the British during the Revolutionary War, and was rebuilt by American forces in 1812–1814. A residential neighborhood eventually developed here, off the grid of the ward plan, nostalgically called the "Old Fort" area.

In 1852 the Savannah Gas Light Company purchased the fort, building a variety of structures for coal-gas generation and storage on it over the course of many years, including furnaces, coal sheds, gasometers, offices, and shops. By the 1940s there were six large gas storage vats and the neighborhood around it was described by newspaper journalist John Chamberlain in 1964 as "some of the worst slums on the Eastern seaboard." With the decommissioning of the gas tanks in 1953, Mary Hillyer, wife of the gas company president Hansell Hillyer, led a campaign to preserve and revitalize the dilapidated structures of this neighborhood, adding lacy ironwork porches to several buildings in an attempt to recall the early history of the site and the utopian origins of the garden. Several nineteenth-century brick structures remain as the complex is being developed by Charles H. Morris as an arts center. The renovated, one-story brick building at 12 Hillyer Place (1881, William Farmer), now called Charles H. Morris Center at Trustees' Garden (2011 renovation, Dawson Architects), is restrained but inventive in its employment of corbeled cornice details and a pilastered facade framing segmental-arched hoods over casement windows with fanlights (now replaced). The original iron rod Pratt trusses remain exposed inside, and its gutted interior now serves as a multipurpose event space.

4.1 Pirate's House Restaurant (House)

1794–1808; after 1871 second story; later additions.
20 East Broad St.

The Pirate's House was so named to celebrate the purported use of the building in the colonial era as a tavern frequented by sailors and pirates. Inside, marked for all to see, are the entrances to two tunnels about which many tales have been told. Regardless of the legitimacy of these claims, in its current use as a themed restaurant the Pirate's House has played a prominent role in the revitalization of the Trustees' Garden and in the development of the tourist industry in Savannah since the 1930s. Various dates have been suggested for the original structure, which has been added to and modified many times. Adjoining the Pirate's House is the so-called Herb House (26 East Broad Street), claimed by some to be the oldest surviving structure in Savannah, but which likely dates to around 1853.

4.2 Kehoe Iron Works

1873–1883, with later additions; 2013–2015 machine shop and smithy renovation, Lominack Kolman Smith Architects.
656 E. Broughton St.

What began as the Phoenix Iron Works took its more familiar name when William Kehoe bought out his partner in 1883. Kehoe extended the main building on Broughton Street eastward, adding to the brick foundry and constructing a three-story entrance pavilion with a mansard roof and cupola and a two-story pattern shop. Several other buildings once occupied the factory campus of less than one acre. The only other extant structures, however, are the smithy and the basilica-shaped machine shop that abut the east end of the brick pattern shop. The impressive machine shop (before 1916) is a 165-foot-long, steel-framed structure clad with galvanized corrugated iron sheets and a long monitor roof. The Kehoe works relocated to a shipyard site during World War II.

WASHINGTON WARD

Washington Ward and its square honor George Washington, who came to Savannah in 1791 on his "Southern Tour." During the nineteenth century, the ward had a working-class demographic with a large Irish population. The northeast tything lots were occupied by workshops, warehouses, and light industry in the later nineteenth century. Today, some commercial buildings occupy the northern half of the ward, which is mostly residential.

4.3 Washington Square

1790–1791; 1963–1964 relandscaped, Clermont Lee

Typical of the eastern expansion wards, Washington Square is roughly half the size of the squares planned by Oglethorpe, due to limitations imposed by the size of the eastern common. The threat of fire led to the establishment of the Savannah Fire Company with twenty firemen in 1825 and construction of twelve wooden underground cisterns, each holding at least eight hundred gallons, here and within the other squares in 1830. In the latter part of the nineteenth century the square was sometimes known as "Firehouse Square," because a small, brick firehouse occupied its south end from 1847 until 1875. During the early twentieth century it hosted a playground and other recreational activities.

4.4 Norris Hall, SCAD (Abrahams Home)

1856–1858, John S. Norris; c. 1900 addition; 1989, 2002, 2014 renovations. 548 E. Broughton St.

Upon her death in 1853, Dorothea Abrahams left most of a considerable estate for the establishment of a home for indigent or widowed ladies. Under the direction of George Wymberley

Jones De Renne (see **18.1**) and Joseph Connerat, Norris was selected to design the building on two tything lots facing Broughton Street. Construction began on the three-story, 90 × 40–foot building in 1856 and was complete by 1858. It was described in a local newspaper as having "32 chambers, each with a fireplace and closet." Four bays were added to the west c. 1900. The building was acquired by SCAD in 1989.

4.5 Hampton Lillibridge House

1796–1799, Hampton Lillibridge, builder; 1963 moved; 1981 rear addition. 507 E. St. Julian St.

In March 1796, planter Lillibridge from Newport, Rhode Island, purchased tything lot 15 of Warren Ward. There he built two wood-frame, gambrel-roofed houses, which are unusual in Savannah. This house, the larger of the two, was moved from 310 E. Bryan Street to its present location in 1963 and heavily restored. The other was demolished.

WARREN WARD

Warren Ward and its square are named for General Joseph Warren, president of the Massachusetts Provincial Congress, who was killed in the Battle of Bunker Hill in 1775.

4.6 Warren Square

1790–1791; 1962 relandscaped

Warren Square follows the pattern of the eastern expansion wards in being roughly half the size of the squares of the original town. Perhaps inspired by the precedent of the two-level parking deck erected on Ellis Square (**2.39**) in 1955, a trilevel, concrete parking garage was erected over the two western trust lots of Warren Ward.

4.7 John David Mongin House

1797; 1964 moved; 1964 restored, John C. LeBey.
24 Habersham St.

John David Mongin was a wealthy Sea Island cotton planter at Haig Point plantation on Daufuskie Island who made several investments after moving to Savannah. Mongin purchased the empty half trust lot directly across from the present site in August 1797 and built this two-and-a-half-story, five-bay, central-passage clapboard house. Mills B. Lane Jr., who carried on the leadership of C&S Bank established by his father, had the Mongin House moved across the square when plans were made to build the parking garage. The landscape construction plan, which included the rear yard and surrounding sidewalks, was designed by local landscape architect Clermont Lee in 1966 and revised in 1967. The new basement is lower than the previous one and the porch is not original. On the trust lot to the north, the smaller Spencer-Woodbridge House (c. 1795; c. 1830, c. 1960 additions; 22 Habersham Street) is similar in appearance, remains on its original site, and has a rare, though likely modern, side garden.

4.8 Paul Hamilton Wilkins House

1791–1794. 7 Habersham St.

Wilkins was a carpenter-builder who purchased this property in the initial city auction for lots in Warren Ward in January 1791 and sold the property with "improvements" (namely the house) to Henry C. Jones in December 1794, a typical pattern of real estate development in the early days of the republic. It is a restrained five-bay, clapboard house resting on a tall one-story raised basement, unusual both for its early date and use of brick and ballast stone (similar to the warehouses at 202–206 W. Bay St. [**1.12**]), no doubt benefiting from its proximity to the port. The round-arched fanlight over the door reflects the simple elegance of the Federal style. The elaborate central dormer is a modern modification.

4.9 John Berrien House

c. 1810; 1917 altered; 2013–2015 restored, Cowart Group Architects. 322–324 E. Broughton St.

Revolutionary War hero Major John Berrien built this house, bequeathing it to his son, John McPherson Berrien, who served in the U.S. Senate and also as attorney general under President Andrew Jackson. The three-and-a-half-story wood-frame house is sometimes dated as early as 1791, but the physical evidence of its quirked moldings and early use of cut nails point to a later date. Prominent architectural features include a side-gabled roof, six dormer windows, beaded wooden clapboard, and Greek Revival detailing dating to the 1850s. The cornice ornament is especially fine. Set on Savannah's main commercial street, the house was raised on a high foundation in 1917 to allow for retail space on the ground level. The current restoration undertaken by direct family descendant Andrew Berrien Jones and carried out by J. T. Turner Construction lowered the house back to its pre-1917 elevation. The Kennedy Pharmacy (1890) across the street at 323 E. Broughton was restored (2007–2009) to its nineteenth-century appearance and retains the vestiges of painted advertisements on its east facade.

COLUMBIA WARD

The patriotic theme in the naming of squares and wards continued in the three wards of 1799: Liberty, Columbia, and Greene. The personification of the United States as Columbia had gained currency with the newly established state capital of South Carolina in 1786 and the naming of the District of Columbia in 1791. This ward was the location of one of six town gates built into the palisaded wall erected during the French and Indian Wars to the designs of William G. De Brahm in 1757.

4.10 Columbia Square

1799; 1970–1971 relandscaped, Sam Monk

In the colonial era a town gate stood on this site, at the edge of the East Common, and from 1877 until 1946 a streetcar line passed through the square in line with Habersham Street. In 1970–1971 it was renovated with financing from an Urban Beautification Grant through the federal urban renewal program, with the design by Monk, the director of Savannah's Park and Tree Department. Under the patronage of Eudora and Wainwright Roebling, the Art Nouveau fountain sitting incongruously in a brick pool in the square's center was moved in 1971 from the gardens of Wormsloe Plantation (**18.1**); it honors the memory of Augusta and Wymberley Wormsloe De Renne (son of George Wymberley Jones De Renne).

4.11 Isaiah Davenport House

1821, Isaiah Davenport; 1956 restoration, John C. LeBey; 1975 garden, Cy Paumier, landscape architect. 324 E. State St.

Built by and for a successful carpenter-builder from Rhode Island, this is among the city's most celebrated buildings both for its design and its role in preservation history. Sitting on the

innermost tything lot (closest to Habersham Street) and facing the square, the three-story red brick Federal-style house features a wide, arched front door surround, one full story above the street, accessed by a curved double stair. Paired tall brick chimneys bracket the standing-seam metal roof, which is punctuated by prominent dormer windows. The central-hall plan features an arched columnar screen framing an elegant oval stair, as well as exquisite craftsmanship showcasing Davenport's talents as a builder. In 1955 a group of seven women saved the building from demolition, founding at the same time the Historic Savannah Foundation (HSF). Following an initial restoration, which eliminated features added during its longtime use as a boarding house, the Davenport House was opened to the public in 1963; it also served as the HSF headquarters for many years. An early-twentieth-century brick two-story apartment building that filled most of the rear yard was demolished in 1973. Although the original house had no formal garden, the Trustees' Garden Club commissioned the side and rear garden, designed in 1975 by Paumier of Land Design/Research in the manner of antebellum gardens of coastal Georgia. The plantings were modified in 1998 by British landscape designer Penelope Hobhouse. Across the square at 321 E. York Street is the current HSF headquarters, which occupies the former Abraham Sheftall House (1818; 2000 restored), a building that was aggrandized with the addition of a full-height raised basement and accompanying covered high stoop after being moved from its humbler original location facing Jefferson Street in Elbert Ward in 1968 when that neighborhood was being razed to make way for the construction of the Civic Center (**5.14**).

4.12 Kehoe House Bed-and-Breakfast (William Kehoe House)

1892, DeWitt Bruyn; 1990–1992 renovation, Kolman and Smith, Architects. 123 Habersham St.

A fulsome statement of Gilded Age grandeur, the Kehoe House showcases the work and aspirations of its owner, an Irish immigrant whose ironworks had become one of the city's most productive industries. The house is a romantic assemblage of architectural forms, motifs, and elements, including a projecting two-story polygonal bay to the right of the central entrance and a two-story corner cylindrical turret to the left, and a grand double gallery on the south facade abutting another multistory polygonal bay. A majority of the ornamental features are, of course, cast iron, though there is also a considerable amount of terra-cotta. Originally, a cupola capped the house. Before establishing his solo practice, Bruyn had worked for John S. Norris and Calvin Fay. Substantial modifications were made in converting the residence from a funeral home into its current use as a bed-and-breakfast, including the addition of an elevator shaft to the rear. The project, completed in 1992, was the first to receive the state historic preservation tax credit in Georgia.

4.13 Timothy Bonticou Double House

c. 1815; 1971 moved. 418–420 E. State St.

At one and one half stories and originally facing the lane behind its present location, this double house illustrates both the density and modesty of worker housing along Savannah's lanes, characteristics often erased with subsequent development. Having five plastered rooms in each unit, three of which were heated, and a double-pile plan featuring front rooms with wood-paneled wainscoting, speaks to the notable pretensions of this particular example. Moved in 1971 from 419–421 E. Broughton Lane to the site of the previous formal house on the front of the lot, this building attests to the interests of preservationists to showcase characteristic Savannah architecture even if in an uncharacteristic location.

4.14 Frederick Ball House

c. 1809–1815, Frederick Ball; 1989–1990 restoration, Jones and Herrin Architecture with Cowart Design Group Architects. 136 Habersham St.

Frederick Ball was a builder of classicizing taste from Newark, New Jersey, who named his five children Tuscan, Doric, Corinthian, Ionic, and Annulet. Ball was able to build three narrow houses on this 60 × 90–foot tything lot, including the neighboring houses at 138 and 140 Habersham, which defy local convention by facing the side of the lot (on Habersham) rather than the square. The side-hall, double-pile house with its four-bay facade is efficiently heated by an interior chimney centered between the two rooms (unusual in Savannah), while an abundance of windows provides cross-ventilation for summer cooling. Built for Ball's own family, the house showcased his preferences for classical style, particularly on the interior, where elaborate composition mantels feature scenes from Greek mythology. Their mixed themes of liberty, peace, and bounty suggest a date following the War of 1812. The 1990 exterior and interior restoration, commissioned by Mills B. Lane IV (son of Mills B. Lane Jr.), involved removing later additions and reconstructing the portico; the houses at 138 and 140 were also restored as part of the project.

GREENE WARD

Named for Revolutionary War hero Nathanael Greene, who is also commemorated by the monument (**2.2**) in Johnson Square, Greene Ward was platted in 1799 and was home to a significant population of free African Americans during the antebellum period. It is filled with small wooden houses that recall the scale and materials that characterized all of Savannah in the colonial era.

4.15 Greene Square

1799; 1967–1968 relandscaped, Clermont Lee

The small size of Greene Square reflects the constricted space afforded by the East Common for expansion of the town. Small flower gardens, including raised brick planting beds, anchor the corners of the modestly landscaped square. The sidewalks employ concrete with oyster shell aggregate, evoking the tabby commonly used in the eighteenth and early nineteenth centuries in Savannah.

4.16 Susannah R. Clarke House

1801–1808. 517 E. York St.

About thirty feet wide, the Clarke House is an asymmetrical, one-story, central-hall cottage with a loft lit by a single dormer. The roof, originally wooden shingles, is now covered with standing-seam metal. On the adjoining lot to the east, the Edward White House (1812) is similar but smaller. Smaller yet, the John Dorsett House across the square (1845; 536 E. State

Street) was moved to its present site from Crawford Ward and of the three houses most closely approximates the size, and even the intense color, of the colony's earliest houses, such as those appearing in the famous Gordon View print of 1734 (see page 6).

4.17 Second African Baptist Church

1926; 1999 restoration, Gunn Meyerhoff Shay Architects. 123 Houston St.

The congregation of Second African Baptist church has met at this location since its founding in 1802. The original wood church building was raised a full story in 1889, following the trend of Savannah's churches set on trust lots to have elevated sanctuaries with multipurpose spaces below. The present plain brick structure was built when the wooden superstructure burned in 1926. William Tecumseh Sherman read Field

Order No. 15, offering freed slaves forty acres, in the original building, and Martin Luther King Jr. gave his "I Have a Dream" sermon here in 1963 (as he did elsewhere) prior to the March on Washington later that year. The restoration of 1999 included the installation of an elevator in the foyer.

West Side Expansion and Oglethorpe Wards

The western wards are the most fragmented in the historic district in terms of their architectural and urban integrity. The only "lost squares" of the twenty-four-ward Savannah plan were located here. This section of the city has been shaped by significant changes in land use, transportation, and industry, and diverse communities of people, including some of the city's wealthiest citizens, Native Americans, African Americans, Orthodox Jews, and Irish Catholics have left their mark on this area over the past three centuries. Fractured though they appear, the western wards of the historic district are home to civic, governmental, and cultural institutions that play vital roles

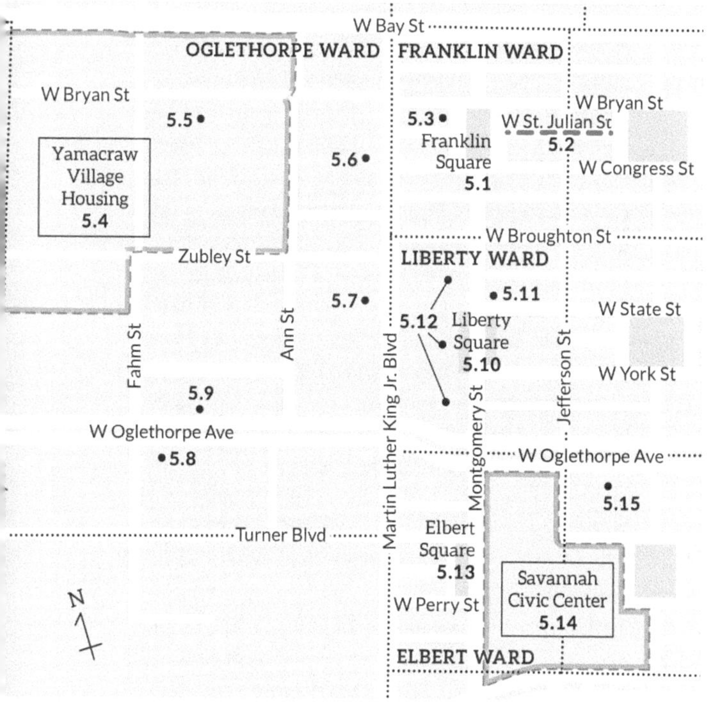

in Savannah, and among their empty lots, generic retail structures, and residual green spaces are some architectural gems and historically rich sites.

FRANKLIN WARD

The laying out of Franklin Ward in 1791, concurrent with Washington and Warren wards on the eastern side of the original six-ward plan of the city, ratified the Savannah plan ward established by Oglethorpe as the incremental unit by which the city would grow until 1854. Franklin, like the east expansion wards, is narrower than the standard colonial ward due to the limited space within the West Common. Its tything blocks had only four rather than five 60 × 90–foot house lots across, reducing the east–west dimension of the ward by 120 feet. Like the other 1790s expansion wards, its name commemorates a hero of American independence: Benjamin Franklin, who had numerous ties with the Georgia colony and died in April 1790, just a month before the city council initiated plans to lay out new wards.

5.1 Franklin Square

1790–1791; 1935–1937 partially destroyed; 1985 restored, Gunn Meyerhoff Shay Architects

In keeping with the squares in the eastern expansion wards, Franklin Square is roughly half the size of those within Oglethorpe's original six wards. From 1853 to the early twentieth century it was marked by an 87-foot-tall brick and iron water tower. Franklin, Liberty, and Elbert squares were largely obliterated by the transformation of Montgomery Street into U.S. 17 between 1935 and 1937, but Franklin Square—a gathering place for day laborers for decades, both before and after its destruction—was restored in 1985. In 2007 a monument to Haitian Volunteers (James Mastin, sculptor) who fought in the Battle of Savannah in 1779 was erected in the center of the square.

5.2 St. Julian Street Pedestrian Mall and City Market

1985, Gunn Meyerhoff Shay Architects. St. Julian St., between Franklin and Ellis sqs.

In conjunction with the reclamation of Franklin Square, the City closed a two-block section of St. Julian Street to automobile traffic in 1985 and, in a successful attempt to lure shoppers to return to the downtown, leased the street to a retail management company that calls the outdoor mall "City Market"—invoking the spirit of the lamented market structure in nearby Ellis Square, which was demolished in 1954. The commercial buildings lining this mall date from the 1840s to the early twentieth century. Unlike many conversions of main streets to pedestrian-only spaces in the 1970s, City Market has been highly effective in attracting both locals and tourists to its shops, outdoor cafes, and informal performance spaces.

5.3 First African Baptist Church

1855–1859; 1888 additions; 1995 steeple, Gunn Meyerhoff Shay Architects. 23 Montgomery St.

First African Baptist claims to be the nation's oldest African American Baptist congregation (originally called First Colored Baptist), dating its founding to 1773 under the Reverend George Leile. The congregation's first building was erected on the site of the current First Bryan Baptist Church (**5.5**) in 1794. Following extraordinary church growth, a doctrinal split sent more than 2,000 congregants looking for another facility in 1832. In that year they purchased a building on the present site from the white Baptist church, which had recently relocated to its present site on Chippewa Square. Incorporating the 1832 pipe organ from the congregation's previous home, the current church was built in 1859 by members of the congregation, many of whom were enslaved laborers who earned time off from their plantation duties to work here. Following another revival in 1888, the building was expanded by 28 feet to the west, and a pulpit, baptismal pool, and stained glass windows were added, as was a multistage, 125-foot wooden steeple (which was destroyed just five years later in a hurricane). The building, a simple box (35 feet tall) with a gable roof, is made of Savannah Grey brick, which remained exposed until covered with stucco in the mid-twentieth century. The sanctuary is raised on a half basement and is entered via two doors flanking the central tower. Below the basement level is a 4-foot-high crawl space that is said to have been used to hide escaping slaves as part of the Underground Railroad. Holes drilled into the floorboards in geometric patterns—described in church literature as a Congolese Cosmogram—provided ventilation for the crawl space. The ministerial platform in the main auditorium is framed by a kind of chancel arch flanked by paired Corinthian columns, and a wraparound gallery is supported by iron columns with gilded capitals.

OGLETHORPE WARD

Oglethorpe Ward was established by the newly formed state government in 1787 as the city's seventh ward. It is ironic that this ward—an anomaly within Oglethorpe's urban and regional plan—should carry his name. This area west of the original town common was never divided into garden lots, but instead seems to have been part of what was set aside as "Indian Lands." In 1760 lots of varying sizes in the area adjoining the West Common, then referred to as "Yamacraw" (a name the area retains), began to be granted to prominent merchants and planters. Most important were those of John Joachim Zubly and William Ewen, whose names are commemorated in the later designation of portions of this area as the hamlets of St. Gall (Zubly's birthplace in Switzerland) and Ewensburg. Streets were laid out by the end of the eighteenth century. In 1856 Oglethorpe Ward was divided into three sections (North, Middle, and South), each subdivided by numerous narrow streets, almost all of which have disappeared. Over the course of the nineteenth century, the area gained a reputation for squalor. Flanked by industrial sites, the neighborhood attracted Russian, Norwegian, and Irish immigrant workers and free African Americans. More than two thousand small and predominantly one-story freestanding and attached wooden houses, similar to those that survive on the east side of downtown in the Beach Institute area (see **9.5**, **9.6**), filled the neighborhoods between the river and Turner Boulevard (the northern edge of the Central of Georgia complex), along with several industrial buildings catering to the railroad. Various redevelopments have destroyed all of these houses.

5.4 **Yamacraw Village Housing**

1938–1941, Cletus W. Bergen, Morton H. Levy, William B. Clarke, Walter P. Marshall, and John C. LeBey. Bounded by W. Bay, Ann, Zubley, and York sts., and the Ogeechee Canal

A year after the Housing Authority of Savannah was formed in 1938, work began on a "slum clearance and low-rent housing project," with the U.S. Housing Authority administrator Nathan Straus presiding. Built exclusively for African Americans, four hundred and eighty subsidized rental units form widely spaced parallel rows of two-story, multifamily housing blocks. These blocks feature porches, pediment-shaped roof vents, and a rather abstract form of quoining, all suggestive of high- style, traditional architecture. Hot water was originally supplied by solar collectors on the roof of each unit, which functioned until 1968. The architecture and urban layout seem to be a cross between Congrès Internationaux d'Architecture Moderne (CIAM)–inspired Zeilenbauen (linear blocks) and historic Savannah row house design, set in a green parklike setting with pedestrian paths replacing the former streets. The community house (Yamacraw Administration Building), completed in 1941 at 349 W. Bryan Street, is a replica of the nearby celebrated Hermitage plantation house that had been demolished just six years earlier. The recollection that the "big-house" at the Hermitage was once flanked by rows of slave quarters is eerily invoked by the community house's axial alignment onto a grassy mall flanked by housing blocks. Contrary to perceptions of public housing today, Yamacraw (one of first housing projects in the country to use cement blocks) and other subsidized housing projects in Savannah were celebrated modern additions to the city and promoted as tourist destinations.

5.5 First Bryan Baptist Church

1873–1893, John B. Hogg. 575 W. Bryan St.

Andrew Bryan purchased this lot in 1793, making it, according to the church's account, the nation's oldest property continuously owned by African Americans. This location served as the First African Baptist Church until 1832 when doctrinal differences prompted a large group of members to form a new church at the current site of First African Baptist (**5.3**), leaving a smaller congregation at the Bryan Street location. The present building was designed by architect and city engineer Hogg and built by members of the congregation. The distyle in antis portico is similar to Hogg's 1848–1850 design for Trinity Methodist Church (**2.37**). The choir loft and organ, purchased from the Independent Presbyterian Church, were added in 1945.

5.6 Ships of the Sea Museum (William Scarbrough House)

1818–1819, William Jay; 1972–1978 restoration; 1975–1977 landscape gardens, Clermont Lee; 1980 gate reconstruction; 1994–1997 renovation and rear alteration, John Deering for Hansen Architects; 2012 north garden, Daniel E. Snyder Architect. 41 Martin Luther King Jr. Blvd.

With its austere Doric portico protruding from a massive but simple cubic block, this is the boldest of Jay's surviving Savannah houses. The abstract classical design confidently uses dramatic lighting effects, inset arched windows, and elliptical interior walls. Particularly striking is the adjoining carriage gate, a triumphal arch flanked by pairs of squat, archaic Doric columns with exaggerated entasis. The side porch on the south features cast-iron columns and a balustrade, while a cast-iron anthemion-like cresting runs across the rear cornice.

Scarbrough was president of the Savannah Steam Ship Company when he built the house and hosted President James

Monroe here in 1819 (on the occasion of the launching of the SS *Savannah*, the first steamship to cross the Atlantic), but he lost everything to bankruptcy in 1820. The grand house was then used as an orphanage, and became a school for African Americans from 1878 to 1962. It has undergone significant modification and restoration, including the 1836–1837 addition and subsequent removal of a third story as part of the extensive 1970s restoration carried out under the direction of the Historic Savannah Foundation, which was headquartered here from 1976 to 1990. Further renovations in 1995, under the ownership of Mills B. Lane IV's Beehive Foundation, added a new roof and a rear main entrance, transforming the building into a maritime museum. The adjacent 1.25-acre north garden is its most recent addition.

5.7 **The Grey (Atlantic Greyhound Bus Depot)**

1937–1938, George D. Brown; 2015 restoration, Parts and Labor Design with Felder and Associates. 109 Martin Luther King Jr. Blvd.

With a blue-and-white Vitrolite and Vitrolux facade, as well a curved, stainless steel–clad, cantilevered canopy above a curved glass window, and a neon sign, this former Greyhound Station is exemplary of the bus company's exuberant proto-streamlined designs and the work of one of its leading designers in the 1930s. Significantly smaller than today's buses, coaches would enter through the opening on the right, pull into one of three loading bays, and exit through the rear. The front room originally served as a restaurant. The recent restoration, carried out by Bloomquist Construction, included replicating the lost and damaged Vitrolite facade and vertical blade sign.

5.8 Thunderbird Inn

1964, John Knox Stacy; 2004–2005 restoration, Ramsay Sherrill Architects. 611 W. Oglethorpe Ave.

Noteworthy for its eye-catching neon sign, the Thunderbird Inn was one of several motels built in the region in the 1960s by Stanley Fulghum. Its strategic location on Oglethorpe Avenue, just outside of the historic district, conveniently served automobile tourists traveling across the first Talmadge Bridge (completed 1954; see **1.14**) on U.S. 17 to or from South Carolina. The two-story, concrete-block structure follows a simple, L-shaped plan with forty-two guest rooms connected by covered walkways opening onto an asphalt parking lot. Yellow, teal, and red panels below the windows of each room and the boldly cantilevered canopy above the office entrance enliven the design.

5.9 **Joe Murray Rivers, Jr. Intermodal Transit Center (Greyhound Bus Station)**

1965, Greer, Holmquist, and Chambers; 2013 restoration and expansion, Cogdell and Mendrala Architects, with Wendel Duchscherer Architects and Engineers. 610 W. Oglethorpe Ave.

Recently renovated and expanded to serve as the Chatham Area Transit Authority headquarters, the center's dynamic steel canopies evoke the spirit of mid-twentieth-century Googie architecture. The original building has a sturdy concrete frame filled with brick walls and roofed with precast, prestressed concrete T-beams. More exuberant is the Gray Line Tour pavilion (built in 1963 as the state's second Georgia Welcome Center, attributed to Eugene Maxwell) to the west at 215 W. Boundary Street, where clusters of opposing concrete half arches support billowing thin-shell concrete vaults.

LIBERTY WARD

Liberty Ward was laid out in 1799, simultaneously with Columbia and Greene wards and squares. The name refers to the Sons of Liberty, a Revolutionary group which had an active chapter in Savannah.

5.10 **Liberty Square**

1799; 1935–1937 partially destroyed

Like the other squares of the 1790s, Liberty was roughly half the size of the Olgethorpe-era squares. The straightening of Montgomery Street as U.S. 17 in 1935 obliterated most of the square (together with Elbert and Franklin), leaving only a patch of green space in front of the Chatham County Courthouse (see **5.12**) and another in front of the city parking garage across the street.

5.11 **Student Center, SCAD (B'nai B'rith Jacob Synagogue)**
1907–1909, Hyman W. Witcover; 2002–2006 rear addition and renovation. 112 Montgomery St.

Congregation B'nai B'rith was founded in 1861 to serve the needs of Eastern European Jews worshipping in the Ashkenazic tradition. After meeting for five years in the Georgia Hussars' armory hall on Wright Square, the congregation built a wooden synagogue on the present site, which was replaced in the early twentieth century by the current red brick, Moorish Revival synagogue, characterized by the prominent use of horseshoe arches. A new, modernist synagogue, B'nai B'rith Jacob, was built in 1963 about three miles to the south on Abercorn Street, a move that depopulated the historic district's Orthodox Jewish community. The vacated building on the present site then served as a church before it became the Student Center of the Savannah College of Art and Design in 2006.

5.12 **Chatham County Courthouse, Parking Garage, and Jail**
1978, Helfrich and Grantham. 133 and 145 Montgomery St.

These three concrete buildings sit in a minimally landscaped superblock covering the entire western half of Liberty Ward, obliterating blocklong segments of three streets and two lanes. The project provided much-needed courthouse and office space, as well as increased parking and a detention center to accommodate the rapidly growing prisoner population, the result of the decade's rising crime rate and an increased pattern of incarceration for minor offenses. Together, they constitute a late expression of "blank-slate" urban renewal, which cleared the site of all previous structures and made scant efforts to respect the historic surroundings. The six-story courthouse employs horizontal strip windows and Brutalist cladding of rough-surfaced precast concrete panels with unusual vertical scoring.

ELBERT WARD

When Elbert Ward was laid out in 1801, it initiated the first expansion of the Savannah plan in a southward direction. The ward was named after Samuel Elbert, a Savannah-born Revolutionary War hero and governor of Georgia. By the early twentieth century Elbert Ward was home to orphanages, boarding houses, a Salvation Army hotel, and warehouses, replaced by automobile-related service buildings after Montgomery Street became U.S. 17 in the 1930s.

5.13 Elbert Square

1801; 1935–1937 partially destroyed

Following the model of the expansion ward squares to its north, Elbert Square was roughly half the size of the squares created by Oglethorpe. A decorative mound (one of at least four erected in the city's squares in 1872) stood here until at least 1897. A paltry strip of grass, azaleas, and some trees are all that remains on this site, victim of the 1935 straightening of Montgomery Street to accommodate U.S. 17, which also destroyed Liberty and Franklin squares.

5.14 Savannah Civic Center

1968–1971, Nowell and Ritzert. 301 W. Oglethorpe Ave.

Funded by a public bond and federal urban renewal program, the Civic Center answered the city's need for urban revitalization and large-scale event space. Tied to the construction of an overpass, which allowed I-16 direct access to the historic district, the project followed the national pattern of urban renewal. Work began in 1968 with the clearing of approximately seven-and-a-half acres, half of Elbert Ward, along with the southwest tything and western trust lots of Jackson Ward, and

necessitated the demolition of Municipal Auditorium (1911–1916, Henrik Wallin), which faced Orleans Square. The Civic Center comprises two principal parts—the Martin Luther King Jr. Arena and the Johnny Mercer Theatre. These spaces are connected by a tall lobby aligned with McDonough Street, which it blocks. Although its size is formidable, attempts were made to make the building appear compatible with the traditional language of the city's architecture. Its monumental arcade clearly evokes the New Formalism popular during the 1960s, typified by the 1962–1968 ensemble of buildings at Lincoln Center in New York City. The concrete-frame structure is clad in modern Savannah Grey brick and embellished with a colossal blind arcade surrounding the arena and an arcaded porch wrapping the theater. The entire building is enveloped by a margin of green space, with a formal garden on the north side and an asphalt parking lot of nearly two and a half acres to the east. The axis of the former McDonough Street is marked by an allée of magnolias on a swath of grass leading to the east entrance of the lobby. Although much criticized for disrupting the scale and refinement of Savannah's urban and architectural fabric, the Civic Center has played a vital role as a venue for public events.

5.15 Oglethorpe House, SCAD (Downtowner Motor Inn)

1964; 1990, 1996, 2002 renovations. 201 W. Oglethorpe Ave.

Although located just east of Elbert Ward, the Downtowner Motor Inn preceded the large urban renewal projects to its west in bringing an automobile-oriented modernity to Savannah's historic district. Founded in Memphis in 1958, the Downtowner Corporation was a small national chain that sought to bridge the gap between suburban and urban motels by creating mid-rise, hovering, concrete-frame blocks surrounded by parking lots. Apart from a pair of internal elevators, the external staircases and balcony corridors, which are enlivened with traditional ornate ironwork, dramatize a sense of movement. When it opened the building was described as having "204 ultramodern rooms or suites designed to give the utmost comfort and luxury." It was converted into a SCAD dormitory in 1990.

Between the Boulevards

Majestic allées of live oaks run along the parklike median strips of Oglethorpe Avenue and Liberty Street. Bracketed between these boulevards, a third row of wards developed between 1801 and 1847 that introduced subtle and not-so-subtle modifications to the ward plan formula conceived by Oglethorpe. Oglethorpe Avenue, originally called South Broad Street, first appears on a 1796 map as the southern border of the original six-ward town. At the intersection of Bull Street and Oglethorpe Avenue, a sarcophagus-shaped granite monument (1983) marks the original Jewish burying ground established here in 1733. The cemetery was officially closed by the colonial council in 1770, but it was also protected against displacement. The city reaffirmed protection of this site in 1790 as expansion of the town plan was being contemplated. It is possible, therefore, to explain the great width of the avenue and the presence of its median strip (originally planted with chinaberry trees) as an accommodation for this sacred ground.

Oglethorpe Avenue and Liberty Street (the latter named in 1801) are, at 140 and 130 feet respectively, the widest streets in the downtown historic district. It seems clear that both were conceived as multilane boulevards with central allées for public promenading, a fact sadly documented in an ordinance of 1827, which stated that "no negro or mulatto [shall] appear on the Public promenade on South Broad Street." Liberty Street, which was never quite as elegant as Oglethorpe Avenue and provided a connection between the city's two primary railroad depots, was bordered by a military barracks and factories, some stately houses, and, in the twentieth century, apartment buildings and hotels. A streetcar line ran down its length beginning in 1881. Both Oglethorpe Avenue and Liberty Street were significantly realigned in the 1980s between Montgomery Street and Martin Luther King Jr. Boulevard in order to facilitate the flow of automobile traffic. These realignments further degraded the integrity of the Savannah plan in its western neighborhoods. The Distillery (1902, Kentucky Distilling Co.) at 416 W. Liberty Street offers a vivid reminder of the realignment as the sole surviving building on the former edge of the street, facing an anomalous spur north of the rerouted street.

JACKSON WARD

The names of Jackson Ward and Orleans Square reveal the date of their development in June 1815, roughly five months following Andrew Jackson's victory in the Battle of New Orleans (although several surveyor maps show that Jackson, Brown, and Crawford wards were being planned before the War of 1812). A grand house built in 1820 for Archibald Bulloch to the designs of William Jay occupied the southwest trust lot until it was replaced by the Municipal Auditorium in 1916. Most of the western half of the ward, along with its streets, was replaced by a vast surface parking lot as part of the Civic Center (**5.14**) urban renewal scheme in 1968–1971.

6.1 Orleans Square

1815

Commemorating the Battle of New Orleans in the War of 1812, Orleans Square reflects the dramatic changes that have occurred in the western area of downtown Savannah. Matthew Lufburrow constructed the city's first brick cistern here in 1833, with a capacity of 12,000 gallons of water, to replace the small 800-gallon wooden cisterns built just three years earlier. From 1877 until 1946 streetcar tracks crossed the middle of the square

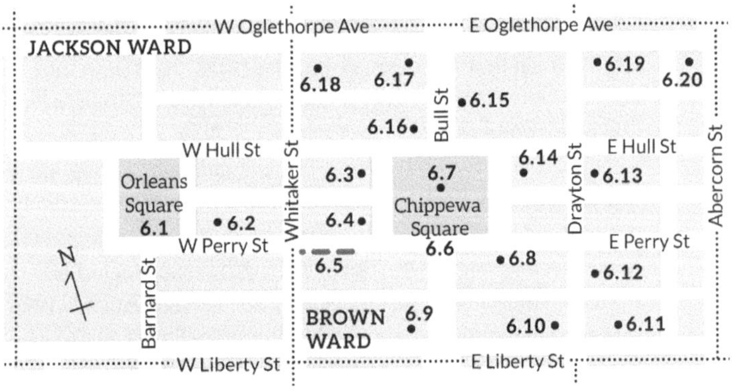

in line with Barnard Street. The walls of the Civic Center's large parking lot now line two sides of the square, and the fountain in its center was added in 1989 to commemorate Savannah's early German immigrants.

6.2 **Harper Fowlkes House (Aaron Champion House)**
1842–1845, Charles B. Cluskey and Henry McAlpin; 1895 additions; 1995 restoration, Gunn Meyerhoff Shay Architects.
230 Barnard St.

This inventive, central-hall house is a magnificent example of a trust-lot mansion. It was erected for Aaron Champion, a banker from Massachusetts, by Hermitage Plantation owner Henry McAlpin, whose son married Champion's daughter and thus inherited the house. The design, commonly attributed to Cluskey, features a colossal Greek Revival portico with four Tower of the Winds columns standing in antis between channeled corner piers. Set back behind an elegant iron fence, the house rests on a partially raised basement and is accessed by a double curved stair. Classicizing details abound in the interior, which features an oval oculus between the first- and second-floor hallways, aligned with a rectangular opening and monitor above to facilitate convection ventilation. First-floor rooms were lit by grand gasoliers made by Cornelius and Company in Philadelphia. The 1895 modifications added a third floor, built into a mansard roof, and relocated the main stair to the rear where the double gallery was filled and fronted by an exuberantly swooping iron and copper canopy. The Society of the Cincinnati took possession of the house in 1988 and commissioned the 1995 restoration, carried out by Sterling Builders and Restoration, which uncovered the magnificent faux bois (false wood) paintings on the walls and ceiling of the dining room. The carriage house at the back of the lot is a reconstruction by the Spriggs Group (1999–2002), placed atop the original building's foundations, and the modern garden was designed by John F. McEllen.

BROWN WARD

Brown Ward has more blocks than the typical Savannah ward, extending to the edge of Colonial Park Cemetery (**6.21**) on Abercorn Street. The "excess" blocks were added in 1853, whereas the core of the ward was laid out in 1815. Brown Ward and Chippewa Square memorialize the 1813 victory of American troops under the command of Major General Jacob Brown in the War of 1812 battle near Niagara Falls, Ontario.

6.3 First Baptist Church

1831–1833, Elias Carter; 1839 enlarged; 1921–1922 remodeled, Henrik Wallin; 1966 and 2010 restored. 223 Bull St.

Soon after it was chartered in 1800, the Savannah Baptist Society built its first meetinghouse on Franklin Square, on the site now occupied by First African Baptist Church (**5.3**). The present church, designed as a Doric in antis structure with a square cupola, was similar to Carter's Central Congregational Church in his hometown of Worcester, Massachusetts, which he was designing at the same time. (Both are also reminiscent of plate 57 in *An Improved and Enlarged Edition of Biddle's Young Carpenter's Assistant* [1833].) In 1921–1922 the steeple and interior gallery were removed, the former portico was transformed into a narthex, the hexastyle unfluted Corinthian portico (with Tower of the Winds capitals) was added, and the entire exterior reclad in limestone. Both the 1966 and 2010 restoration campaigns involved installing steel beams in the roof structure; the latter, by J. T. Turner Construction, also revealed that the interior originally had decorative stenciling along the upper walls.

6.4 Eastman-Hull-Stoddard-Barrow House (Moses Eastman House)

1844–1847, Charles B. Cluskey; 1911 additions, Henrik Wallin. 17 W. McDonough St.

The Eastman House cogently responds to the urban plan of Savannah. Its original stout single-story Doric front portico faces the wide expanse of McDonough Street (diverging from trust-lot convention of facing the square), while its eastern facade is more monumental with a semicircular, colossal Ionic portico dramatically addressing Chippewa Square. The semicircular portico was originally one story high, but was rebuilt in 1911 along with other changes by Wallin, including a third-story addition. Moses Eastman, a Savannah silversmith, sold the house to merchant and planter John Stoddard before it was completed in 1847. The iron fence featuring medallions with busts of statesmen and poets on the outside of the sidewalk dates to 1857 and was salvaged from the Wetter House after its demolition in 1950.

6.5 Stoddard Row Houses

1854–1855. 19–25 W. Perry St.

Restrained and precise, these four three-story Greek Revival row houses reveal their interior spatial hierarchy by the progressively lower heights of the windows as they rise up the facade. Shallow iron balconies extending from the first floor windows add a delicate accent to these otherwise austere buildings. The houses rest on a partial basement of channeled masonry, which is accessed by an external stair in the manner of English or New York City row houses, a rare configuration in Savannah. Stone stairways, set perpendicular to the house, lead to the principal floor of each dwelling, where the entrance is capped by pedimented lintels set against the scored masonry facades.

The distinctive, front-gabled, asymmetrical Italianate house next door at 15 W. Perry is thought to have been built by William Hunter for General Alexander Robert Lawton in 1867. It is raised to the same height as the adjoining row houses and features a similar front stairway, channeled masonry basement, and first-floor iron balconies. Cast-iron hoods cover the wide, segmental-arched windows. The facade of number 19 was renovated in 1978 and a cast-iron balcony added to number 25 in 1987.

6.6 Chippewa Square

1815

The dimensions of Chippewa Square are the same as those of Johnson Square—one hundred and twenty feet wider than the other central squares—which results in smaller trust lots. Prior to the addition of the Oglethorpe Monument, a fountain (erected 1871) occupied the center of the square, flanked to the north and south by portrait bust monuments commemorating Savannah's Civil War heroes, Major General Lafayette McLaws and Brigadier General [Colonel] Francis S. Bartow (1901–1902, G. J. Zolnay, sculptor), which were relocated to Forsyth Park (**10.1**) in 1909 when the fountain moved to Thomas Square.

6.7 Oglethorpe Monument

1909–1910, Daniel Chester French and Henry Bacon. Chippewa Square

The Oglethorpe Monument Association was chartered in 1901, initiated by a private coalition of patriotic societies but later supported by the City. Dedicated in 1910 and constructed by the Dixie Stone Company, this monument was an early collaboration of these two designers. French's statue is a nine-foot bronze representation of the colonial founder dressed in the uniform of a British general. A speech made at the dedication described the statue's "defiant and fighting look toward the south," in the direction of his Spanish enemies. In addition to the pedestal, Bacon designed the hardscape plan of the square, including the gryphon-footed limestone benches.

6.8 Bryson Hall (T. A. Bryson Automobile Garage)

1904. 5 E. Perry St.

Thomas Archer Bryson commissioned this substantial Romanesque Revival–influenced brick structure in 1904 as a Packard Motor Car Company showroom and parking garage, and it remains the oldest such showroom in the South. As is evident from surviving curbstones that curve towards the entrance, automobiles were driven into the three-story unheated garage through the central ground-floor arch. The garage had a concrete floor and a capacity of seventy-five cars, and lettering of the surviving original copper signage reflects the influence of Art Nouveau. The building is currently used as an event space, but retains parking in the basement, accessed from the lane via a ramp.

6.9 **Henry Brigham House**

1879, Francis Grimball; 1987 south facade restoration. 4 W. Liberty St.

Brigham came to Savannah in 1835 from Southborough, Massachusetts, making a name for himself in commerce and banking. This Second Empire house by local builder Grimball replaced his previous residence on the same site. A newspaper account describes it as having thirteen bedrooms and two baths and costing $16,000, a considerable amount at the time. The five-bay facade is noteworthy for its perpendicular stair facing Liberty Street, but its side porch also makes a grand gesture toward the corner of Bull Street.

6.10 **De Renne Apartments**

1920, Henrik Wallin. 20–30 E. Liberty St.

Financed by Wymberley Wormsloe De Renne (son of George Wymberley Jones De Renne), this eight-story, forty-four-unit building secured a place for modern apartment living in Savannah. Its U-shaped courtyard plan follows a building type popular in many American cities of the pre–World War II era. The steel-frame building supports thin, precast concrete slabs cantilevered over the sidewalk, providing each unit with a balcony. An inventive decorative tile frieze with a colorful lattice pattern is topped with acroteria. Unfortunately, Savannah's economy turned sour soon after completion of the De Renne, bankrupting its owner.

6.11 **Drayton Tower (Drayton Arms Apartments)**

1949–1951, Cletus W. Bergen and William P. Bergen Architects; 2005–2007 renovation and restoration, Greenline Architecture; 2013 renovation, Hansen Architects. 102 E. Liberty St.

The contrast in formal typology, composition, and scale between the Drayton Arms Apartments and the majority of Savannah's buildings seems as startling today as it did when the former was new. This FHA-backed experiment in modern living featured an early expression of postwar International Style design with green-tinted Solex glass arranged in alternating bands of limestone veneer hanging onto a concrete frame, and Pittsburgh Plate Glass Company (PPG) used Drayton Arms in their 1951 national advertising campaign promoting the product. The ground floor, notable for its angled concrete and glass end walls, acts a base for the slightly smaller apartment block, whose horizontal bands seem to float above. The reinforced concrete cantilevered canopy is a tour de force of engineering. The building was allegedly designed as a thesis project by Georgia Tech student William P. Bergen, who actually created it with his father, a leading architect in Savannah in the mid-twentieth century. It was the first air-conditioned apartment building in Georgia. Recent renovation efforts have returned the building close to its original condition, but as market-rate housing.

6.12 Commercial Building (George Summerell Texaco Service Station)

1936. 236 Drayton St.

This relatively well-preserved example of a 1930s full-service station was built by Texaco for George Summerell, who managed it for forty-six years. It is a stripped classical design with two service bays, a car-wash bay, and an integrated canopy. Subtle Art Deco details, such as the stepped tops on the piers, further refine the design. Unlike the two other remaining service stations (both built earlier) on Drayton Street, this one steps back from the street line to provide more space for cars to maneuver.

6.13 Parker's Market Urban Gourmet (Blum Dimmit Company Autos)

1912; 1920 renovation, Arthur F. Comer; 1998–2000 renovation, Hansen Architects. 222 Drayton St.

Initially a livery occupied this site. It was modified or replaced in 1912 by an automobile sales and service facility. The building took its present form in 1920, proving adaptable to changing times while remaining true to its original use (the only historic gas station in downtown still serving that purpose). Comer was a Savannah architect, formerly in partnership with Henrik Wallin; the recent renovation was carried out by Renaissance Restorations.

6.14 Savannah Theater

1818, William Jay; c. 1890 facade altered; 1906 rebuilt; 1948–1950 rebuilt, Helfrich and Grantham; 2001 and later renovated. 222 Bull St.

Purporting to be America's oldest continually operating theater (a claim also made by the Walnut Street Theater in Philadel-

phia), this building was designed by Jay as a large, three-story box occupying the entire trust lot. It was largely rebuilt after it burned in 1906 and again in 1948, though portions of the north and east walls of the 1818 building survive (covered on the exterior by stucco). The exuberant Art Moderne marquee, terrazzo pavement evoking wave patterns, and cylindrical glass ticket office attest that the rebuilt theater was emulating a "modern look" to compete with the recently opened Weis Theater (**3.10**) on Broughton Street, while an exterior stair, designed to admit African Americans, speaks to the backcast legacy of racial segregation. Historic seats from the SCAD Trustees Theater (**3.10**) were salvaged and installed here in 2013.

6.15 Chatham County Board of Education (Chatham Academy)

1901, 1908, Henry Urban. 208 Bull St.

The northeast tything of Brown Ward was never subdivided into house lots, but was instead set aside for the use of the Chatham Academy, a charity school dating back to 1788, when the site was still part of the common. The first academy was built here in 1813 (prior to the sale of lots in Brown Ward), together with the Pavilion Hotel on land granted them by the Union Society. Following the destruction of the old building by fire in 1899, the current Beaux-Arts classical structure was built in two parts. The grammar school was constructed in 1901, its bold triumphal arch entrance addressing Oglethorpe Avenue. The 1908 temple-fronted high school, facing Bull Street on axis with Oglethorpe Lane, is even grander in its decoration, with a carved stone pediment representing allegories of education.

6.16 Independent Presbyterian Church Sunday School Building

1894, Charles Henry. 207 Bull St.

This is the third Sunday School building to sit on this innermost tything lot nearest Bull Street. The first was an 1833 one-story temple-like structure and the second a Victorian Gothic school built in 1884, but destroyed in the same fire that burned the adjoining church just five years later. Identified in a pamphlet as an Akron plan, this simple but classical structure is similar but deferential to the church across the lane. The two chamfered corner entrances, each with single colossal Doric columns, subtly engage both the church and Chippewa Square. Between them an overscaled pediment with a dramatic radial sunburst pattern crowns the building.

6.17 Independent Presbyterian Church

1817–1819, John Holden Greene; 1891 rebuilt, William G. Preston. 25 W. Oglethorpe Ave.

Chartered by George II in 1756, the independent Presbyterians—identified as "dissenters" and "professors of the doctrines of the Church of Scotland"—built their first meeting-house on Ellis Square soon after. A new meetinghouse on Telfair Square was completed around 1800. Less than two decades later, however, following rapid growth of the congregation, they acquired five contiguous lots within the northwestern tything of Brown Ward to build the present church. This building closely follows the design of Greene's own First Congregational Church in Providence, Rhode Island, completed in 1816; apart from the portico and interior dimensions, the two are remarkably similar. When this church was destroyed by fire in 1889, the session voted to rebuild it exactly as it had been. The reconstructed church differs from the original in having granite columns rather than brick, as well as a taller and more slender steeple, made possible by using steel and iron rather than wood above the masonry base. The steeple is 227 feet high, the tallest structure in the downtown. Among the most monumental buildings in the city, the church's capacious interior is remarkable for its suspended wooden dome, mahogany pulpit, and exquisitely crafted classical details—though it lacks any representational art or symbolism, consistent with Puritan and Reformed traditions. The wide central aisle accommodates tables and benches used for the celebration of the Lord's Supper. The massive split-case design of a new organ (the fifth in the church), built by Rieger-Kloss of the Czech Republic and installed in 2005, required the construction of a centrally placed choir loft.

6.18 Axson Memorial Building

1928, Cram and Ferguson; 2015–2016 modifications, Sottile and Sottile. 25 W. Oglethorpe Lane

The demolition of the John S. Norris–designed Italianate manse on this site was not without controversy, especially because its parlor had hosted the wedding of Ellen Axson (granddaughter of the former minister of the Independent Presbyterian Church [**6.17**]) and Woodrow Wilson in 1888. (A replica of this room was included inside the new building.) Although plans by the New York firm of Ludlow and Peabody were already underway, famed Boston architect Ralph Adams Cram offered an alternative design. Cram's building ties directly into the church, forming an enclosed garden on the northern side, and his restrained English classicism defers to the church in its materials, ornament, and scale. Modifications currently underway will transform the auditorium into a multipurpose space with direct access to the garden courtyard via a new door and stairway, which will also lead to the fellowship hall in the basement level.

Out-of-Town Designers in Savannah

Savannah's buildings speak in a distinctive local dialect, but one colored by the blending of multiple foreign accents. Lacking a program in architectural education until the Savannah College of Art and Design (SCAD) established one in 1985, the rapidly growing port city naturally attracted the talents of out-of-town architects. Nationally and even internationally known architects, builders, and artists, including John Holden Greene, William Strickland, Henry Van Brunt, Alexander Doyle, Henry Bacon, Daniel Chester French, Ralph Adams Cram, John Nolen, Pietro Belluschi, and Moshe Safdie have worked here. More significant, however, are the designers who left a lasting mark by relocating their practices to Savannah or by accepting multiple commissions in the city. In each case they brought with them their own traditions, styles, and even materials, but adapted them to local forms and practices. Moving from his native Rhode Island in 1809, master builder Isaiah Davenport, for example, established a benchmark for craftsmanship and typology in Savannah. Englishman William Jay, one of the earliest professionally trained architects to arrive in the United States, designed at least six of the city's most innovative and influential buildings in his brief three-year career here starting in 1818. Working with Jay was New Jersey builder Amos Scudder, who spent nine years in Savannah. Irish architect Charles B. Cluskey greatly amplified the city's Greek Revival accent through numerous buildings in the 1830s. Buffalo-born architect Calvin Fay came to the city to work on St. John's Episcopal Church (**8.6**), but stayed to develop a flourishing practice in partnership with New York native Alfred S. Eichberg, one of Savannah's first Jewish architects.

The Whitaker Street Building across the lane (2010, Hansen Architects; 210 Whitaker Street) was built to serve as additional Sunday school space. Following the stylistic example of the other two supporting structures, it contributes to a multisite campus for the church.

Architectural drawing (1893) of the Savannah Volunteer Guards Armory

After John S. Norris, another New Yorker, came to Savannah to design the U.S. Custom House (**2.9**) in 1848, he worked on many of the city's most celebrated public and private buildings before returning North in 1860, fleeing the rumblings of war. Boston architect William G. Preston likewise left a vivid imprint on Savannah's architecture, designing at least five landmark buildings (including the Savannah Volunteer Guards Armory, now SCAD's Poetter Hall; **8.10**) between 1887 and 1894. One of the most prolific and influential architects of early-twentieth-century Savannah was South Carolina native Hyman W. Witcover, who trained under Eichberg and designed many public and private buildings. Working briefly for Witcover was Henrik Wallin, a Swedish architect trained in France and Italy, who came to Savannah from New York to work under Henry Bacon on the Oglethorpe Monument (**6.7**) in 1910, becoming one of Savannah's most accomplished classicists.

6.19 John Hunter Row Houses

1821–1822; later alterations; 2012–2014 renovation at number 101. 101–105 E. Oglethorpe Ave.

Savannah merchant Hunter commissioned this elegant pair of houses and lived in number 101 until his death in 1825. The

Federal houses are three stories atop partially excavated basements, which retain their original kitchens. The Ionic porticos of limestone fronted by perpendicular stairs and topped by a balustrade balcony are relatively unusual. The portico of number 105 seems to have been rebuilt, and the rear of number 101 was recently altered with a new carriage house added. The imported hard-pressed red bricks are laid in Flemish bond. Modifications over the years have produced differences in fenestration.

Next door, the row houses (1820–1822) at 107–109 E. Oglethorpe, which are named after their builders, Thomas Clark and Matthew Lufburrow, are also raised, but have a shared central perpendicular stair. Number 107 features an elegant Ionic door surround and fanlight, while number 109 has undergone numerous modifications, including gaining an extra story.

6.20 Savannah Fire Station No. 3

1937, Walter P. Marshall, with W. H. Armstrong, structural engineer. 121 E. Oglethorpe Ave.

This lot has been used for a fire station since 1855, when Central Station and Firemen's Hall was erected and subsequently expanded four times between 1884 and 1908. By the early twentieth century, it was renamed Station No. 3. The original building was replaced by this one with the assistance of the Works Progress Administration (WPA). Red brick piers capped with limestone crenellation rhythmically mark the square-grid module of this building, which is a blend of Romanesque Revival and Art Deco.

CRAWFORD WARD

This ward is named after William Harris Crawford (1772–1834), a U.S. senator, cabinet member under two presidents, and foreign diplomat. Laid out between 1841 and 1847, Crawford Ward is an anomaly in the historic district's systematic pattern of streets, blocks, and squares and, like Brown Ward, has more blocks than a conventional Savannah plan ward. In order to accommodate the anomalous Colonial Park Cemetery (**6.21**), it covers an area equivalent to two and a half times the typical Savannah ward, stretching from Abercorn Street to East Broad Street. With several vacant lots, strip mall–type retail development, and a few recent row houses, Crawford Ward seems less intact than most of the others, but historic maps suggest that it has always been more random in its urban texture than the central wards. It never seems to have attracted grand or high-style residences, and the maps record numerous vacant properties, many small residences (some called "shanties" by the 1880s), brothels (at least forty-two in this area by 1916), and industrial areas, including the entire southwest tything lot. The ward was fairly described as a ghetto by Lou Rivers, who grew up in this neighborhood, in his memoir *Remembering Crawford Square* (2005).

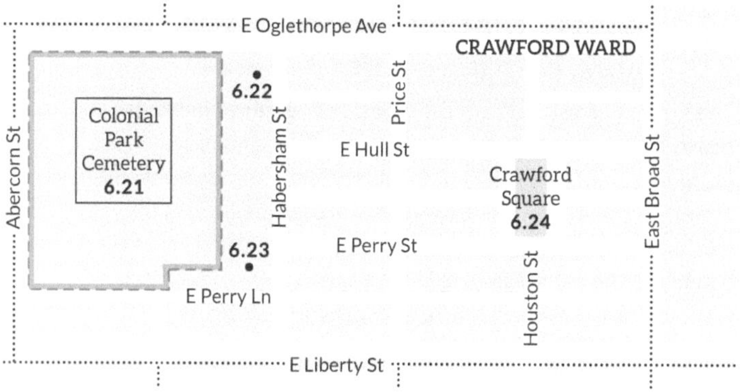

6.21 Colonial Park Cemetery

1750; 1768, 1789 expansions; 1897 relandscaped, P. J. Berckmans Company; 1967–1970 restored. 201 Abercorn St.

The Public Burial Ground, as it was referred to by the colonial town council, was officially the cemetery of Christ Church parish until 1789, when it became a city property for the use of all Protestant sects, with separate burial grounds established for Jews, African Americans, Catholics, and indigents. By the early nineteenth century Colonial Park Cemetery's 500 × 500-foot walled enclosure presented a significant impediment to the regularized development of new wards in the South Common. It may be that the 140-foot width of Oglethorpe Avenue was dictated by the northern edge of the cemetery. In 1853 the Old Cemetery (as it came to be called) was closed to new burials, and replaced by Laurel Grove Cemetery (**11.9**) on the southwestern edge of town. Several graves were moved to Bonaventure Cemetery (**17.1**) in 1873 with the hope of opening up this land to new development, but a scant number were relocated before opposition curtailed that plan. Initiatives to maintain and preserve Colonial Park Cemetery prompted the City to declare it a public park in 1896 and commission its relandscaping a year later. The Daughters of the American Revolution built the corner gate in 1915. The Trustees' Garden Club completed a comprehensive three-year restoration of the cemetery in the late 1960s and continues to supervise its maintenance to the present day.

6.22 Savannah-Chatham Metropolitan Police Department Headquarters (Police Barracks)

1869–1870, J. H. Boggs; 1936–1937 and 1949 additions, Cletus W. Bergen; 1965 new entrance, Ralph S. Thomas. 201 Habersham St. (formerly 323 E. Oglethorpe Ave.)

The Police Barracks, one of the oldest actively used police facilities in the country, occupies a residual strip of land between the eastern edge of Colonial Park Cemetery (**6.21**) and Habersham Street. Its tripartite, three-story Italianate facade echoes the rhythmic patterns of nearby row houses. The building was expanded to the rear beginning in 1936 and in 1965 a new entrance was built facing Habersham Street, with the historic front entrances filled in with brick.

6.23 Habersham Hall, SCAD (Chatham County Jail)

1887, McDonald Brothers and DeWitt Bruyn; 1898 alteration; 1984 roof demolition; 1989, 2007 renovations.
235 Habersham St.

Described as "large and costly" by celebrated Georgia historian Charles C. Jones Jr. in 1890, the old Chatham County Jail is noteworthy for its exuberant Moorish-influenced tower (106 feet high) which replaced the original octagonal Byzantine style tower (93 feet high) following a fire in 1898. The McDonald Brothers Jail Building Company of Louisville, Kentucky, constructed the brick and iron 117-cell jail with the assistance of local architect DeWitt Bruyn and contractor W. F. Bowe. The jail was closed in 1978 with the completion of the new Chatham County Jail on Montgomery Street and the building gradually became a largely ruined shell. The Savannah College of Art and Design acquired the old jail in 1989, restoring only the jailer's residence and tower.

6.24 Crawford Square

1841; 1981 relandscaped, Edward Pinckney/Associates; 2005 altered

Crawford Square is unique in several ways: its basketball court provides space for active recreation not found in the other squares, and it is the only one surrounded, at least in part, by a fence, a feature that originally typified most of the others. Pinckney's design included the gazebo and a playground (removed in 2005) set atop a sunken square area lowered to reveal the original brick cistern (dating from 1850). The reason for these anomalies may stem from its sociopolitical history as the only square accessible to African Americans during segregation. In 1946 the City sponsored a basketball tournament among four low-income neighborhoods, and Crawford Ward was granted the basketball court to mark its victory. Recent efforts to have it removed have been blocked by those for whom it remains a symbol of community pride.

Central of Georgia Railroad Complex and Savannah-Ogeechee Canal

The west side of Savannah was the terminus for several railroad lines as well as the Savannah-Ogeechee Canal. The city's main industrial quarter during the nineteenth and early twentieth centuries developed adjacent to these transportation facilities. The largest rail facility was the Central of Georgia, which in 1976 was designated and preserved as a National Historic Landmark district. The Central was founded in 1833 to link the port of Savannah with Georgia's interior, primarily to facilitate the export of cotton. Rail operations began in 1837 and the 190-mile main line to Macon was completed in 1843 (creating one of the longest rail lines in the world at the time). By 1851 the line had expanded to some 295 miles of track with a substantial increase in locomotive power and rolling stock. Such rapid growth made the original 1840s railroad depot, located on the site of the passenger terminal (**7.1.1**), inadequate and led to the creation of the present railroad complex. The nearby Savannah-Ogeechee Canal, though theoretically superseded by the railroad, proved

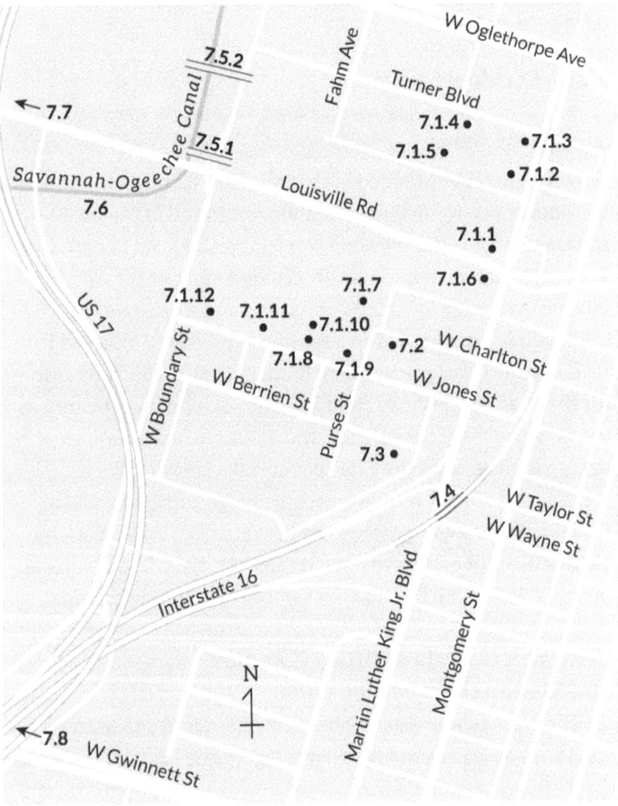

to be very successful and facilitated additional cargo shipments from the interior. The area would also support the development of early industrialized water works facilities for the city.

7.1 Central of Georgia Railroad, Savannah Shops and Terminal Facilities

1851–1855 and later

The Central of Georgia complex is not only noteworthy as one of the most complete historic railroad facilities worldwide, but is also significant for its integrated design, incorporating passenger, freight, and repair service as well as design and corporate offices into a single 33.2-acre site. Construction of the integrated facility began in 1851 under William Wadley, superintendent and self-taught engineer (and later president of the Central). Wadley had previously served as superintendent of public works on Cockspur Island during construction of Fort Pulaski (**15.4.2**) in the 1840s. Many of the Central's buildings and structures are attributed to Augustus Schwaab and Martin P. Muller, although their work can be verified in only a few cases.

The complex includes the Central's repair shops (1851–1946), which were capable of fabricating parts and making repairs, including construction of new rolling stock, passenger cars, and even several steam locomotives. The only operation not handled here was iron and steel casting, which was outsourced to Savannah's foundries. Most of the buildings and structures are contemporary with the integrated plan of the 1850s. The compact layout was designed for line shaft technology and steam locomotive maintenance. With the advent of electrification and the shift to diesel locomotion, the shops became outdated and were gradually eclipsed by larger, more modern facilities at the Central's Macon depot. The complex was acquired by the City of Savannah in 1989 and is now maintained by the Coastal Heritage Society as the Georgia State Railroad Museum.

Despite alterations and additions, and reuse of the buildings for new functions, the Central of Georgia complex is essentially unchanged from its mid-nineteenth-century form and remains largely accessible to visitors.

7.1.1 Savannah Visitors Center (Central of Georgia Passenger Depot)

1860–1876, Augustus Schwaab; 1901 addition; 1974 restoration and renovation, Gunn and Meyerhoff. 301 Martin Luther King Jr. Blvd.

The Central's passenger depot is one of the oldest surviving train stations in the nation. It is a head or terminal-type station, more common in Europe, which employs a high-style headhouse for passenger services that is connected to a train shed with platforms. The passenger depot headhouse was begun in 1860 but not completed until 1876 (due to the disruption of the Civil War). The classically inspired design, employing Savannah Grey brick, includes round-arched windows separated by pilasters and a Doric frieze with grilled vents separated by triglyphs. The main floor housed the ticket office and baggage room as well as separate waiting rooms and lavatories for white and black patrons. Offices were located on the second floor and the lower level housed a restaurant. The passenger train shed behind the depot, completed in 1861, displays impressive rows of brick arches on the exterior and now houses the Savannah History Museum. The shed is noteworthy for its long-span trussed roof, which is the earliest surviving U.S. example of a tricomposite truss, consisting of cast-iron, wrought-iron, and wood components. The cast-iron struts connect to the wrought-iron tension rods via spoked disks that resemble pulleys, visually tying the structure together (as is evident from across Louisville Road to the west as well). The passenger shed "umbrella" extension was added in 1901 to accommodate longer trains. The adjacent Visitors Center parking lot was originally the cotton freight yard; the crenellated cotton-yard gates facing Martin Luther King Jr. Boulevard were completed in 1856 and include guard rooms for sentries protecting the valuable freight. Along with the adjacent wrought-iron Wickersham fence ornamented with cast-iron cast-ons, the gates were part of a series of walls and fences that surrounded the entire thirty-three-acre complex.

7.1.2 Eichberg Hall, SCAD (Red Building, Central of Georgia Railroad)

1887, Fay and Eichberg; 1901, 1905 additions; 1988, 2003 renovations. 229 Martin Luther King Jr. Blvd.

The Red Building, now SCAD's Eichberg Hall (acquired in 1988), housed the Central of Georgia's engineering department. The eclectic design incorporates a blend of classical elements with a variety of materials, including the rusticated granite foundation beneath the smooth, pressed-brick facade with terra-cotta accents, and the inset columns. The building was lengthened by fifteen bays in 1901. The interior is mostly large open-framed studios suitable for large-scale drafting, with abundant lighting from the large windows that are crowned by squares of colored glass. A two-story fireproof vault was added to the north side in 1905 to preserve the plans and drawings created here. The exterior iron shutters can be seen from the SCAD courtyard.

7.1.3 Kiah Hall, SCAD (Gray Building, Central of Georgia Railroad)

c. 1851–1856; 1992, 1999, and 2002 renovations; 2013 restoration. 227 Martin Luther King Jr. Blvd.

The Gray Building with its columned portico supporting a classical pediment—now SCAD's Kiah Hall—was described as Roman Doric (unusual in lacking bases) when it was constructed as the Central's administrative headquarters. The completion date is recorded in the painted central coffer above the entrance. The heavily altered interior retains Italianate fireplaces that recall its original corporate opulence. J. T. Turner Construction oversaw the thorough restoration in 2013. Between the two buildings is a stairway descending to the SCAD Museum of Art. The landscaped courtyard beside the museum was originally the Dooley Freight Yard with rail spurs accessing the adjacent up-freight and down-freight warehouses.

7.1.4 SCAD Museum of Art (Up-Freight Warehouse, Central of Georgia Railroad)

1853; 2008–2011 adaptive rehabilitation, Sottile and Sottile, Lord Aeck Sargent, and Dawson Architects. 601 Turner Blvd.

The up-freight (export) warehouse, primarily constructed of Savannah Grey brick, provided through-storage for freight

transferred from the building's north side on Turner Boulevard (formerly New Street) to rolling stock in the freight yard. The warehouse was divided into sections by demising walls (visible between the museum galleries) that provided structural support, impeded the spread of fire, and allowed each section to be leased to separate shippers with their respective products. Vestiges of the different companies' painted advertising survive on the Turner Boulevard exterior wall. In 1988 SCAD acquired the building, which was already a partial ruin.

Significant donations of art to the college in the early 2000s prompted the creation of a new museum. Atlanta architects Lord Aeck Sargent, collaborating with local firms Sottile and Sottile and Dawson Architects, employed a modernist design principally using concrete and glass that consciously contrasted with the surviving brick fragments of the warehouse. All standing brick walls were retained and stabilized, while bricks from parts of the building that had collapsed were utilized for landscaping features. No historic bricks left the site and no new bricks were added. The museum's main entrance on Turner Boulevard is marked by an 86-foot steel and glass rectangular tower that signals the building's civic role and landmark ambitions. Former arched doorways to either side are framed by projecting glass display cases. An unpretentious staircase leads to second-floor classrooms above the galleries and a terrace overlooking the courtyard. A 250-seat theater, unusual for its broad and shallow proportions, fills the area west of the lobby.

Savannah Grey Brick

Part of the distinctive urban character of Savannah derives from the prevalence of a building material peculiar to the city—the so-called "Savannah Grey" brick (spelled "grey" likely because their manufacture began before the adoption of the more common American spelling "gray" in the 1820s). Historically made by hand, Savannah Grey bricks are larger, softer, and more porous than conventional hard-pressed bricks. The name refers to the color of the clay harvested from the Savannah River and adjacent areas prior to being fired, after which the bricks are typically a reddish brown. Prior to the Civil War, the majority of bricks were produced at the now-demolished Hermitage Plantation, located three miles northwest of the city (site of the International Paper mill today). Scottish-born Henry McAlpin, who acquired the plantation in 1815, built a brick manufacturing plant in 1819 to make use of the rich clay on the site. This plant was operated by as many as 227 slaves living on the plantation in 52 cottages built of Savannah Greys produced on the grounds. (Only two of these cottages survive, having been moved in the 1930s by Henry Ford to Greenfield Village in Michigan.) In the aftermath of the large urban fire in 1820 that devastated more than half of the city, increased demand for brick construction in Savannah prompted McAlpin to expand his operation to several kilns and an early horse-drawn railroad facilitating the movement of materials. The production of Savannah Greys continued after the Civil War, principally by the Savannah Brick Manufac-

---

7.1.5 Eichberg Hall Shed, SCAD (Down-Freight Warehouse, Central of Georgia Railroad)

1859; 1887 roof modified; 1988, 2003 renovated. Rear of Eichberg Hall (7.1.2)

The down-freight (import) warehouse, attached to the rear of the Red Building, was constructed in 1859 for handling produce. Its wide, overslung roof is an addition contemporary with the Red Building. Timber brackets supporting the roof have chamfer

Historic stereoscopic photograph of slave cottages on Hermitage Plantation

turing Company, followed by the Lovell Brick Company, the last manufacturer of Savannah Grey bricks (ending production in 1910), whose site is marked by Brickyard Street and Clay Street off Louisville Road. From the 1950s through the 1970s, downtown Savannah buildings were demolished in order to reclaim their highly valued Savannah Grey bricks, which were used for suburban houses. Reproduction Savannah Greys have been used in new downtown construction, such as the Hampton Inn on Bay Street.

---

cuts that eliminate their squared corners, an aesthetic detail that also served to retard the spread of fire since the corners would catch fire first. The two-story addition at the western end of the warehouse contained an office and equipment storage for track maintenance. Both warehouses originally had floors pitched in the direction that freight was transferred so that it always moved downhill. SCAD acquired the building in 1988 and it now serves as classrooms and studios.

7.1.6 Battlefield Memorial Park (Central of Georgia Railroad Freight Yard)

2005–2007, Coastal Heritage Society Design Group. Martin Luther King Jr. Blvd. at Old Louisville Rd.

Battlefield Memorial Park commemorates one of the bloodiest battles of the American Revolution, whose combatants reflected the international nature of the conflict. Here on October 9, 1779, a combined force of 5,500 American, French, and Haitian soldiers (as well as Swedish, Polish, and German troops), advanced on the British at Spring Hill Redoubt in a failed attempt to recapture the city, resulting in some 800 American and allied casualties (commemorated by squares of Georgia granite) compared to roughly 100 for the British. The site was later used by the Central as a freight yard for lumber, resin, and turpentine. The nearby repair shops were reached by a branch from the main line that crossed Louisville Road over an iron bridge (demolished in 1974) near the bottom of the hill. The (British) Spring Hill Redoubt was reconstructed by the Coastal Heritage Society in 2007 based on archaeological remains of the original structure identified by a marker to the west.

7.1.7 Engine House/Roundhouse (Central of Georgia Railroad)

1855; 1888–1889, 1926, 1946 alterations. 655 Louisville Rd.

The roundhouse with its central turntable enabled service and repair of multiple steam locomotives under one roof. The original 250-foot-diameter facility, constructed in 1855 of Savannah Grey brick, consisted of forty stalls around a small, 50-foot hand-operated turntable. The building was partly demolished and enlarged with reinforced concrete construction in 1926, destroying its circular form to accommodate larger locomotives in thirty-four stalls. Only a segment of the original building, comprising seven stalls, survives west of the turntable. This section of the old roundhouse was dedicated to repair operations and includes an operational electric drop table for removing wheel assemblies. The central turntable was enlarged several times, culminating with the current functioning 90-foot motorized table installed in 1946 (restored in 2004).

Unless an engine was shut down for major repairs, it was

necessary to keep steam locomotive boilers alive, which required continuous stoking and service, and the original roundhouse included water faucets in each stall for filling the tenders. In the expanded section, smoke hoods (or jacks) above each stall vented smoke from locomotives while the large, triple-hung sash windows provided light and ventilation, with additional ventilation from the monitor roof above. Each stall of the enlarged section was also provided with compressed air for pneumatic tools, acetylene for torches, and electrical outlets. The floors are surfaced with end-grain wood blocks treated with creosote which absorbed oil, providing a nonslip surface that yielded more readily to cast-iron tools when dropped. Pits beneath the tracks provided maintenance access to locomotives from below. All interior walls were originally painted white to enhance light levels.

7.1.8 Boiler Room (Powerhouse, Central of Georgia Railroad)

1854; 1907 interior alterations. Behind the Roundhouse (7.1.7)

The elaborate brickwork and crenellated parapet of this building heralded its importance in supplying power to the site. It was originally fitted with a single-cylinder, beam steam engine with ornamental Gothic tracery (according to an 1855 description) manufactured by the A. N. Miller Foundry in Savannah. The present single-cylinder, horizontal steam engine, manufactured by the Findley Iron Works in Macon, is authentic to the period but was installed in the 1990s. The boiler opposite the engine is also not the original. An interior wall once divided the engine room from the boiler room, while the space along the south side of the building was used to store wooden mold-making patterns for casting iron parts. The steam engine powered the line shaft system for the repair shop complex. The line shaft exited through openings visible at the tops of the east and west walls, and the entire system, which operated continuously, extended east through the blacksmith and machine shops and west through the carpentry shop to power machinery from the shafts via individual drive belts. The steam engine remained in service until 1907 when the line shaft was motorized and an electrical power plant was installed in the adjacent lumber storage shed to the west. The boiler continued to power the steam hammer in the blacksmith shop (**7.1.9**) and a compressor that supplied air to the shops and engine house. Machinery was gradually motorized with individual motors until the line shaft system was finally retired in 1923. A powered line shaft display with drive belts running the machinery is located in the blacksmith shop.

7.1.9 Blacksmith Shop (Central of Georgia Railroad)

1851. Behind the Roundhouse (7.1.7)

The blacksmith shop is a classic example of nineteenth-century industrial building type. The long, narrow structure makes efficient use of the line shaft along its long south wall, while its tight width permits ample lighting and ventilation through the large sash windows with splayed jambs along the walls. The wooden trussed roof allows for an open, flexible plan without internal supports, and its monitor roof provides additional lighting and ventilation. Openings for the line shaft are visible in each end wall and rectangular yellow patches of sulfur grouting reveal the locations of its bearing foundations. The shop housed seven forges along the walls that were naturally vented into the floor through a remarkable system of underground conduits to the smokestack; the foundation of one forge is still visible in the floor. Iron and steel heated in the forges were handled by jib cranes, one of which survives, and worked by a ten-ton steam hammer. The present operational example, which is not the original, was installed in 1996. Rough forgings from the blacksmith shop were finished in the machine shop (1855; 1878 rebuilt with additional story and modified roof; 1979 collapsed), now in ruins abutting the east wall. From there, the completed parts could be installed in the adjacent roundhouse (**7.1.7**).

7.1.10 Smokestack (Central of Georgia Railroad)

1855; 1992 restoration, David Philips. Behind the Roundhouse (7.1.7)

The 123-foot-tall smokestack is the most richly ornamented element of the repair complex, not surprising given its landmark prominence. The polygonal shaft of the stack with its flared mouth evokes the form of a fluted classical column. In addition to exhausting smoke from the site, it provided a natural draft for the powerhouse boiler and the forges of the blacksmith shop. Surrounding the stack is a 40,000-gallon cast-iron water tank decorated with Perpendicular Gothic tracery that was cast at the D. and W. Rose Foundry in Savannah. The tank supplied water to the powerhouse boiler and to each stall of the roundhouse, preheated to some extent by the hot exhaust of the central flue. The sixteen brick barrel vaults supporting the tank housed latrines that were also ventilated by the stack and emptied into a sewer line directly below. The partial demolition of the prominent top of the stack in the 1960s prompted locals to call for the site's preservation.

7.1.11 Savannah Children's Museum (Carpentry Shop, Central of Georgia Railroad)

1853; 1923 rebuilt; 2008–2012 renovated, Coastal Heritage Society Design Group. Beyond the Boiler Room (7.1.8)

The 1853 carpentry shop was destroyed by fire, rebuilt in 1923, and burned again in 1984. Today only brick walls and basement-level transverse vaults survive but they suggest that the line shaft system continued through this building at basement level to power machinery from below. The basement level now incorporates a playground as part of the Savannah Children's Museum, which opened in 2012.

7.1.12 Coach Shop and Paint Shop (Central of Georgia Railroad)

1907; 1924–1925 rebuilt; 2013 renovation begun. Next to the Children's Museum (7.1.11)

The largest surviving building in the complex, the new coach shop and paint shop were constructed at its southwest corner concurrent with the introduction of electricity. The paired buildings were farthest from the line shaft system, and thus required electrical power, employing an electrical transfer table to the north of the buildings (now largely hidden from view by lawns and trees) that moved rolling stock laterally on short sections of track for access into the shops. Both buildings were destroyed by fire in 1923 and rebuilt on the same foundations with updated fireproof technology, including automatic, self-closing fire doors and a sprinkler system. The coach shop, with some forty-five-thousand square feet per floor, comprises a reinforced concrete basement level that included testing laboratories, storage, and latrines, and a main floor with built-in tracks corresponding to the twelve bays accessed from the transfer table outside the building's north elevation. The sawtooth roof provided abundant natural lighting. Today both shops are under renovation for a second phase of the Savannah Children's Museum.

7.2 Houses

Before 1888. 535–537 W. Charlton St.

Beyond the repair shops, the areas east (Railroad Ward) and south comprised numerous blocks of modest housing—mostly single-story, clapboard cottages—used by railroad workers. Of the more than three hundred houses standing in the early twentieth century, only four examples survive, at Charlton and Purse streets. This pair remains on its original site and is privately owned. The two other worker cottages, at 539 W. Charlton (moved from across the street) and at 342 Purse Street, are preserved by the Coastal Heritage Society.

7.3 Frogtown Lofts

2008, Lominack Kolman Smith Architects. 545–555 Berrien St.

The area south of Jones Street to the present I-16 entrance ramp was known historically as Frogtown, so named from the sound of croaking frogs in the low-lying area. This housing development is part of a larger effort to revitalize the area west of Martin Luther King Jr. Boulevard. The design employs exposed concrete and glass in a starkly modern manner well suited to the industrial traditions of the area, but softened by sections of stained wood. The north side exemplifies a modern interpretation of Savannah elevated town houses with the characteristic raised stoops, while the east end reflects the architects' inspiration from the Dessau Bauhaus. The project sensitively incorporated and restored the 1940s modernist Central of Georgia Switching Station. To the southwest, behind Savannah Station, stand two small historic colonial Jewish cemeteries, each enclosed by a stone wall. The Sheftall Family Cemetery was established in 1773 by Levi Sheftall and the Jewish Burial Ground in 1773 by Mordecai Sheftall.

7.4 Interstate-16, Montgomery Street Exit Ramp

1963–1967. Spanning Martin Luther King Jr. Blvd. between W. Taylor and W. Wayne sts.

The construction of I-16 and its Montgomery Street exit ramp necessitated the destruction in 1963 of one of the city's landmarks, the Spanish Renaissance–style Savannah Union Station

(1902, Frank P. Milburn; see page 16), jointly operated by the Seaboard Air Line Railway, the Atlantic Coast Line Railroad, and the Southern Railroad, consolidating all passenger service except for the nearby Central of Georgia passenger depot (**7.1.1**). This diagonal tract of land, which sits in juxtaposition to Savannah's city grid, is a vestige of the diagonally oriented garden lots from Oglethope's original plan. The station was built at 601 Cohen Street alongside Union Station's train shed as the Southern Express Co. stables, with the long, low brick wall along the north side of Selma Street its only standing evidence. Since 1998, multiple studies and revitalization plans for Martin Luther King Jr. Boulevard have proposed removing the I-16 flyover.

7.5.1 Main Line Viaduct for the Central of Georgia Railroad

7.5.2 Dooley Yard Viaduct for the Central of Georgia Railroad

1853 and 1859, Augustus Schwaab. W. Boundary St., north of Louisville Rd.

The two Central of Georgia railroad viaducts that cross W. Boundary Street near Louisville Road were designed by Schwaab and constructed of Savannah Grey brick. The southern, Main Line Viaduct, with access to the passenger depot, cotton yard, and repair shops, was completed in 1853 and employs semielliptical arches. Small arched openings between the spandrels provide drainage in times of flooding. The northern, Dooley Yard Viaduct, accessing the up-freight and down-freight warehouses, was completed in 1861 and employs wider segmental arches. The westernmost arch of both viaducts spans the

Savannah-Ogeechee Canal. The infill structure from the 1960s that occupies one of the arches of the Dooley Yard Viaduct, originally a construction materials business and then Olde Arch Antiques, was acquired by SCAD in 2002.

7.6 Savannah-Ogeechee Canal (Savannah, Ogeechee, and Altamaha Canal)

1826–1830; 1836 modifications. West of W. Boundary St.

Receiving its charter in 1824, the Savannah-Ogeechee Canal connected the Ogeechee watershed with the port of Savannah. Construction on the sixteen-mile route began in 1826 and was completed in 1830, and employed six locks between the canal terminals and an aqueduct (still visible west of Stiles Avenue on private property about five hundred feet south of Louisville Road) that crossed over a drainage canal. A number of industries once fronted the canal; most processed lumber brought from the Ogeechee River. Canal operation continued despite growth of the railroads, but its stagnant waters were increasingly viewed by city officials as a health liability. Finally, during the 1880s, the Central of Georgia acquired canal property adjoining the Savannah River to create a subsidiary—the Ocean Steamship Company, now the Georgia Port Authority's Ocean Terminal—located just west of the Talmadge Memorial Bridge (**1.14**). Near the opposite end of the canal, the Savannah-Ogeechee Canal Museum at 681 Argyle Road documents the canal's history and includes a well-preserved lock.

7.7 Commercial Building (Midland Railway Freight Depot)

1916. 307 Stiles Ave.

Originally built for the Midland Railway, the Savannah and Atlanta Railway freight depot at Stiles Avenue was in operation until at least the mid-1950s, after which various supply and distribution companies used the building. Its conventional headhouse-and-shed configuration includes a porte-cochere with exaggerated compound brick piers. To the east stands the later and simpler Seaboard Air Line Railway Freight Station (1929; 703 Louisville Road). A mile to the west along Louisville Road stood the Ten Broeck Race Course, where in 1859 the largest slave sale on U.S. soil took place, involving 436 slaves in an event often called "The Weeping Time."

7.8 **City of Savannah Water Works Pump House**
1891–1892, Thomas T. Johnston, engineer, and G. L. Christy. Gwinnett St. at Stiles Ave.

The first city waterworks sat just west of the Savannah-Ogeechee Canal and pumped water from the Savannah River to a large tower in Franklin Square. That system, used by the city since 1854, had become polluted by 1887. After new wells proved inadequate, in 1890 the City invited Chicago civil engineer Johnston, who recently had designed a water system for Memphis, Tennessee, to inspect the old waterworks system. He recommended building a new plant. The red brick pump house (which the *Savannah Morning News* described as "quite a handsome and imposing structure" in 1892) stands as an iconic monument to what was only a brief solution to the city's insatiable desire for fresh water. Built by Savannah contractor W. F. Chaplin, the pump house drew more than sixteen million gallons a day from twelve wells dug five hundred to one thousand feet deep running along Stiles Avenue. The architecture and landscape of the pump house were a testament to Savannah's technological advances, and by 1895, just two years after the building's completion, city ordinances prohibited the use of surface wells in any area where municipal water mains were accessible. By 1896, however, there was sufficient need to again draw water from the Savannah River. The plant closed in 1940 and became a storage warehouse for the city.

Between Liberty and Gaston Streets

With the establishment of the Central of Georgia Railroad (**7.1**) in 1833, Savannah entered a period of rapid growth. Nine new wards were laid out between 1837 and 1854, bringing the number of Oglethorpe-type wards with squares to its final tally of twenty-four. In the fourth and fifth rows of wards (comprising the eight wards south of Liberty Street), adjustments were made to the standard formula, as tything lots were lengthened to one hundred feet deep, rather than ninety feet, and the new east–west streets become a uniform sixty feet in width. Larger lots permitted increased building setbacks, producing something akin to front yards. Between these two final rows of wards, Jones Street, at ninety-five feet wide, became a tree-lined, residential avenue, distinct from the multilane boulevards of Oglethorpe Avenue or Liberty Street, or the main street retail corridor of Broughton Street.

JASPER WARD

This ward honors Sergeant William Jasper, who died saving the American colors (battle flags) during the Battle of Savannah in October 1779. The entire northeastern tything of Jasper Ward was already occupied by the Oglethorpe Barracks, a military outpost built in 1834, when the first part (north of Harris Street) was platted in 1837; the remainder of the ward, along with the square, was laid out in 1839. Of the three wards created that year (the other two were Pulaski and Lafayette), Jasper Ward has always been the most monumental in its architecture. In 1890, the eleven army buildings of Oglethorpe Barracks on this superblock were replaced by the enormous Hotel Desoto, which was, in turn, replaced by Desoto Hilton Hotel complex in 1968.

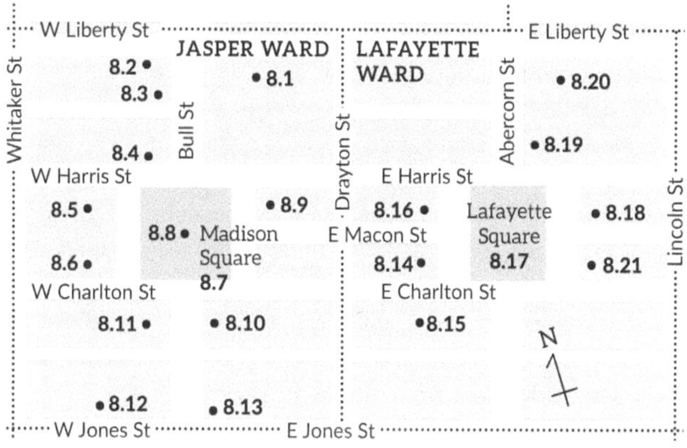

8.1 **Desoto Hilton Hotel and Condominiums (Desoto Hilton Hotel and Citizens and Southern Bank)**

1966–1968, Richard Aeck; 1968 pool plaza and landscaping, Clermont Lee, landscape architect; 2008 entrance canopy, Gunn Meyerhoff Shay Architects. 15 E. Liberty St.

Mounting maintenance and repair costs and an increased demand for modern comforts including air-conditioning brought the wrecking ball to the venerable Hotel Desoto in 1966. That building had been the center of Savannah's social life from 1890 until it was replaced by this mixed-use megastructure composed of two tall boxes atop a horizontal base that covers the entire tything. The hotel's 264 guest rooms and suites are housed in a sixteen-story concrete-frame high-rise clad with colossal brick arches that are punctuated irregularly with precast concrete balconies. The similarly New Formalist seven-story block running parallel to Bull Street served as a bank and office park. A tall lobby connects the vertical boxes and also provides room for conference spaces, a restaurant, an outdoor terrace, and what was originally described as a lush indoor tropical garden lit by Plexiglas skylights. A massive precast concrete canopy that once protected the primary entrance on Liberty Street was replaced by the arched glass canopy in 2008. Underneath the entire structure, which is raised several feet above street level, is a three-level parking garage. A few ornamental red terra-cotta details from the old hotel were preserved and incorporated into the new structure. Atlanta architect Aeck, together with city officials and investors, promoted this project as an attempt to reinvigorate Savannah's economy, and it remains a vital and popular hotel in the heart of the historic district.

8.2 Knights of Columbus Council Building (Joseph S. Fay House)

1849, John S. Norris; later modifications. 1–3 W. Liberty St.

Massachusetts-born merchant Joseph Fay purchased these two tything lots in 1847, hiring Norris to design this impressive but curious hybrid of country villa and town house. Encumbered today by subsequent additions, it was originally a tall, freestanding, three-bay, three-story Italianate building raised on a half basement and surrounded by a walled garden on three sides. In 1871 the property was purchased by George Wymberley Jones De Renne, who extended it to the west, adding a carriage house and servants quarters along Liberty Street and hiring J. J. Cadogan to create a formal garden of camellias, roses, and cypress trees. The building was further modified after it was sold to the Georgia Hussars in 1890, serving as their armory until 1925. The attached restaurant, The Public Kitchen and Bar, was constructed before 1916 for use as stores and recently redesigned (2011–2012, Dawson Architects).

8.3 Commercial Building (Desoto Pharmacy)

1897. 307–309 Bull St.

Built on the back of the property of the Fay House while it was owned by the Georgia Hussars, this loggia-like pavilion clad in terra-cotta, with its ogee-arched arcade supported by spiral fluted columns, adds an exotic touch to the Bull Street corridor. Serving briefly as a pharmacy, it was turned into an automobile showroom in 1910.

8.4 **Sorrel-Weed House (Francis Sorrel House)**

1839–1843, Charles B. Cluskey; 1996–1998 reconstruction of east and north verandahs, John Deering for Hansen Architects. 6 W. Harris St.

Dominican-born merchant Francis Sorrel clearly intended to make an impression when he paid a premium for two prominently positioned tything lots in the newly begun Jasper Ward and hired Cluskey to design this grand mansion straddling them. Its bright orange-colored stucco—discovered through historic paint analysis—enlivens its severe Greek Revival forms and details. Porches project from all four sides, conferring a sense of spaciousness. Raised on a half basement, the first floor features a wide central hall punctuated by a columnar screen and terminated by a dramatic curved staircase. Cluskey also designed the adjacent handsome pair of Greek Revival Savannah elevated town houses at 14 and 18 W. Harris.

8.5 **Green-Meldrim House (Charles Green House)**

1853, John S. Norris. 14 W. Macon St.

Serving as the parish house and rectory of St. John's since 1943, this rare example of Gothic Revival domestic architecture in Savannah features exquisite ornamental details both inside and out. The main house is a two-story rectangular block wrapped on three sides by an ornate ironwork porch and sits about twenty-five feet back from the "front" edge of the trust lot to accommodate a formal garden protected by an iron fence (with

a Warwick Vase that was originally in Madison Square; **8.7**). This garden was restored with a new planting plan in the "style of 1855–1861" by Clermont Lee in 1978. A service wing extends from the main house along the northwestern edge of the property. The front entrance, a canopied cast-iron Gothic Revival pavilion with an oriel window above, eschews the trust-lot norm for mansions by facing Macon Street, which was closed and converted by the church into a formal garden (1960–1961, Clermont Lee). Green was an English cotton trader whose most noteworthy deed was to offer his house to General William Tecumseh Sherman for use as headquarters during the Union occupation of the city in the winter of 1864–1865; meetings with leaders of local African American churches here resulted in Sherman's Field Order No. 15, which famously promised each freed family forty acres.

8.6 St. John's Episcopal Church

1852–1853, Calvin N. Otis with Calvin Fay, with Daniel L. Cohen, builder; 1914 chancel addition. 1 W. Macon St.

St. John's was organized in 1840 as part of a new Episcopal diocese. Holding services in a temporary wooden structure beginning in 1841, the wardens and vestry began plans for a new church on the southwest trust lot of Jasper Ward in 1848. Working under Buffalo architect Otis, Calvin Fay (also from Buffalo but by then based in Savannah) supervised the former's design. With its buttresses, finials, lancet windows, and single central tower and spire, the stucco-covered brick building takes the form of a medieval English parish church and makes evident the rapid spread of the American Ecclesiological movement to the South. Its hammer beam roof is similar to that of St. John's

Church in Buffalo, designed by Otis in 1846 but no longer extant, which was considered the earliest example of such a roof in America. The chancel was added in 1914 and the central panel of the reredos was made by Calvert, Herrick and Riedinger of New York City, following drawings by the rector, William Dakin. The final statues were not completed until the 1980s. The parish house behind the church was built in 1881, but significantly modified when it was transformed for its present use as a Lady Chapel and office space in the 1950s. Across Charlton Street is Cranmer Hall, the educational building constructed in 1953 in a strikingly modernist style with ribbon windows but radically reconfigured to its present Gothic Revival form in 2005 by Greenline Architecture.

8.7 Madison Square

1839; 1986–1987 relandscaped, Clermont Lee

The square commemorates President James Madison, who died in 1836. To the south of the Jasper Monument (**8.8**), an 1848 city cistern cover (the oldest example in Savannah), emblazoned with an American eagle, marks the location of one of the brick cisterns installed in the city's squares between 1833 and 1850, this one constructed by local contractor and mason Adam Short. A pair of bronze 1860s field cannon (Model 1857, 12-Pounder Napoleon) stands at the square's southern edge; these were donated in 1920 by the Savannah Volunteer Guards to commemorate the starting points of Georgia's first two highways, Augusta Road leading to Augusta and Ogeechee Road leading to Darien. From 1872 to 1879, a decorative earthen mound crowned by a Warwick Vase (modeled after the famous Warwick Vase discovered in 1771 at Hadrian's Villa and eventually owned by George Grenville, the 2nd Earl of Warwick)—now in the garden of the adjacent Green-Meldrim House (**8.5**)—occupied the center of the square.

8.8 Sergeant William Jasper Monument

1879–1888, Alexander Doyle, sculptor. Madison Square

With its cornerstone laid on the one hundredth anniversary of the Siege of Savannah in October 1879, Doyle's colossal bronze statue, dedicated in 1888 in the presence of President Grover Cleveland, commemorates the heroism of William Jasper, who lost his life carrying the American colors in the Battle of Savan-

nah. Adorning the tall granite pedestal are four bronze reliefs cast by the Henry Bonnard Bronze Company in New York City. The statue was cast by the Ames Manufacturing Company in Chicopee, Massachusetts.

8.9 Eliza Jewett House

1843. 326 Bull St.

North Carolina native Eliza Ann Jewett was among the most successful entrepreneurs in antebellum Savannah. Widowed three times, she became one of the city's leading slave traders and real estate developers, building at least twenty-two residential units in nine different building projects before her death in 1856. Most are nearby, including the handsome row of four Savannah elevated town houses (1855–1856, 18–24 E. Macon Street) behind her own house. Jewett owned the entire northeast trust lot of Jasper Ward. Her tall, three-story, side-hall house once had a walled side- and backyard with a narrow, two-story carriage house running across the rear. A bookstore and garage now fill these spaces. The stucco surface, bracketed cornice, curved stair leading to a covered porch, tripartite windows, and iron balconies make this house a model of refinement and decorum facing Madison Square and Macon Street. Inside, elegant Greek Revival decorative details and early built-in closets attest to Jewett's taste and innovation.

8.10 Poetter Hall, SCAD (Savannah Volunteer Guards Armory)

1892–1893, William G. Preston; 1978 and later, adaptive rehabilitation; 2001, 2008, 2012 partial restoration. 342 Bull St.

When Jasper Ward was laid out, the City granted two lots to the Female Orphan Asylum, which built a highly publicized structure on this site in 1838 and added another lot to accommodate a garden in 1846. When the orphanage was reorganized and relocated to the now-demolished Wetter House on West Broad Street in 1888, the Savannah Volunteer Guards bought the property and replaced the building with this castlelike armory. Preston's design (see page 115) is a romantic mélange of red brick towers and rounded arches, suggestive of a fortress but also reflective of his exuberant Hotel Desoto, which formerly stood across the square. The 24-pounder cannon flanking the entrance, which were discovered buried under the previous Volunteer Guard Armory during its demolition, are the oldest extant cannon forged by the U.S. government. At the rear stands the original drill hall; along its north side there was once a rifle range and then an indoor swimming pool. In 1978 the armory became the first of many derelict buildings in Savannah to be renovated and adaptively reused by SCAD, for which it remains the flagship building.

8.11 Scottish Rite Temple

1912–1923, Hyman W. Witcover. 341 Bull St.

At six stories tall, this colorful and richly decorated Masonic Temple appears somewhat out of context in this neighborhood.

Using Georgia marble, glazed terra-cotta, and yellow brick over a steel-frame, Witcover, himself a 33rd Degree Scottish Rite Mason, saturated the building with Masonic symbolism. The interior has three ceremonial meeting rooms above the ground floor, originally occupied by a pharmacy known as Solomon's Drugstore, with elaborate cabinetry still visible in the Gryphon Tearoom managed by SCAD. The block of houses extending westward along Charlton Street from the Scottish Rite Temple vividly illustrates the role proximity to the square had on property value, with the most lavish houses being closer to Bull Street and progressively simpler and shorter houses marching down the block.

8.12 Houses

1891, Alfred S. Eichberg. 12–14 W. Jones St.

Built for Morris Sternberg, a Savannah jeweler, Eichberg's elaborate and eclectic Queen Anne interpretation of the Savannah elevated double house shows what could be done to modernize and monumentalize the building type at the end of the nineteenth century; see 10 W. Jones Street (1857, attributed to John S. Norris) by way of comparison. His most creative touch was in adapting the scrolling forms of a Flemish gable to the symmetrical exterior staircases. The front porch was modified in 1920, and the carriage houses behind the house date to 1847.

8.13 Morris Hall, SCAD (Alexander Smets House)

1853, John S. Norris; 2013 renovation, Dawson Architects. 24 E. Jones St.

Bank president, art collector, bibliophile, and French immigrant, Alexander Smets commissioned this austere cubic house as

Jones Street was developing into a street of elegant homes. Although the channeled masonry signifies that the ground floor is to be understood as a basement, the front door opens at grade, unlike most other grand houses. A writer for the *Southern Literary Messenger*, assessing Smet's extensive and famous collection of rare books held within this house, observed that "the first emotion on entering and casting the eye around upon the magnificent display of the ample shelves, is that of surprise, that the visitor has not before heard of so extensive and luxurious a collection." The pyramidal roof is capped by a tall cupola accessed by a freestanding spiral stair. The doors were modified in 1879 when the building housed Savannah's first Jewish social club, the Harmonie Club, whose monogram is etched in the glass. The Smets House was acquired by SCAD in 1988.

LAFAYETTE WARD

Named in 1837, Lafayette Ward and its square commemorate the Marquis de Lafayette, who visited Savannah to much fanfare in 1825 (and who died in 1834). Like Jasper and Pulaski wards, Lafayette Ward was developed incrementally. Only the northwestern tything was actually auctioned in 1837; lots in the remaining western half were sold beginning in 1839 and the eastern half in 1854. From 1801–1846, before the final laying-out of the ward, the city jail occupied what would become the northwestern trust lot.

8.14 Andrew Low House

1849, John S. Norris. 329 Abercorn St.

This is one of Savannah's best-preserved houses, having passed directly from the Low family to its current owner, the National Society of Colonial Dames, in 1928. It has been open to the public since 1952. An early example of Norris's residential architecture, its elegant cubic form is dramatically set off by an iron-fenced garden in front that declared the owner's wealth (prominent private gardens are rare in downtown Savannah). The garden, with its double-hourglass parterres, has been well preserved since it was established. The house sits in a shallow sunken well, granting light to the semi- raised basement and making it seem that the building is rising from below ground level. A bold but simple double gallery covers the entire rear elevation of the house and an elaborate covered iron balcony faces

Charlton Street to the south. The carriage house served as the first national headquarters of the Girl Scouts, whose founder, Juliette Gordon Low, lived in the main house. The adjacent courtyard garden was designed in 1969 by Clermont Lee.

8.15 William Battersby House

c. 1852. 119 E. Charlton St.

Andrew Low's business partner, English cotton trader Battersby, built this rare example of a Charleston single house in Savannah, featuring a "false" front door that accesses a two-story side verandah facing a walled side yard and to which the central hall plan is oriented. True to its Charleston spirit, the house does not have an elevated basement in the Savannah manner. The Greek Revival street facade is, by contrast, opaque and severe. The carriage house behind was modified in 1971 to connect it to the main house.

8.16 Lafayette Condominiums (Southern Bell Telephone and Telegraph Company Building)

1928, Hentz, Adler and Shutze; 1954 expansion, Shutze and Armistead; 1985 conversion. 321 Abercorn St.

Occupied first by the city jail and then by the grand house of Octavus Cohen, this trust lot was acquired by Bell Telephone in 1928 for use as a switching station and offices. Schutze's muscular but graceful Georgian Revival mid-rise building demonstrates the telephone company's commitment to civic architecture in the early twentieth century. The building originally faced Drayton Street and covered only the western two-thirds of the lot, but was seamlessly expanded in 1954 to its present size. In 1985 condominium developers Lafayette Square

Corporation acquired the building and, remarkably, excavated an underground parking garage.

8.17 Lafayette Square

c. 1837–1840; 1940 relandscaped

Streetcar tracks passed through the square from 1877 until 1946 in line with Abercorn Street. The three-tiered, cast- iron Semiquincentenary Fountain in the center, produced by the Robinson Iron Company in Alexander City, Alabama, was erected in 1982–1983 by the Colonial Dames of America to commemorate the 250th anniversary of founding of the colony.

8.18 Cathedral Parochial School

1954, Benjamin P. Ritzert. 324 Abercorn St.

The compact horizontality of this modernist building's tight assemblage of boxes and planes contrasts with the Gothic verticality of the cathedral across the street. Even so, the school clearly echoes the church in its color palette and the relief portraying Our Lady of Grace over the glass entrance, which repeats the church's southern entrance portal dedicated to the Virgin Mary as "Regina Coeli" (Queen of Heaven). Savannah architect Ritzert's careful use of glass block, aluminum sun screens, and outdoor walkways makes this a sophisticated, regionally specific functionalist composition.

8.19 Cathedral Basilica of St. John the Baptist

1872–1876, E. Francis Baldwin, with W. G. Butler, supervising engineer; 1896 spires and stucco; 1900–1914 interior rebuilt; 1959–1963 renovated; 1999–2000 restored, DPK&A Architects. 222 E. Harris St.

Set back on a raised, open forecourt facing Abercorn Street, the cathedral's white stuccoed brick facade with twin 214-foot towers stands in stark contrast to all other buildings in Savannah and yet seems comfortably at home here in this Southern port city. Catholics, who were originally banned from the colony, had become numerous enough by 1850 for Pope Pius IX to establish the Diocese of Savannah. The second site of the church of St. John the Baptist (founded c. 1796), a brick building on Drayton and Perry streets, originally served as the cathedral until the present Gothic Revival building was completed in 1876. The interior, almost totally destroyed by fire in 1898, was rebuilt

between 1898 and 1914. Although there is no clerestory, the Latin cross-plan interior is bright and lively with polychrome stenciled decoration mainly on the ceiling and along the upper walls. The nave rises 66 feet on marbleized cast-iron columns to false ribbed vaults of iron- and wood-truss construction. The Renaissance-styled murals of biblical scenes, installed in 1912, were designed by Savannah artist Christopher Murphy and painted by Paul Gutsche and a team of artists in New York. The stained glass windows are mostly Austrian made. A Noack tracker organ was installed in 1987 in the gallery below the rose window, which is dedicated to St. Cecelia. Connected to the apse of the cathedral by a loggia-like bridge is the bishop's residence (1888, W. F. Chaplin), which incorporates forms and motifs modeled directly from those of the cathedral. The most recent and extensive restoration, conducted by Kansas City–based J. E. Dunn Construction and Savannah's Rives E. Worrell Company, installed a new slate roof and a monumental baptismal font, carved in Carrara, Italy, with a design modeled on details of the cathedral's reredos and high altar.

8.20 Convent and Academy of St. Vincent DePaul

1845, Charles B. Cluskey; 1855, 1869, c. 1955, and 1960 additions. 207 E. Liberty St.

Securely set about twenty feet behind an iron fence, the convent and academy occupy two tything lots granted by the

City in 1842. Additions were made in 1855 and again in 1869, doubling the length of the original building. Cluskey's stucco-covered brick building is sober yet sophisticated, with stripped-down colossal pilaster strips on the central and end pavilions and simplified Doric piers on the two one-story entrance porticoes. Between 1955 and 1960 a cluster of modernist structures was attached to the eastern edge of the academy (replacing the original Sisters' Chapel), extending the building line the entire length of the tything and forming a courtyard on the rear.

8.21 Hamilton-Turner Inn (Samuel Pugh Hamilton House)

1873, John D. Hall; 2000 restoration. 330 Abercorn St.

In 1883 this house became the first in the city to be electrified. Hamilton was a founder of the Brush Electric Light and Power Company, which installed its first electric streetlight in Lafayette Square that same year. In contrast to the more sober classicism of the Andrew Low House (**8.14**) across the square, this is the city's grandest Second Empire residence, with ornate quoining, window hood molds, lintels, and a crowning mansard roof. Converted to an inn in 2000 (work by J. T. Turner Construction), the building benefits from its celebrated role as the house of Joe Odum in John Berendt's book *Midnight in the Garden of Good and Evil* (1994). Across the street at 207 E. Charlton (1856) is the childhood home of the noted writer Flannery O'Connor.

TROUP WARD

Named after George Michael Troup (Georgia's governor from 1823–1827), Troup Ward was developed in 1851 as one of three final wards to follow the Trustee-era formula. Like the other eastern wards, it is compressed, with only four 60 × 90–foot lots across each tything. The land for Troup Ward was taken mostly from the town common, but the eastern edge was made possible by the City's acquisition of two garden lots in 1852. Troup Ward was rather slow to develop, with most of the lots remaining empty until after the Civil War. The ward has a high percentage of small- to-medium-size row houses built in the late nineteenth century.

8.22 Unitarian Universalist Church (Unitarian Church)

1850–1851, John S. Norris; 1860 moved and rebuilt, John B. Hogg; 1999–2000 restored. 321 Habersham St.

Founded in 1831, the Savannah Unitarian Society dedicated its first building in 1834 on Wright Square. Funded by a bequest of the "recently deceased silversmith Moses Eastman" (May 24, 1850), the cross-plan church was originally built on the north-

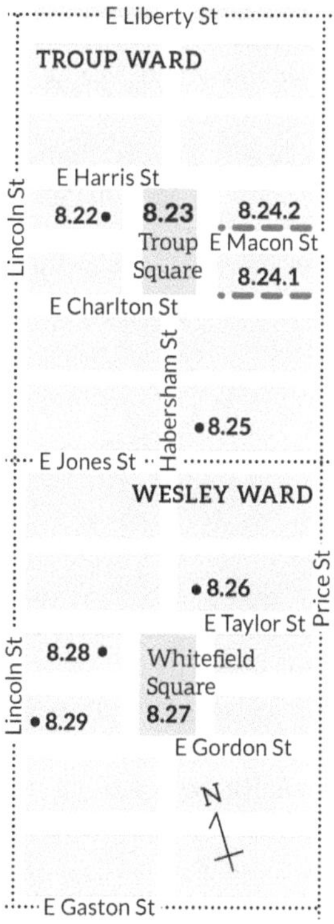

west trust lot facing Oglethorpe Square. The congregation was disbanded in 1858, apparently because of the unwelcome abolitionist stance taken by the minister, John Pierpont Jr. whose brother, James L. Pierpont, served as the organist and music director and is remembered for his song "Jingle Bells, or The One Horse Open Sleigh," possibly composed here. The building was dismantled and rebuilt in 1860 on its present site as St. Stephen's Episcopal Church for free people of color. It became the Savannah Baptist Center in 1958, but in 1997 a different Unitarian-Universalist congregation purchased the property and restored the building with support from local philanthropist and preservationist Mills B. Lane IV.

8.23 Troup Square

1851; 1967–1969 relandscaped, Clermont Lee

From 1877 until 1946 streetcar tracks crossed this square in line with Habersham Street, and it is ornamented today by a bronze armillary sphere manufactured by Kenneth Lynch and Sons of Oxford, Connecticut, donated along with the surrounding landscaping by Mills B. Lane Jr. and his wife, Anne (Waring), as part of the Troup Square Conservation Project in 1968. The small cast-iron water fountain for use by pets was cast from parts of a larger bronze fountain originally placed in Forsyth Park in 1897.

8.24.1 John J. McDonough Row

1882–1885, John J. McDonough, builder. 410–424 E. Charlton St.

8.24.2 Edward Kennedy Row

1855, J. J. Dooley, builder; 1872, John J. McDonough, builder. 410–424 E. Macon St.

The two trust lots east of Troup Square are each occupied by eight row houses oriented to the south. The four units on the western half of Kennedy Row, built in 1855 for Edward Kennedy, established the form for the rest of this row, which was completed by McDonough with similar units to the east. The westernmost house sports an iron balcony and has a central entrance facing the square. Kennedy Row is unusual in its use of ground-level entrances and its lack of carriage houses, attributes that seem to attest to a humbler social standing in its peripheral location relative to the city's social focus along

Bull Street. McDonough later built the more southern row facing Charlton Street, instead of the conventional orientation toward the wider central street of the ward, E. Macon Street, thereby also facing away from Kennedy Row. Reflecting the air of prosperity and confidence of the 1880s, the McDonough row houses are set on a fully raised basement and enlivened by the rhythmic three-dimensional effect of alternating curving stone stairs and angled projecting one-and-a-half-story bays. McDonough, who became Savannah's mayor in 1891, owned a sawmill and an iron foundry in nearby Bartow Ward.

8.25 Jerry Lominack House

1972–1973, Jerry Lominack. 400–402 E. Jones St.

This house is startling in its deviation from the traditional Savannah row house typology dominant on Jones Street, in its picturesque massing of abstract cylindrical and rectangular forms, and in the numerous diagonal wall-ends evoking gables that frame small portions of steeply sloping standing-seam copper roofs. This use of abstracted traditional forms represents the flight from modernist dogmatism and the attempt to create the sense of place that characterized Postmodern architecture of the early 1970s. Zoning laws at the time required the house be set back from the street line. The much simpler and more recent Brower House (2007, Daniel E. Snyder Architect) across the street at 320 E. Jones is an abstract reinterpretation of a Charleston single house for the twenty-first century, with an at-grade side-porch entrance and, facing the side garden to the west, colossal abstract piers (suggestive of a traditional double gallery) that frame a second-floor verandah and floor-to-ceiling windows.

WESLEY WARD

Two of the most influential ministers of the Great Awakening, John Wesley and George Whitefield, served as Anglican ministers in the early Georgia colony. Both left legacies considered worthy of commemoration by Savannah's city council a century later. Wesley Ward was another of the three "final" wards to be named and laid out following the Trustee-era formula in 1851, though very little building occurred here until the late nineteenth century and only one antebellum house survives. Impeding the development of Wesley Ward was the Negro Burial Ground, a 300 × 650-foot fenced cemetery established by the City in 1813 in this part of the common. As with the white Church Burial Ground, the Negro Burial Ground was closed in 1852 and the internments relocated to the newly established Laurel Grove Cemetery (**11.9**), a gruesome task that was still not completed by 1855. Victorian-era wooden houses, most with ground-floor entrances and full-width front porches, confer on this ward an aura of domesticity and intimacy not found in most of the other squares. Those at 405–419 E. Gordon Street were erected by the Home Building Company and the Workman and Traders Loan and Building Association. Despite its domestic quality, the square has been home to large-scale medical facilities since its founding. The most notable was St. Joseph's Hospital, which occupied the northwest tything until it was replaced by a twelve-story housing block.

8.26 Madonna Hall

1954–1955. 418 Habersham St.

Built in 1954 as Madonna Hall, this International Style building served as a nursing school and dormitory for St. Joseph's Hospital until 1970. The building's buff-brick six-story cubic massing is attached to a two-story entrance pavilion and education wing that matches the scale of the neighboring houses along E. Taylor Street. The dormitory features cantilevered concrete balconies on the Habersham (west) elevation and sun canopies on the south side shading horizontal bands of aluminum windows that illuminate the nurses' rooms. A brick-walled courtyard completes the tything-lot site.

8.27 Whitefield Square

1851; 1973 relandscaped, Cy Paumier

This site had been occupied since c. 1759 by an African American cemetery, which was moved when Whitefield Square—the final one created in downtown Savannah—was laid out and named to honor George Whitefield, second minister at Christ Church (**2.4**) and founder of Bethesda Home for Boys (**19.4**). From 1877 until 1946 streetcar tracks crossed here in line with Habersham Street; when they were removed the Office of City Engineer proposed a 32-foot-wide roadway that would have cut through the square (akin to the disruption of Franklin, Liberty, and Elbert squares along Montgomery Street in 1935–1937), which fortunately was not implemented. In 1973, the center of the square was relandscaped by Cy Paumier, followed in 1975 by the addition of a small octagonal gazebo, commissioned by Mills B. Lane Jr. and designed by John C. LeBey, now frequently used for weddings and other semiprivate gatherings.

8.28 First Congregational Church

1895; 1979 rear annex; 1991 steeple reconstruction, Lee Meyer. 421 Habersham St.

Organized in 1869, this church was an outgrowth of the Beach Institute (**9.1**), a school where white missionary teachers taught African American children shortly after the Civil War. The congregation acquired this property in 1878 and later built this modest Gothic Revival brick meetinghouse, which has a front-gabled facade and square corner tower with a short spire.

8.29 Beth Eden Baptist Church

1893, Henry Urban. 302 E. Gordon St.

In 1890, the Reverend Alexander Ellis left his position as pastor of the Second African Baptist Church (**4.17**) to organize the Beth Eden Baptist Church. Urban's compact, Lombard Gothic red brick building differs from Savannah's typical church architecture in being located on the rear half of a trust lot instead of facing a square. Also unusual is the building's corner entrance framed within the stout tower crowned by a broach spire. The church's compact interior features a gallery with broad pointed arches resting on metal columns. A block south, at 304 E. Gaston (1867), stands an unusual cruciform variation on Andrew Jackson Downing's popular "bracketed cottage," reflecting a suburban character appropriate for its location then on the edge of downtown, yet boasting Savannah Grey brick and an elevated two stories typical of urban townhouses.

CALHOUN WARD

Calhoun Ward was laid out and named in 1851, one year after the death of its namesake, South Carolina statesman John C. Calhoun. Like Wesley Ward, portions of Calhoun Ward had previously served as part of the Negro Burial Ground, and its southern tything blocks were also not laid out until 1854. Once those lots were platted the practice of replicating the Trustee-era ward would come to an end, leaving the city with twenty-four squares surrounded by tything blocks and trust lots. More centrally located than Wesley and Troup and enjoying the full size of the original wards, Calhoun Ward also developed more rapidly and more grandly.

8.30 Calhoun Square

1851; 1937 relandscaped

Calhoun Square long served as a playground for the adjacent Massie Common School, including annual May Day celebra-

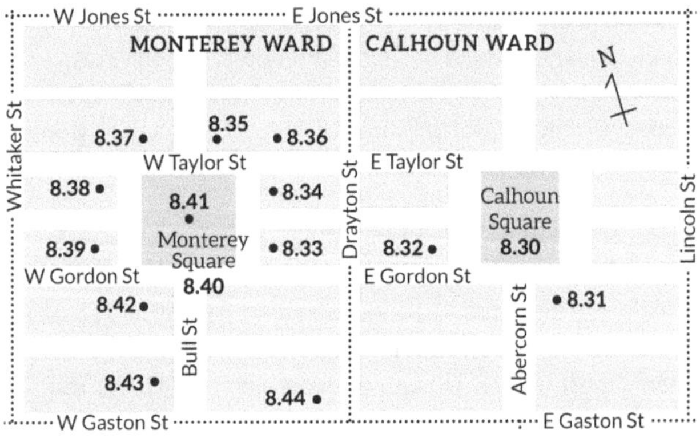

tions, with student dancing around a maypole that continues today. Despite this, a streetcar line passed through the square from 1877 until 1946 in line with Abercorn Street. In 1937 half of the square was beautified.

8.31 Massie Heritage Center (Massie Common School)

1856, John S. Norris; 1872, 1886 wings; 2010–2012 restoration, The Spriggs Group. 201–213 E. Gordon St.

In 1841, Peter Massie, a Scottish planter who had settled in Glynn County, Georgia, left a bequest to Savannah for the education of the poor. The City hired Norris to design this austere, two-story pedimented building after the invested funds had matured. In what appears to have been a planned phased development, the eastern wing was added in 1872 and the western wing in 1886, producing a three-part pavilion plan connected by upper and lower walkways, with playgrounds behind the two wings. Unifying all three pavilions are abstract colossal pilaster strips carrying segmental arches below the cornice. The building served as a public school until 1974, and has remained part of the Savannah Public School system as a museum and learning center for the teaching of local history and architecture. The recent extensive restoration carried out by Sterling Builders and Restoration included correcting sagging queen-post trusses in the attic by means of shoring jacks, a solution devised by David Franchetti of DCF Engineering.

8.32 Wesley Monumental United Methodist Church

1875–1890, Dixon and Carson; 1895 spires and stucco, Charles L. Carson. 429 Abercorn St.

In 1854 an octagonal German church, known as the "Coffeepot," was built on the western end of this trust lot. A mission group from Trinity Methodist Church purchased the property in 1868

and hired Baltimore architects Dixon and Carson in 1874 to design a new church filling the east two-thirds of the trust lot and fronting Calhoun Square. Construction began in 1875 and although the ground floor was finished in 1878, insufficient funds delayed completion of the church until 1890, when it was dedicated. The spires and exterior stucco were added in 1895. The taller north tower follows the pattern of emphasizing the front corner of the trust lot closest to the middle of the ward. The sanctuary, raised above the ground floor, features side galleries supported by iron columns, fifteen double-lancet stained glass windows depicting a pantheon of Methodist church leaders, and a false hammer beam truss constructed of steel. The Sunday school building attached to the rear of the church was built in 1926–1927, at the same time as the exterior stair to the sanctuary.

MONTEREY WARD

In March 1847, one year after the American victory at the Battle of Monterey, the City laid out this final ward and square on the Bull Street axis, and Monterey Ward quickly became one of the most fashionable addresses in antebellum Savannah. In 1851 some of the residents successfully petitioned the City to increase the length of the southernmost tything lots fronting Gaston Street from 100 to 120 feet, setting a pattern for the other wards in this row (Chatham, Calhoun, and Wesley) that developed soon after. Many of the houses built on these lots facing Gaston Street and the newly established Forsyth Place (now Forsyth Park; **10.1**) are, unsurprisingly, larger with more generous yards and setbacks than those on the older lots. The buildings around Monterey Square possess the richest concentration of cast- and wrought-iron work in Savannah.

8.33 Temple Mickve Israel

1874–1878, Henry G. Harrison; late 19th century, steeple alteration. 20 E. Gordon St.

Congregation Mickve Israel is the third-oldest Jewish congregation in America, tracing its origins to forty-two Sephardic and Ashkenazi Jews who sought asylum in the Georgia colony in 1733. The congregation had no permanent building until 1818, when it constructed the first synagogue in the state, at the corner of Perry Lane and Whitaker Street. Plans were begun by 1874 to build a new synagogue on the present site, a task for which Harrison, an English immigrant architect working in New York City, was hired. Consecrated in 1878, Harrison's Gothic Revival synagogue took inspiration from the similarly styled First Presbyterian Church that stood on the neighboring trust lot to the north until 1941, following the custom of Reform Judaism congregations emulating Christian models. Its T-shaped basilican form with a nonstructural rib-vaulted ceiling, clustered piers, and stained glass lancet windows give the synagogue a remarkably churchlike appearance. Only the small Star of David atop the entrance gable and the Byzantine-influenced octagonal belfry with a copper dome that crowns the massive square front tower suggest the building's true function. In 1956 a modernist brick building, Mordecai Sheftall Memorial Hall, was completed behind the sanctuary, only to be replaced in 2003 by the present Sheftall Building (Levin/Brown and Associates), the design of which attempts to harmonize with the synagogue.

8.34 Herschel V. Jenkins United Way Building (Thomas Gamble Hall)

1941. 428 Bull St.

Although it was criticized for being poorly proportioned by architect and urban planner Edmund Bacon in his book, *Design of Cities* (1967), this modest brick building, constructed to house science laboratories and lecture halls for Armstrong Junior College, exemplifies the civic spirit of the trust lot, politely addressing the public square with its semicircular portico. The lot was previously occupied by the Gothic Revival First Presbyterian Church of 1872, whose congregation was the first to leave downtown Savannah for the suburbs, eventually building a new church at 520 Washington Avenue in 1956.

8.35 Hugh Moss Comer House

1880. 2 E. Taylor St.

The Comer House, built for the president of the Central of Georgia Railroad, is a late but fulsome example of the standard Savannah elevated town house with a full-height basement and parallel exterior stair married to a Charleston single house–inspired triple-height side gallery overlooking a side garden. The garden is especially remarkable because it adjoins a reciprocal garden belonging to the neighboring house at 10 E. Taylor Street (built for William Hunter in 1872), which nearly identically mirrors the Comer House design, including its own triple-height side gallery facing west.

8.36 Daniel J. Purse and Daniel Thomas Houses

1869; 1897 remodeled. 12–14 E. Taylor St.

This Reconstruction-era double house was remodeled for department store owner B. H. Levy in 1897, adding a fourth story fronted by a metal (faux tile) mansard roof and robust dormers

that boldly punctuate the floor level below. A mid-level decorative frieze and elaborate, curved window bays faced in marble project over the arched entrance stoops to produce a decidedly theatrical and exuberant effect.

8.37 Nicholas Crugar House

1852; before 1888 addition; 2007–2010 restoration, Daniel E. Snyder Architect. 4 W. Taylor St.

Crugar, a cotton merchant and planter from a wealthy New York family, built this imposing house on the innermost tything lot facing the square, but placed it thirty feet from Bull Street, allowing for a walled side garden. The house is also slightly recessed from the Taylor Street lot line, to allow the entrance staircase to be perpendicular to the facade, in a manner unusual for Savannah town houses on tything lots. The front stair boasts magnificent cast-iron newel posts adorned by pelicans. The lot was expanded to the west and the recessed western wing was added before 1888. The facade displays high-quality hard-pressed imported red bricks with meticulously narrow mortar joints, while the west elevation shows the use of less-refined local bricks. Architect Daniel E. Snyder designed the laser-cut metal fence (2008) as part of the restoration, completed by Bloomquist Construction. The neighboring house at 10 W. Taylor (1852; 1904 and 1916 remodeled) introduces an exotic note to the square with its Spanish Colonial Baroque gables and Florentine-style ironwork.

8.38 Charles Rogers Houses

1858, John S. Norris. 423–425 Bull St.

This large double house epitomizes the height of refinement of its type. It also bears a striking resemblance to 3 and 4 Gramercy Park W. in New York City, an 1840s double house attributed to Alexander Jackson Davis, which Norris is likely to have known. In both cases, a pair of wide sandstone stairs carry visitors a full story up and across an iron-fenced garden to high front stoops. Lacy wire ironwork (by J. B. Wickersham) simultaneously ornaments and obscures the private realm behind the covered balconies and porches. The houses were built for Rogers, a Presbyterian minister who had inherited a fortune. He lived in the southern unit with his family and fourteen slaves, while his daughter lived in the northern house with her husband, Dr. Joseph West.

8.39 Mercer Williams House (General Hugh Weedon Mercer House)

1860, John S. Norris; 1868–1871, Muller and Bruyn, with John R. Wilder. 429 Bull St.

One of Savannah's most celebrated buildings, primarily because of its association with the colorful and notorious Jim Williams (whose story was recounted by John Berendt in his 1994 book, *Midnight in the Garden of Good and Evil*), the Mercer House is also renowned for its connection with songwriter Johnny Mercer (who never lived here), the best-known descendant of Confederate general Hugh Mercer. Apart from these associations, it stands as Norris's final work in Savannah, before he left the South for New York City on the eve of the Civil War. Left unfinished, the house was completed after the war under the supervision of the Savannah firm of Muller and Bruyn and

John R. Wilder. The Mercer House is similar to the Andrew Low House (**8.14**), another of Norris's trust-lot mansions. Both houses are set back far from the street, with heavy cornices, semibasements that sit in moatlike wells, and double porches extending across the back. The Mercer House has a larger setback and overall size; it also differs in its more exuberant expression of Italianate style, featuring a three-bay facade with large Florentine-style *bifora* (double-light) windows crowned by ornate cast-iron hood molds and a projecting cast-iron Corinthian portico. The nearby town house at 7 West Gordon Street (1884, Augustus Schwaab) was restored by J. T. Turner Construction as part of "This Old House" in 1996.

8.40 Monterey Square

1847

The fifth square along the Bull Street axis from City Hall, Monterey quickly acquired a status rivaling Johnson Square as Savannah's most prestigious with the construction of the city's second monument, dedicated to Casimir Pulaski (**8.41**). Attesting to its prominence, the square was the subject of a handsome view entitled *Savannah, Ga., 1855,* drawn by J. W. Hill and published by Endicott and Company of New York a year later.

8.41 Casimir Pulaski Monument

1852–1855, Robert E. Launitz, sculptor; 1996–2001 restoration, James Wermuth, conservator. Monterey Square

Casimir Pulaski, a Polish nobleman and cavalry officer who died in the Battle of Savannah and became one of the city's most celebrated heroes, was to have been honored by a monument in Chippewa Square. A cornerstone was laid there in 1825 by the Marquis de Lafayette, but owing to financial constraints Pulaski was instead memorialized in 1830 along with his fellow Revolutionary War hero, Nathanael Greene, by the obelisk (**2.2**) in Johnson Square (where the cornerstone was first moved in 1835 and languished until it was relocated for use here). This slightly taller (fifty-five feet) and more elaborate monument in Monterey Square was set on Pulaski's cornerstone, leaving the Johnson Square obelisk to commemorate just Greene. Similar in its design to other examples of his work, Launitz's marble shaft is crowned with a statue of personified Liberty. The carved relief panels are the work of Polish sculptor and political activist Henryk Dmochowski (also known as Henry Sanders). The cast-iron fence continues the military theme. A restoration by conservator Wermuth saw the monument completely dismantled and moved to a remote site. As part of this work, copies of Lady Liberty and the capital were installed, with the originals now displayed at the Savannah History Museum (see **7.1.1**).

8.42 Alex Raskin Antiques (Noble Hardee House)

1860–1869. 3 W. Gordon St.

Cotton merchant Noble Hardee began building this sizeable Italianate mansion just prior to the outbreak of the Civil War, and, like the neighboring Mercer House, it remained unfinished until after the war and under a new owner. Being set back about twelve feet from the other buildings on the block allows a grand front stair to lead to a bold but simple portico. A richly ornamented cast-iron balcony, possibly added in the 1880s, wraps across the front and eastern facades. Large segmental-arched windows with Baroque-like cast-iron frames add a dramatic effect. Other features include a wide central hall, a rear double gallery (recently restored), and a tall cupola with a deep cornice perched on top of the pyramidal roof.

8.43 Bouhan and Falligant (George Ferguson Armstrong House)

1916–1919, Henrik Wallin. 443–451 Bull St.

This regal Beaux-Arts classical house built for a shipping tycoon during World War I has little to do with the traditional residen-

tial building typology of Savannah. The house, its dependencies, and gardens originally occupied two 60 × 120–foot tything lots like a vast estate, eschewing the modest scale of the old city plan. It can also be seen as the fitting if not inevitable spatial and temporal conclusion to the southward thrust of Bull Street. In fact, the asymmetrical, curved colonnade cleverly widens the Bull Street axis to announce its termination at Forsyth Park across Gaston Street. Axial vistas abound in the house's floor and site plan.

The stately two-story rectangular mass of glazed white brick frames the Ionic limestone frontispiece. Here the bronze front doors open to a wide hall that originally led straight through the rear doors to a fountain in the garden, which once occupied the back half of the double lot. That larger garden was replaced by a large auditorium building (1938; demolished) for Armstrong Junior College, which was established in 1935 through a donation by Armstrong's widow. The house then served as the central building for what became a "campus" of eight buildings in Monterey Ward. Continued expansion and talk of demolishing the 1919 mansion prompted Mills B. Lane Jr. in 1962 to donate two hundred and fifty acres on the far south side of Savannah to build a modern campus for the college. In 1966 what is now Armstrong State University (**21.3**) moved to its suburban location. The Armstrong mansion was subsequently restored by Jim Williams (see **8.39**) and then sold to a local law firm. Across from the mansion at 450 Bull Street, the Oglethorpe Club (Edmund Molyneux House, 1857) also occupies a double tything lot.

8.44 Mills Bee Lane House

1909, Mowbray and Uffinger; 2001–2004 restoration, Hansen Architects. 26 E. Gaston St.

After Mills B. Lane Sr., president of the Citizens and Southern National Bank, hired the New York City firm of Mowbray and Uffinger in 1907 to design his bank (**2.5**) on Johnson Square, he engaged them to create this magnificent red brick Colonial Revival house. Mounted on a balustraded plinth with a massive swan-neck pediment atop a ponderous Ionic portico as its compositional focal point, the house presents a commanding figure to the voluminous traffic that enters the historic district via Drayton Street. The front and west gardens, including the brick retaining walls, were designed by Clermont Lee in 1972. A comprehensive four-year restoration of the house by J. T. Turner Construction garnered local and state preservation awards.

CHATHAM WARD

Named for William Pitt, First Earl of Chatham, an important British politician during the Trustee era, Chatham Ward was laid out together with Monterey Ward in 1847. Like Pulaski Ward to its north, the western edge of Chatham Ward is significantly compressed because of prior development in the adjoining garden lots. Thus, the western tythings comprise three rather than five lots, and the western trust lots are less than seventy feet deep. Yet from within the ward and especially the square, the orderly symmetry of the Savannah plan masks its truncated nature.

8.45 Gordon Block

1853. 101–129 W. Gordon St.

With fifteen identical units creating an urban wall along an entire three-hundred-foot-long tything, the Gordon Block (see page 47) could be seen as the quintessential Savannah elevated town house development. Each house is three stories above a fully raised basement and has an identical carriage house behind a service yard. Large sandstone lintels over the doors and windows contrast with the light-colored stucco surface of their facades. Each has a curved sandstone staircase with a cast-iron railing leading to the elevated main entrance, adding a lyrical note to their impressively repetitive effect.

8.46 Chatham Square

1847

Densely planted with live oak trees, Chatham Square has long provided a shady setting for residents and students, serving as a playground during the early twentieth century for the adjacent elementary school. Occupying the northwest trust lot is a row of four houses, disguised as a grander pair by having the entrance stairs to the middle two houses on the front and the stairs to the outer houses on the flanking north and south sides.

8.47 Pepe Hall, SCAD (Barnard Street School)

1906, Gottfried L. Norrman; 2001 roof replaced; 2009 renovated and restored, Dawson Architects. 212 W. Taylor St.

The first Barnard Street School, built in 1847, faced Barnard Street and occupied only one tything lot. The 1906 building that replaced it faces Taylor Street straddling all three lots of this tything block. The Mediterranean Revival school features a battered basement, tapered central tower, and tall hipped red-tile roof (the current tiles are modern replicas). Following a German elementary school model, it has lateral double-loaded corridors. During the twentieth century, the Board of Education enclosed the grand symmetrical interior staircases in the interest of fire prevention. SCAD acquired the building in 1988 and dramatically restored the interior in 2009, reopening the staircases and the interior ventilation windows between the classrooms and hallways and returning the building to its airy original state, as well as adding a rear elevator for handicapped accessibility.

PULASKI WARD

Pulaski Ward, like Chatham Ward, is lopsided in its plan, cut off on the western side by the preexistence of Tattnall Street when the new ward was laid out beginning in 1837 (north of Harris Street) and completed by 1839. The western tything blocks have only three lots rather than five and the western trust lots are shallow.

8.48 Pulaski Square

1839

Commemorating the Revolutionary War hero, Pulaski Square is a quiet, residential park with no monument or fountain. Facing the square are two infill replica houses, one at 209 W. Charlton Street (2005, John Deering) and the other at 200 W. Harris Street (1993), both built by the Beehive Foundation under the direction of Mills B. Lane IV.

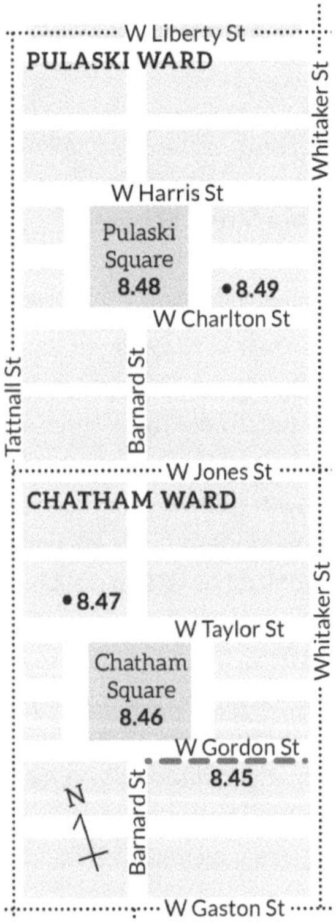

8.49 Pulaski House, SCAD (Jewish Educational Alliance)

1915–1916, Hyman W. Witcover; 1988 renovation.
328 Barnard St.

The Jewish Educational Alliance (JEA) was organized in 1912 to promote education, physical fitness, and community life for the growing Jewish immigrant community. Contained in this rather plain four-story red brick building was a gymnasium, library, meeting rooms, banquet hall, kindergarten, and swimming pool. Yellow-brick details at the cornice create the illusion that the building has square corner towers. In 1955 the JEA moved to a new facility three miles to the south, and after serving a variety of functions this building was purchased in 1995 by SCAD, which converted it into an apartment-style dormitory.

The Beach Institute Area

Originally laid out as garden lots, the Beach Institute neighborhood today comprises thirty-three acres of land divided into eleven blocks bordered by Liberty, East Broad, Gwinnett, and Price streets. In the late eighteenth century, the property passed from Sir James Wright, the last royal governor of Georgia, to Josiah Tattnall. Revolutionaries confiscated and then sold it in 1782 as Fair Lawn Plantation. In 1853, the Savannah and Albany Railroad (later the Savannah, Florida and Western and then the Atlantic Coast Line Railroad) established a terminal at Liberty and East Broad streets and neighborhood development began. Five tracts between the railroad complex and Price Street were developed. Planning took the form of long blocks with streets and lanes aligning with those of the wards to the west, but did not continue the pattern of squares used in the rest of the historic district.

The Beach Institute's development primarily involved frame housing for railroad workers. Tax rolls show that African Americans, Irish, and Germans developed twenty-two lots between 1854 and 1861 and a total of fifty-one by 1866. Progress was slow until 1871, when city officials allowed frame construction south of South Broad Street (Oglethorpe Avenue) and east of Price Street. The neighborhood includes large numbers of double tenements with shared chimneys, row houses, and Savannah's greatest concentration of single-story side-gabled cottages.

The neighborhood population declined in the second half of the twentieth century from 1,500 in 1970 to half that number twenty years later. Ethnic diversity declined as well, and by 1990 the neighborhood was 96 percent African American. In 1978, preservationist and African American local civil rights leader W. W. Law called for an effort to save the neighborhood. The preservation of a few key buildings, new infill construction, and the rise of property values in the historic district have all helped rejuvenate this area.

South of this neighborhood was one of Savannah's first segregated black communities. As emancipation and transportation systems increasingly fostered large-scale racial segrega-

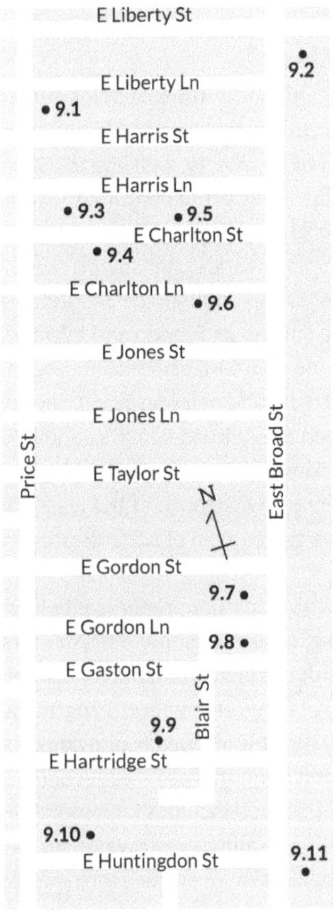

tion, black professional families moved to what originally was called Waringville, named for its founder, Savannah alderman and physician James J. Waring, who purchased the land in 1866. Waring's platting of this area innovated with twenty-five-foot setbacks allowing for ample openness and greenery, as well as paving using a variety of materials. Having experienced many years of yellow fever epidemics, Waring (no known relation to the eminent New York sanitation engineer of this period, George E. Waring) also promoted water and sewage systems, which were incorporated as the neighborhood became Waring Ward in 1871. Waring's health concerns also led to the dredging of the Bilbo Canal just to the east of Waringville in 1874. The neighborhood's centerpiece came in 1906 when the City purchased a group of lots and created Dixon Park as a recreational square, eventually giving its name to the neighborhood.

9.1 Beach Institute African American Cultural Center (American Missionary Association Building)

1868, John Boutell; 1878 reconstruction; 2000–2004 restoration, Lominack Kolman Smith Architects. 502 E. Harris St.

The American Missionary Association (AMA), a Northern aid society, occupied this property from 1866, providing a school for newly freed blacks. With the help of the Freedmen's Bureau, the AMA enlisted the financial support of Alfred Ely Beach, an inventor, publisher, and patent attorney. Atlanta architect Boutell constructed the school from plans used for a Freedmen's Bureau school in his home town. The design featured eight rooms, serving eighty students each, and a chapel for five hundred. Completed in 1868, the two-story frame building on a raised basement rose abruptly on its Price Street frontage and featured wooden pilasters and a hipped roof with a pedimented front gable facing E. Harris Street, and was accessed through stairwells on each end of the building. A fire in 1878 led to the building's reconstruction, which included a louvered ventilator rising from a tin roof instead of the original wooden shingles, without the Harris Street pediment. The AMA ran the school until 1939, when the Chatham County Board of Education purchased it and used it until 1970. In 1988, SCAD bought the vacant Beach Institute building and donated it to the King-Tisdell Foundation; it reopened in 1990 as an African American cultural center.

9.2 Commercial Building (Atlantic Coastline Railroad Company Administrative Offices)

1926, Dwight P. Robinson and Company, engineers.
601 E. Liberty St.

A testament to the prominence of the rail yard complex once lining East Broad Street, this four-story Colonial Revival railway office, veneered in brick and stone over a reinforced concrete frame, served as the Catholic diocese of Savannah Pastoral Center from 1989 to 2015. The building is now vacant and awaits new use. Equally impressive as the building is the large swath of former railroad yard now occupied by the East Broad Street School (1990) and Mother Matilda Beasley Park, named in honor of Georgia's first black nun. The house she lived in from the mid-1880s until her death in 1903, originally located at 1511 Price Street, was moved here in 2014.

9.3 Frank Callen Boys and Girls Club

1960. 510 E. Charlton St.

Juvenile probation officer Frank Callen organized a club for boys in 1917 in the Beach Institute, which became one of oldest and most revered of several community-based after-school children's centers. Aided by the donation of a site and building, it became part of the national Boys Clubs of America in 1922 and expanded into a full community center, providing a variety of children's and adult services. Despite its simple appearance, the current concrete-block construction is a significant landmark in this area.

9.4 Simon Mirault House

1862, attributed to Simon Mirault, brickmason.
511 E. Charlton St.

The 500 block of E. Charlton Street dates to 1852, when the City purchased land for the street's extension from Price Street to East Broad Street. The goal was to provide sites for worker housing to serve the adjacent railroad complex across East Broad. This lot was sold in 1861 to Elizabeth Mirault, a free woman of color whose ancestors immigrated to Savannah from Saint-Domingue during the Haitian Revolution of the 1790s. Her husband, Simon, was a brickmason in Savannah and prominent in Reconstruction politics. Simon Mirault probably designed and constructed the brick house himself, illustrating how this livelihood was one of the skilled professions that many blacks (free and enslaved) worked at in the South.

9.5 Harry Hays and William Lattimore Row

1906–1907. 520 E. Charlton St.

The north side of E. Charlton Street was developed by John J. McDonough in 1866 for a building and lumber business, which was demolished by the twentieth century, when the lots were redeveloped by Harry Hays and William Lattimore. The result is an impressive series of single-story side-gabled four-room houses built for railroad workers.

9.6 Railroad Worker Cottages

c. 1866. 535 and 537 E. Charlton Lane

Located behind 540 E. Jones Street, these remarkably intact single-story side-gabled worker cottages follow a saddlebag plan with a large central fireplace serving the kitchens in both of the separate units. Each unit's kitchen serves as a passage from front to back with a door at each end, and also has openings into two unheated rooms at the outer sides. Interior walls are simple thin wooden partitions.

9.7 **The Clarence Thomas Center for Historic Preservation, SCAD (Orphanage and Convent for the Missionary Sisters of the Franciscan Order)**

1908; 2009–2010 restoration and renovation, Dawson Architects. 439 East Broad St.

The former orphanage and convent is a three-story brick building with a chapel on the first floor and a cupola with a cross on the roof. After the building was closed in 1944, SCAD restored it to house classrooms, computer labs, and a state-of-the-art conservation lab. The current name honors Clarence Thomas, associate justice of the U.S. Supreme Court, who served as an altar boy in the adjacent church. He is also the most famous alumnus of St. Benedict the Moor School (1916; closed 1969) at 556 E. Gordon Street, which replaced the original 1907 school for black children that the Missionary Franciscan Sisters had opened in the basement of the church.

9.8 **St. Benedict the Moor Church**

1949, Cletus W. Bergen. 441 East Broad St.

Established in 1874 as the second oldest Catholic parish in Savannah, St. Benedict's flourished because of community need and the patronage of Mother Matilda Beasley. A New Orleans native, Beasley was the second wife of prosperous African

American merchant Abram Beasley, who died in 1878. Beasley took Franciscan orders and founded the St. Francis Orphanage for Colored Children in 1887. Replacing the original church built in 1889, St. Benedict the Moor Church combines a brick front-gabled hall and traditional basilica plan with midcentury modernism. The East Broad Street facade features a central projecting bay containing a recessed entrance at its base and an inlaid glass-block cross in the upper wall below a two-tiered gabled parapet. The lower gable roof covering the sanctuary is buttressed by angled walls extending beyond the edge of the building, and a bell tower is tucked to the side.

9.9 St. John Baptist Church

1891; 1993 interior rebuilt. 522 Hartridge St.

Nicknamed the "Mighty Fortress," this massive red brick building houses one of the largest congregations in Savannah. A 1993 electrical fire destroyed its original nineteenth-century sanctuary, but the congregation chose to rebuild, greatly boosting the neighborhood's resurgence. The church also contributed to restoration efforts of houses along the street, and there is perhaps no more dramatic combination of neighborhood housing benefiting from a supporting institution in the city.

9.10 King-Tisdell Cottage

1896, W. W. Aimar, builder; 1980 moved and altered.
514 E. Huntington St.

Originally located at 516 Ott Street, this one-and-a-half-story house has an integral front porch featuring elaborate turned brackets and balusters. The side-gabled massing, the porch, and

the plan of the house are characteristic of a Creole cottage, a common house type found in the Southeast and the Gulf Coast. Eugene King, a black entrepreneur who owned a pressing business, was its second owner; his widow, Sally King, married Robert Tisdell, a longshoreman. The proposed demolition of this building became the focus of public outcry in 1978. W. W. Law and others proposed that the cottage be moved and used as a center for black heritage, thereby facilitating neighborhood renewal. In 1979, at the urging of Georgia's governor, George Busbee, the Historic Savannah Foundation purchased the current lot and the house was moved the following year (though it was set on a full basement that did not previously exist). To its east extends a row of railroad worker cottages typical of the area.

9.11 Prince Hall Masonic Lodge and Order of the Eastern Star

1904. 602 East Broad St.

This prominent classicizing two-story brown brick and terracotta lodge, divided into five bays by simple pilaster strips, represents the foundation of African American Freemasonry in Savannah. Due to segregation, Prince Hall, an immigrant from Barbados to Boston, Massachusetts, along with about fourteen African Americans, were denied admission to existing lodges in that city. They applied to the Grand Lodge of England to establish their own lodge, and the first African Lodge was chartered in Boston in 1784. After the Reverend J. M. Simms, a black Baptist minister from Savannah who had moved to Boston and become a Mason, returned in 1870 as a District Deputy Grand Master, he established this lodge, incorporating the Order of Eastern Star for African American women in 1898.

Forsyth Park and the Victorian District

In 1851, the City allocated most of the remaining portion of the common south of Gaston Street for a large municipal park. The areas flanking Forsyth Park accommodated the first true suburbs of Savannah, marked by detached houses set back from the sidewalk with front gardens and iron fences defining the edge of the property. The outward growth of Savannah was facilitated by the installation of the city's first streetcar line on Whitaker Street, along the western edge of Forsyth Park.

The Victorian District was platted between 1868 and 1872 as far south as Anderson Street with the majority of building

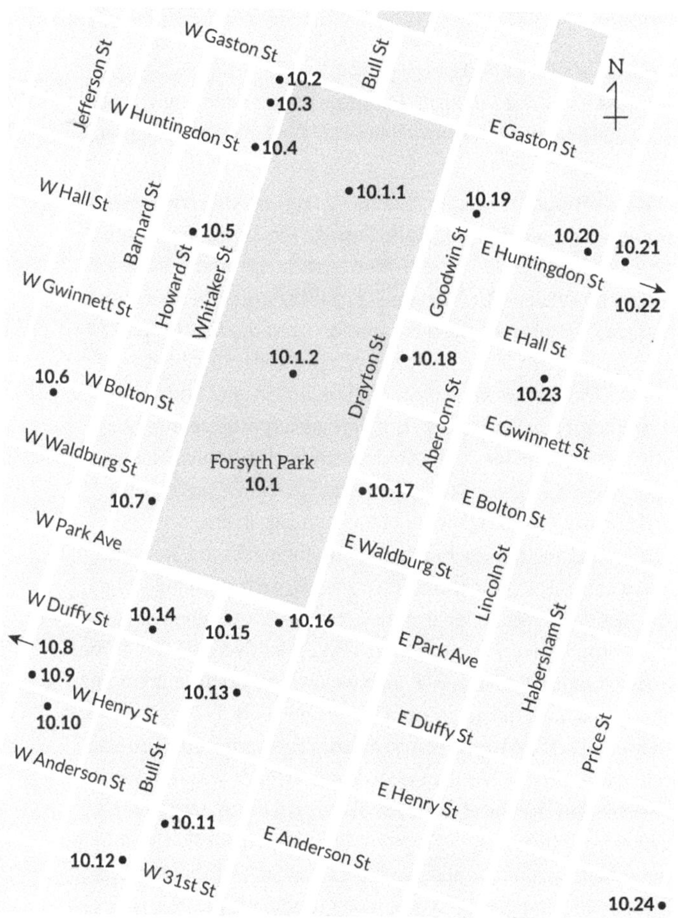

occurring between 1870 and 1897. This extension was less a walking city than a streetcar suburb of individual houses built on open lots. Set outside the city's fire limits and regulations, most of these were wooden and relatively inexpensive, catering to a rising middle class flush with cash readily available through the nineteenth-century innovation of savings and loan associations. The area along Barnard Street between Hall and Waldburg streets, as well as the blocks of streets that cross it in this area, offer one of the best-preserved concentrations of late-nineteenth-century wooden architecture in Savannah. Italianate detached and row houses predominate, many with distinctive projecting polygonal bays rising the full height of the building.

10.1 Forsyth Park (Forsyth Place)

1851, Wilhelm Bischoff, landscape designer, and John B. Hogg; 1853 expanded. Bounded by Gaston, Whitaker and Drayton sts. and Park Ave.

Named after John Forsyth, Georgia governor, U.S. congressman, senator, and secretary of state, Forsyth Place was one of the first municipal parks in the United States. The land had been leased by William B. Hodgson, a prominent member of Savannah society, who received permission from the City in 1846 to enclose it with a fence and open it as a park accessible to the public. The City reclaimed title to the land in 1851 and formally designated it a public park. The first design was created by visiting Bavarian landscape architect Bischoff, whose daughter was married to Louis Knorr, a librarian at the Georgia Historical Society. His design included a main axis in line with Bull Street, picturesque asymmetrical curving paths to each side, and a central circular focus. Responsibility for implementing the design passed to local architect Hogg. Over time the paths have progressively straightened, and the native pine forest that once covered the Savannah area was largely obliterated by the 1893 hurricane, making room for the wide variety of tree species that have turned the park into a veritable arboretum. The iron fence that originally surrounded Forsyth Place was removed in 1896. The land directly south of Forsyth Place, formerly property of the U.S. government and called the "Old Cantonment," was granted in 1853 to the City of Savannah for use by local militia companies as a parade ground, tripling the park's size. This transaction gave rise to a long-standing question of ownership of the "Forsyth Park Extension," with city ordinances in 1859, 1914, and 1923 identifying the militia companies as the effective titleholder. During the late nineteenth century, it was used principally for military parades. Construction of the pair of poured concrete so-called "Dummy Forts" (1912–1915), designed by U.S. Army draftsman Jacquelin M. Braxton and mounted with dummy guns and searchlights, served the growing need for coast artillery training. The fort to the west was converted into the Garden of Fragrance, designed in 1959 by Georges Bignault shortly before he died; this was his final work as the city's landscape architect, a position he had held since the 1930s. The iron gates were salvaged from Union Station on West Broad Street, demolished in 1963, the year the garden opened. After years of neglect, the site was restored in 2011 (John F. McEllen, landscape architect). Its eastern companion sat derelict until 2008, when the distinctive southern half was restored (and northern half reconstructed), a café was installed, and the permanent outdoor stage was erected to its south (2004–2010, Thomas H. Perdue).

10.1.1 Forsyth Fountain

1858, Janes, Beebe and Company, after Michel Joseph Napoléon Liénard; 1960–1961, 1974 repairs; 1988 restoration. Forsyth Park

Situated at the original center of Forsyth Place, the cast-iron Forsyth Fountain remains the stunning focal point of the enlarged park. The fountain is possibly the first large-scale cast-iron fountain within the United States and is the earliest with zinc statues. It was created and installed in 1858 by the New York firm of Janes, Beebe and Company, which a year later received the contract to cast the structural and decorative iron for the U.S. Capitol dome. The company closely modeled this design on the cast-iron fountain displayed in 1851 at the Crystal Palace in London, which was created by Liénard and manufactured by the J.-P.-V. André Iron Foundry of Paris. Forsyth Park's fountain was originally painted with brown graining to simulate Siena marble. All of the original zinc figures—Cornucopia at the top, the Herons and Water Grasses between the two basins, the Tritons at the base and Swans in the larger pool—were replaced with bronze copies in 1974. Janes, Kirtland and Company (successor to Janes, Beebe and Company) displayed a copy of the fountain at the 1876 Centennial Exposition in Philadelphia, which afterward was erected in Madison, Indiana. Two other copies exist, in Poughkeepsie, New York (1870), and Cuzco, Peru.

10.1.2 Confederate Soldiers Memorial

1874–1875, Robert Reid, sculptor; 1879 altered, David Richards, sculptor; 2006 restored, DPK&A Architects. Forsyth Park

The Confederate Soldiers Memorial culminates the sequence of equally spaced monuments along the Bull Street axis and aligns to the east and west with Gwinnett Street, the former southern city limit. Savannah's Ladies Memorial Association raised $10,000 from 1868 to 1874 for the memorial and stipulated that it could not be made of Northern materials, built by Northern workmen, or travel through any Northern state. Montreal sculptor Reid used Nova Scotia sandstone for the monument, which was shipped by sea to avoid touching Union soil. Dedicated in 1875, the original monument included statues depicting Judgment and Silence that met with such unfavorable public opinion that they were replaced by the lone soldier facing north by New York sculptor David Richards in 1879. (Silence was moved to Laurel Grove Cemetery [**11.9**] in the section for Savannah soldiers killed at Gettysburg; Judgment was moved to a cemetery in Thomasville, Georgia.) The flanking pair of bronze busts representing two Savannah Civil War heroes, Major General Lafayette McLaws and Colonel Francis S. Bartow (1901–1902, G. J. Zolnay, sculptor), which formerly stood in

Chippewa Square and were moved here in 1909 to make room for the Oglethorpe Monument. The 2006 restoration, carried out by Sterling Builders and Restoration, involved conservation work and replacing deteriorated stonework.

10.2 W. B. Hodgson Hall

1873–1876, Detlef Lienau; 1970 annex and 1988 elevator tower addition, John R. Reiter. 501 Whitaker St.

Hodgson Hall is the third home of the Georgia Historical Society, which was established in 1839 and is the tenth-oldest such institution in the nation (after those of Massachusetts, 1791; New York, 1804; Maine, 1822; New Hampshire, 1823; Pennsylvania, 1824; Connecticut, 1825; Virginia, 1831; Kentucky, 1836; and Vermont, 1838). Margaret Telfair Hodgson commissioned the building in 1873 to honor her recently deceased husband, William Brown Hodgson, a leading scholar of ancient languages and a U.S. diplomat. New York City architect Lienau, who had trained under Henri Labrouste in France, loosely modeled this Renaissance Revival block on the Bibliothèque Ste. Geneviève (1838–1850) in Paris, the leading exemplar of library architecture, particularly the decorative arcade and pilasters that wrap around the building. A tall staircase leads to one of the great spaces in Savannah, the double-height research library. The room retains its original bookcases, iron mezzanine railings, handsome long wooden research tables, vintage lights, and, as its focal point, the imposing portrait of Hodgson by Carl Ludwig

Brandt. A discrete storage wing, the Edmund H. Abrahams Annex, was added to the south in 1970 and made handicapped accessible in 1988.

10.3 Magnolia Hall, SCAD (Guerard and Pauline Heywood House)

1883, Alfred Snedeker, builder; 2005 renovation. 503 Whitaker St.

A mélange of Queen Anne and Second Empire styles, this house for cotton factor Heywood and his wife took full advantage of its site across from Forsyth Park, being fronted by a double gallery, a form not common in Savannah for a freestanding house. Its narrow cast-iron columns and rounded ends facilitated panoramic views. Pocket sash windows function as doors to the porches. The building serves SCAD as its official guest house.

10.4 House (Laurence McNeil House)

1903, Gottfried L. Norrman. 513 Whitaker St.

One of the most exuberant residences in Savannah, this house was built for McNeil, president of the Savannah Lighting Company. Architect Norrman employed the muscular forms of Beaux-Arts classicism more typical of public buildings, with a colossal Corinthian colonnade whose circular form contrasts with the cubic mass to the north. Here generous arches, baroque terra-cotta details, and iron balconies enliven the design. The row of houses (1883–1897) facing Forsyth Park in the two blocks to the south at 601–711 Whitaker Street is a veritable textbook of prevailing residential styles during the late nineteenth century—Italianate, Queen Anne, and Second Empire.

10.5 Smithfield Cottage, SCAD (J. P. Williams House)

1888, Fay and Eichberg; 2003–2004 restoration; 2015 interior modifications. 118 W. Hall St.

This is the city's finest Queen Anne residence, exuding eclectic self-confidence, with elements projecting in all directions. The exterior includes a regional variation on the usual stucco that incorporates embedded sea shells. The interior possesses a sumptuous range of materials and exotic design details, including Japonesque and Moorish, that illustrate the full potential of craftsmanship. In 2015 some interior spaces were modified when SCAD converted it into its second guest house. The residence across the street at 126 West Hall (1896) is an elaborate example of Colonial Revival with a rare use of graduated clapboarding, which exposes less of the lower boards to weather.

10.6 House

1870. 213 W. Bolton St.

This L-shaped cottage reflects the influence of Andrew Jackson Downing's pattern books, with its picturesque asymmetrical massing and ornamental bargeboards. The 200 block of W. Bolton Street is one of the most varied yet harmonious ensembles of residential architecture in Savannah, displaying various scales, heights, shapes, and styles. The houses at numbers 210–220 (1872) form one of the handsomest examples of Savannah elevated town houses, illustrating the lyrical effects that the raised stoops and accentuated lintels bring to an otherwise plain set of brick buildings. Dramatic double-galleried houses a block to the south at 209–217 W. Waldburg Street illustrate the diversity of house forms in this area.

10.7 Seacrest Partners (IBM Corporation Regional Office)

1960–1961, Aeck Associates; 2010–2011 restoration and renovation, Greenline Architecture. 1001 Whitaker St.

The sprawling, ground-hugging, single-story modernist building reflects the impact of postwar suburban ideals brought downtown and the high quality of midcentury corporate design. The precast concrete waffle slab-roof structure also forms the interior ceiling, evoking traditional coffering, and dramatically cantilevers over the exterior walls, whose continuous ribbon windows make clear their non-loadbearing character. A central glass and aluminum entrance pavilion with a projecting triple-arched canopy reinforces the classical roots of this abstract design. Seacrest Partners commissioned the building's meticulous restoration. The 1973 landscape design by Clermont Lee has since been considerably altered.

10.8 Corner Store

Before 1888. 224 W. Duffy St.

The intersection of W. Duffy and Jefferson streets is perhaps the most vibrant neighborhood corner in this area. The presence of stores originally on all four corners of an intersection reflects the integration of commercial culture into residential neighborhoods that was essential prior to such technological developments as refrigerators and automobiles, which fostered the spread of supermarkets and the preservation of substantive amounts of food at home. The corner stores inherently housed small and specialized businesses such as groceries, confectionaries, restaurants, or barbershops, and were often operated by a family who lived in the apartment above. This wood-frame building on the northeast corner was initially used as a drugstore, and after 1928 a barbershop opened inside a two-story residential addition (1888–1898) on the Duffy Street side. The West Duffy Café occupies the corner today, the last remaining business on the intersection.

At the southeast corner of the intersection (221½ W. Duffy) is a two-story building (1885) with a grocery store, where two triple windows flank the chamfered corner entrance. Notable features include clapboard siding, a decorative cornice between the first and second story, and bracketed eaves. A recessed porch on Duffy Street serves as a covered entrance to the apartments above. The building at 1201 Jefferson on the southwest corner was constructed in 1913 as a two-story wooden-frame house and bakeshop for Jacob Kraft, who added another bake oven by 1916. The bakery lasted until 1961, after which Joe's Grocery operated until 1972. In 1979 the business became Thompson's Garage and the bake ovens along the rear lane were demolished. The pedestrian energy of the neighborhood lasted into the 1950s when seventeen stores occupied the immediate area. Seventy-five percent of the houses on Duffy between Montgomery and Barnard streets featured front porches. By 1950, however, twenty-seven garages appeared in the lanes. The arrival of supermarkets in the 1940s, which offered lower prices and a wider selection, siphoned business away from such neighborhood stores.

10.9 Streamliner Diner

1938, Worcester Lunch Car Company. 120 W. Henry St.

This Art Moderne Worcester Diner Model 751 is great industrial design masquerading as an elegant roadside restaurant pretending to be a railroad car. Stainless steel, mahogany, marble, and tile are arranged into counters and booths with coat stands and hat drawers, making this an unparalleled opportunity to dine with design. Bobbie's Diner (1952; 1402 Habersham Street), manufactured by Mountain View Diners Company, features more midcentury chrome and Naugahyde. SCAD acquired both in 1989.

10.10 Eckburg Hall, SCAD (Henry Street School)

1892, Gottfried L. Norrman; 1910 additions, Hyman W. Witcover; 1986, 2002, 2012 renovations. 115 W. Henry St.

This three-story building is a premier example of the urban version of Queen Anne, as distinct from the picturesque residential style. Red brick, granite, and terra-cotta combine in a symmetrical composition with a monumental arched entrance under an ornate gabled central pavilion. The projecting end pavilions by

Witcover seamlessly expanded Norrman's original design. The building was one of four schools acquired from the Board of Education by SCAD in 1988 and restored. The others included Wallin Hall (37th Street School, 1912, Henrik Wallin and Edwin Young) at 312 E. 37th Street; Anderson Hall (Anderson Street School, 1896, Gottfried L. Norrman) at 412 E. Anderson Street; and Pepe Hall (Barnard Street School, 1906, Gottfried L. Norrman [**8.47**]) at 212 W. Taylor Street. SCAD later acquired Arnold Hall (Savannah Junior High School, 1920) at 1810 Bull Street.

10.11 Bull Street Baptist Church

1927, Wallin and Comer, with N. Sargent Hamilton. 1400 Bull St.

Massive and uncompromising, this church is strikingly modern in its fundamentally simple Greek temple form and makes a fitting complement to the classical-porticoed St. Paul's Greek Orthodox Church (Lawton Auditorium) of 1897–1898 directly across the street. Over a dozen full-width steps lead to a monumental pedimented porch supported by colossal fluted Doric columns. The virtually bare interior is similarly grand. Administrative spaces fill a two-story complex off the apse. The church erected its modernist Education Building in 1953, designed by architect Ralph S. Thomas.

10.12 St. Paul's Evangelical Lutheran Church

1955–1957, Harold E. Wagoner. 10 W. 31st St.

The finest modernist church in Savannah, the current St. Paul's is the second on the site (replacing a more modest wood clapboarded building) and serves as the centerpiece of a small campus of buildings. Wagoner's stepped steeple, crowned by a

pencil-thin spire, is a beacon by day and by night, when electric light illuminates its strips of stained glass. Narrow rock-faced courses of Tennessee quartzite provide warmth and texture to the walls, while flagstones of the same material pave the surrounding sidewalk. Cast-bronze doors open between cast-stone panels. Traditional stained glass creates a window wall around the main entrance, while more modern colored glass designs light the nave and a side hall. A delicately angled brick apse culminates the interior space with a finely detailed altar railing, an abstract geometric pattern of wooden lattice screening, an altar candelabra made of polyester resin, and a striking aluminum cross. Also part of this church complex are the parish house (1925, Levy, Clarke and Bergen) and Haffner Social Hall (1995, Vernon H. Nowell).

10.13 Sears Building (Sears Roebuck and Co.)

1946, Shutze and Armistead; 1970–1971 alterations, Danielson and Paine, Architects. 2 E. Henry St.

The first suburban location for Sears after it moved from Broughton Street, this was a major early shopping plaza in Savannah and represents a transitional phase in the evolution of retail architecture. The building retains the Art Moderne style and projecting canopy over the Bull Street entrance in the manner of urban stores on Broughton, while exploiting its fully detached form with dynamic asymmetrical massing and incorporating a second entrance, also protected by a canopy, facing the off-street parking lot to the south, anticipating sub-

urban malls of the future. The original sleek windowless facade allowed for expanded interior display space. In 1970 the plan was altered and windows added for an unrealized proposed conversion of the building into a nursing home. Beginning in 1974, the building housed government offices for several years; it is currently vacant.

10.14 House

1890; 2006 rear addition, Dirk Hardison. 14 W. Duffy St.

Constructed along with its near-identical neighbor by the Home Building Company, this house illustrates the Victorian love of complexity within the compact form of a narrow yet detached town house. A prominent turret with a conical roof is balanced by an unusual diagonally projecting corner bay. Decorative scrollwork on the porches and strapwork at the cornice, which differ from the twin next door, provide exuberant texture to the otherwise simple wooden clapboard exterior. A dramatic rear addition accompanied an impressive restoration, both carried out by Bloomquist Construction.

10.15 American Legion Post 135 (Chatham Artillery Armory)

1913–1914, Hyman W. Witcover. 1108 Bull St.

The Chatham Artillery is one of the oldest militia companies in the United States, organized in 1786 (and commemorated by a monument in Emmet Park; see **1.8**). One of several private militia companies located in Savannah by the nineteenth century, Chatham Artillery had its headquarters on the northwest trust lot overlooking Wright Square before moving to this location in 1914. This building reflects the popular use of medieval, castlelike architectural forms for armories in North America during the late nineteenth and early twentieth centuries. This armory, however, lacks a drill hall, presumably because of its proximity to Forsyth Park (**10.1**), which had long been used by militia companies. Equally unconventional was the inclusion of rentable commercial spaces flanking the recessed main block that fronts Bull Street. The extension of the building fronting Park Avenue originally was the "Gun House"; when the company vacated this building in 1936, the American Legion Post 135 moved in. The restaurant in the wing to the south acquired a rooftop terrace in 2010 (Tom Hoffman, engineer, with Bloomquist Construction).

10.16 Telfair Arms Apartments (Telfair Hospital for Females)

1886, Fay and Eichberg; 1928 addition; 1995–1997 renovation and restoration, Martin Riley Associates. 17 E. Park Ave.

Erected at the bequest of Mary Telfair to serve as a women's hospital (the first in Georgia), the Telfair took advantage of its site overlooking Forsyth Park, since proximity to fresh air was an important aspect of treatment for a number of illnesses at the time. Fay and Eichberg created a design basically Italianate in style (ornate segmental-arched hood molds, bracketed cornice), but elaborated with Victorian eclectic flourishes like the steep central gable, red brick and terra-cotta decorative details, and originally polychromatic arches (now hidden by paint). A four-story Georgian Revival addition from 1928 partially obscures the original rear galleries. The Telfair Hospital for Women merged with Candler General Hospital in 1960 (**10.19**), and vacated this site in 1980 for its current location midtown. The conversion of the building to fifty-three low-income apartments included painting the exterior, which dramatically altered its character.

10.17 Commercial Building (Independent Life Insurance Company)

1957–1959, Kemp, Bunch and Jackson. 906 Drayton St.

The Pape School, established in 1905 by Nina Anderson Pape, occupied an extravagant Second Empire mansion on this site until 1955 and formed the basis for the Savannah Country Day School established that same year, moving into its present facility on the city's southside in 1960. The current building, occupied by the Independent Life Insurance Company until 1998, was designed by a member of a leading firm in Jacksonville,

Florida, and displays a sophisticated play of abstract modernist volumes and planes that contrasts sharply with traditional, revivalist, and classical structures of its neighborhood.

10.18 Mansion on Forsyth Park (Lewis Kayton House)

1888, Alfred S. Eichberg; 2003–2005 addition, Design Reese Architects and Associates. 700 Drayton Street

The 17,500-square-foot Kayton House was one of the grandest private residences in the vicinity of Forsyth Park. Kayton made his fortune through his business, Herman and Kayton, a large meat-packing company located just east of the city. Eichberg's exuberant Queen Anne design includes picturesque massing, a prominent corner turret, curving Flemish gables, ornamental terra-cotta panels, and elliptical arches. From 1953 until 2001, this building served as the principal facility of Fox and Weeks Funeral Directors (established 1882). Many of the house's features were emulated in somewhat simplified form, but with more than triple the frontage along Drayton, in the hotel developed by Savannah native Richard Kessler.

10.19 Savannah Law School (Candler Hospital)

1819; 1876–1877 redesign, Miller B. Grant; 1884 morgue, John F. Daly; 1941–1942 addition, Walter P. Marshall; 1955 addition, Helfrich and Grantham; 2013–2014 restoration, Lynch Associates Architects. 516 Drayton St.

The oldest surviving institutional building in Savannah was home to the first hospital in Georgia. Tracing its roots back to

1804 as a seamen's hospital, which became the Savannah Poor House and Hospital in 1808, Savannah Hospital in 1872, and finally Candler Hospital in 1930, this is one of the oldest such institutions in the country, and moved to this site on the southern edge of the city common in 1818, nearly half a mile south of the city at the time. The original building received an Italianate makeover in 1876–1877, which included the cast-iron two-story portico, ornate lintels, quoining, and crowning cupola. Grant also adapted the interior to implement what were possibly the first American examples of Nightingale wards, a new approach to hospital practice and ward design based on principles developed by Florence Nightingale during the Crimean War (1853–1856) and published in her influential book *Notes on Hospitals* (1863). He raised floor heights to accommodate the prescribed sixteen- to seventeen-foot-tall ceilings and enlarged window openings to maximize the flow of fresh air and natural light. The hospital boasted three such wards, each a large open room bisected by two parallel rows of decorative load-bearing cast-iron columns, in the east wing of the second floor and in both wings of the third floor. Candler Hospital vacated the building in 1980 for its current location in midtown. After sitting vacant for over a decade, the building was acquired in 2012 by the Savannah Law School, whose restoration (conducted by J. T. Turner Construction) included demolishing a 1968 windowless concrete addition that had blocked Huntingdon Street and obliterated the eastern bay of the portico. The Candler Oak on the northwest corner of the site is at least 250 years old and may predate Savannah itself. The Savannah Tree Foundation was organized in 1982 to save the venerable but ailing oak, which in 1984 became the first individual tree in the nation to receive a protective conservation easement.

10.20 Houses

1890, Alfred S. Eichberg. 226–228 E. Huntingdon St.

Built for businessmen Irwin S. Tiedeman and George W. Tiedeman (who later served three terms as Savannah's mayor), this prominent double house celebrates architect Eichberg's skills in using brick, terra-cotta, and granite as decorative mediums to create many different surface textures and patterns. Additional variety comes from contrasting corner towers and an assortment of chimney turrets enlivening the skyline.

10.21 Houses

1888. 302–304 E. Huntingdon St.

Italianate houses abound in Savannah's Victorian district. This imposing symmetrical stuccoed-brick double house showcases the style's characteristic pronounced bracketed eaves, tall windows with segmental-arched lintels, and projecting polygonal bays at the corners. The developers, the McMillan Brothers, indulged in the Victorian love of eclectic blending, however, by having the bays turn the corner to evoke turrets crowned with tall metal-clad domes more typical of the earlier Second Empire style. In 2001–2004, the rear of number 304 was altered with a two-story addition and porch.

10.22 Houses

1892. 402–410 E. Huntingdon St.

Exuberant eclecticism is a hallmark of Victorian design. Here, bands of red and tan brick form multiple projecting bays and frame Italianate round-arched windows with exaggerated granite keystones. Wide eaves braced by paired serpentine brackets support a lively skyline of boldly projecting gables and pedimented dormers. Below, polylobed and Tudor Gothic arches rest on elaborately turned columns that frame the porch and its quatrefoil-punctuated railing. Ironically, this grandiose ensemble is five traditional row houses in a symmetrical composition, erected by McMillan Brothers, developers of speculative real estate, including 302–304 E. Huntingdon St. (**10.21**) and 318–320 E. Huntingdon St.

10.23 House

1887, William G. Preston. 225 E. Hall St.

This massive house celebrates the business success of Savannah native George Johnson Baldwin, a capitalist and civic leader. Graduated from MIT in 1877, Baldwin began as a chemist, but worked in many companies, especially Stone and Webster of Boston, Massachusetts, a firm of electrical engineers, financiers, and managers of street railway and public utilities companies. Although Baldwin led street railway and electric lighting companies in a number of cities (Savannah and Columbus, Georgia; Jacksonville, Key West, Pensacola, and Tampa, Florida; and Houston, Texas), he was always active in Savannah's civic and philanthropic concerns. One's wealth determined the scale and degree of ornamentation received; Baldwin brought Preston to Savannah from Boston and stamped the city with Richardsonian Romanesque hard-pressed red brick arches and Queen Anne–style terra-cotta ornament.

10.24 Carnegie Library

1914, Julien de Bruyn Kops; 2004 wings, Hansen and Associates. 537 E. Henry St.

The Colored Library Association of Savannah formed in 1906 to establish a public library for African American residents. First using rented facilities and subletting part of that space to pay for subscriptions, the group ultimately received $12,000 from the Carnegie Library Association and, with $3,000 raised locally, hired Savannah architect Kops to design this building. With its textured bricks in red and black and its sandstone detailing, the design reflects Arts and Crafts traditions, as well as Prairie Style with its simple projecting cornice, and features a prominent central stair leading to a large open-space interior. The library fostered the educational enrichment of Pulitzer Prize–winning author James Alan McPherson, state senator Regina Thomas, Floyd Adams and Otis Johnson (two of Savannah's mayors), and U.S. Supreme Court associate justice Clarence Thomas. In continuous use from its opening until 1997, the building was saved from demolition in 2001 by local and national efforts. Its reopening in 2004 was celebrated with two new wings, one of which was dedicated to Justice Thomas.

Historic Suburbs and Near Downtown

Savannah began expanding beyond the downtown area in the second half of the nineteenth century. Facilitated by the installation of horse-drawn streetcar lines beginning in 1867 (electrified from 1888), private residential developments appeared principally south and southeast of downtown. Prior to 1900, all of Savannah's suburbs followed a conventional grid plan, though continuing to incorporate mid-block lanes from the downtown Savannah plan. The less affluent areas to the east and west were populated mainly by African Americans, as racial segregation played a powerful role in shaping the suburban landscape of Savannah. Early-twentieth-century automobile suburbs, notably Ardsley Park, Chatham Crescent, and Gordonston, reflected the grand manner of urban design tendencies that typified the City Beautiful Movement. Such neighborhoods were developed with racial covenants, typically lasting twenty years, ensuring they would begin as purely white enclaves (though often with African American live-in servants). Following World War II, the civil rights movement found fertile ground along Savannah's west side.

Martin Luther King Jr. Boulevard, Cuyler-Brownville, and West Savannah

Former slaves migrated to Savannah following the Civil War and settled in the outlying communities of Brownville in 1867 and Dillontown in 1868. Brownville was platted without squares in a grid with lots oriented toward north–south streets. Dillontown's grid plan included three squares (never created) and lots oriented toward east–west streets. Both tracts were absorbed into the City of Savannah in 1886. Clusters of worker housing indicative of a single-building campaign for an individual patron are common in the eastern and western edges of Savannah's downtown. Many can be found throughout Cuyler-Brownville (also called Cuyler-Brownsville), with perhaps the earliest being the extensive rows of single-story side-gabled houses built for African Americans by a young Peter Wiltberger Meldrim (later the city's mayor) along W. 33rd and W. 34th streets from the late 1880s. Two-story row houses by other speculators followed in the 1910s, with front double porticos, weatherboard cladding, two-over-two double-hung windows, and off-centered chimneys. The predominant house types included single-story shotguns and hall-parlor and Georgian-plan cottages, as well as some two-story side-hall town houses and stacked flats. The neighborhood's name honors the Cuyler Street School.

The area suffered many years of severe decline, prompting the City to implement an urban redevelopment plan in 1997, including thirty new single-family houses. Mercy Housing, founded by the Sisters of Mercy of Nebraska, stepped in to provide a multifamily component and helped serve as a catalyst for continued reinvestment in the neighborhood. Mercy's inclusion of community services enhanced residents' abilities to improve education and life skills and become active participants in their neighborhoods, which in turn allowed for more diverse housing choices in the future. To help guide new development in the area, the City also established the "Cuyler-Brownsville planned neighborhood conservation district" in 1997, complete with development standards and visual compatibility design guidelines.

West Broad Street, now Martin Luther King Jr. Boulevard, first appeared in a surveyor's map of 1777 as a one-hundred-foot-wide street. Its development into the premier African American commercial corridor in segregated Savannah was ironically weakened as integration allowed blacks more business opportunities, and further suffered from heavy-handed urban renewal in the mid-twentieth century. Savannah is currently attempting to balance the successful and diverse part of the street north of Liberty Street with the more challenged southern portion. The weakening of West Broad's economy made the boulevard vulnerable to radical urban interventions. By 1960, I-16 was unanimously approved and by 1963 Union Station was demolished for a flyover off-ramp (**7.4**) to Montgomery Street. This loss exacted a devastating physical, economic, social, and psychological toll on the area. The nearly five hundred identifiable addresses on the street in 1914 were reduced to less than a hundred by 2010. Rental rates to the south of the flyover fell to half those to the north. Revitalization began in 1992 with the newly established Savannah Development and Renewal Authority. One ongoing project promotes removing the I-16 flyover to reclaim Martin Luther King Jr. Boulevard as a major mixed-use economic corridor and a gateway to the

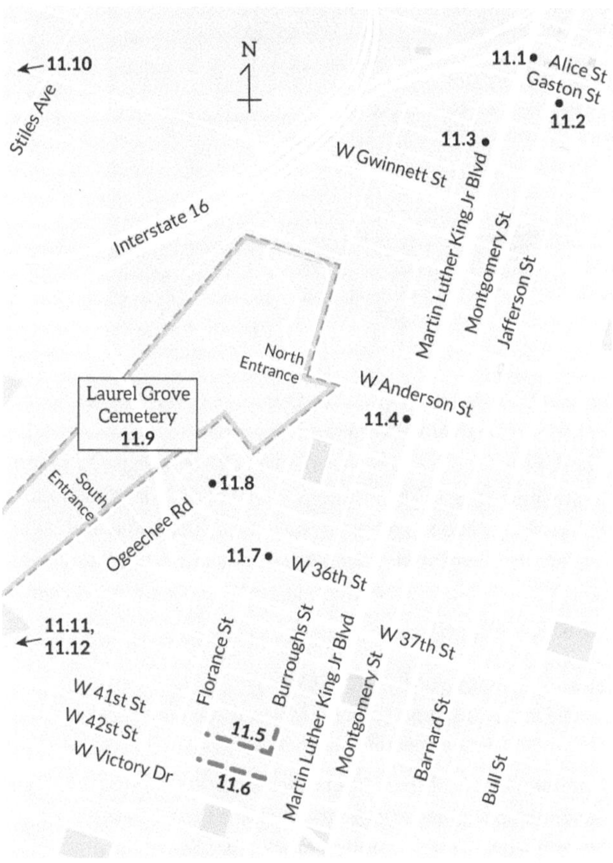

city. Nonetheless, the City of Savannah's 2015 demolition of nineteen of the attached cottages erected by Meldrim on 33rd and 34th streets—to make room for a police precinct—reflects the continued fragility of heritage preservation in this area.

11.1 Ralph Mark Gilbert Civil Rights Museum (Wage Earners Loan and Investment Company)

1914, Robert E. Pharrow, builder; 1995–1996 interior remodeled. 460 Martin Luther King Jr. Blvd.

Once home to the second largest black-owned bank in America, this commercial building served as the Savannah branch of the National Association for the Advancement of Colored People (NAACP) and is now a museum documenting the struggle for

equality. W. W. Law (who served twenty-six years as president of the Savannah NAACP) and the Savannah Yamacraw Association for the Study of African American Life and History worked to ensure its reuse. The museum, which opened in 1996, honors Ralph Mark Gilbert, a religious, political, educational, and social leader who advocated African American voting, organized over forty NAACP branches in Georgia, and was the father of civil rights in Savannah.

11.2 Hollingsworth Auto Services

1917; 1996 carport canopy, Aspinwall and Carter Engineering. 500 Montgomery St.

Although Montgomery Street officially served as U.S. 17 through Savannah beginning in 1935, this building recalls the street's transformation into a service corridor paralleling the grander West Broad a block to the west. While a number of roadside businesses and two decimated squares reflect the impact of this major thoroughfare, Hollingsworth's dramatic lattice girder supporting its canopy and its massive arched and gabled metal-frame workspaces celebrate automotive bravado as do few other remaining automobile-era buildings along the street.

11.3 St. Philip Monumental African Methodist Episcopal (AME) Church

1911, John Anderson Lankford; 1960s parsonage. 613 Martin Luther King Jr. Blvd.

For many years the largest black church in Savannah, this monumental exercise in Romanesque Revival seats 1,400 and was

the setting for black high school commencements and town hall meetings prior to the completion of the Savannah Civic Center. Lankford was supervising architect for the AME denomination, active throughout the United States and South Africa. One of the first African American architects to be licensed in Virginia (only two years after licensing began in that state in 1920) and the first architect to be licensed in the District of Columbia in 1924, he specialized in church, fraternal, and school designs and published *Artistic Churches and Other Designs* in 1916. In 1997 the parsonage was converted into an education center.

11.4 St. Matthew's Episcopal Church

1948, John C. LeBey; 1992 rear addition, William B. Haynes.
1401 Martin Luther King Jr. Blvd.

With its membership dating back to 1855, when nine free blacks organized in a bakery at Perry Lane and Habersham Street, this Greek Revival church represents a familiar story of congregational growth and aspiration. The 1943 merging of St. Stephen's Episcopal on Troup Square with St. Augustine's Episcopal on West Broad Street prompted their move to Savannah's premier African American main street, where they commissioned this refined building designed by an established local white architect.

11.5 Heritage Row Railroad Row Houses

1890s; 2002 redevelopment, Martin Riley Associates with Hussey Gay Bell and Meyer and Associates. 602–642 W. 41st St. and 2415–2419 Burroughs St.

This ensemble of twenty-three wooden single-story side-gabled four-room houses makes up one of the most dramatic rows of worker housing in Savannah. Named Heritage Row as part of Mercy Housing, they are grouped into six buildings with varying numbers of units divided by narrow gaps, except at the center of the 41st Street block. There, a wider space allows a walkway to the gazebo at the center of the interior courtyard, to which all of the houses are oriented. Each house has a covered stoop and short side stair, following the pattern of taller stoops on elevated town houses downtown, with the stair orientation alternating to create a rhythmic effect. Norsouth Construction Corporation was the general contractor for the project.

11.6 Houses

c. 1880s. W. 42nd St. between Burroughs and Florance sts.

The north side of this block is composed of a unique row of late-nineteenth-century single shotgun houses, with their distinctive single-room width and multiple-room depth under a front-facing gable, usually set with a porch. While many such rows once existed, most have been demolished and only isolated examples of single or double shotguns survive.

11.7 Heritage Place Apartments (Charity Hospital)

1931, Cletus W. Bergen; 2002 redevelopment. 644 W. 36th St.

Charity Hospital is a notable architectural and social landmark. Prior to 1893, the only hospital care available to African American Savannahians was the Georgia Infirmary (**12.6**) of 1838 in Thomas Square which was founded and staffed exclusively by whites. In 1893, two West Indian physicians, Alice Woodby McKane and her husband, Cornelius McKane, established an early school for nurses in their home, which led to the McKane Hospital for Women and Children and Training School for Nurses in 1896. Renamed Charity Hospital and Training School for Nurses in 1901, the facility not only served African Americans but was administered and staffed by blacks as well. Constructed in 1931, Charity Hospital's large Colonial Revival building speaks to its success, which was fostered by donations from Savannah's black and white communities and the Rosenwald Foundation. The nurse-training portion of the facility closed in 1937, but the hospital remained open until 1964, serving as a private nursing home from 1967 to 1976. Earmarked for demolition, the property was saved by the Cuyler Community Improvement Association, led by activist Marie Teal Williams, which organized a fundraising drive and bought the building in 1983. A fire gutted the interior in the early 1990s, and Mercy Housing Southeast redeveloped the building in 2002 to provide twenty-five apartments. The 1929 Florance Street School on W. 35th Street between Harden and Florance streets now serves as Heritage Place apartments.

11.8 The United House of Prayer For All People of the Church on the Rock of the Apostolic Faith

1964; 1995 renovation and expansion, Overcash Demmitt Architects. 1805 Ogeechee Rd.

Bishop Charles Manuel (Sweet Daddy) Grace, who immigrated to the United States from Cape Verde off the coast of West Africa, established Savannah's first House of Prayer on W. 31st Street in 1926 (seven years after building the first House of Prayer in West Wareham, Massachusetts), which promoted

emotional worship fueled by marathon preaching and spirited brass bands and often resulted in faith healing. As with evangelical faith in general, this less-restricted religious setting had broad appeal. Grace's visits through the eastern United States from the 1920s to the 1950s always involved long processions, massive tent revivals, and hundreds of baptisms. The 1964 building credits Bishop W. McCollough as Grace's successor and the church's builder. Bishop S. C. Madison renovated and expanded the building to its present form in 1995. This is one of several houses of prayer in Savannah with an overall colorful and creative as well as professional and up-to-date appearance, and features multiple crosses adorning the walls as well as tricross supports acting as columns for the porch. Seated lions flanking the entrance and winged golden angels with upturned hands standing on the roofline further ornament the church.

11.9 Laurel Grove Cemetery

1852, James O. Morse, landscape architect, with Sholl and Fay; 1899 addition. W. Anderson St. at May St. (Laurel Grove North), and west end of W. 37th St. at Kollock St. (Laurel Grove South)

Laurel Grove Cemetery opened when Colonial Park Cemetery (**6.21**) closed, and together with Bonaventure Cemetery (**17.1**) to the east represents the city's contribution to the rural cemetery movement. Overcrowded churchyards and serious health hazards led reformers to promote publicly or privately owned cemeteries that foregrounded picturesque traditions of curvilinear roadways through natural surroundings. This might explain why Morse, a civil engineer from New Jersey contracted to create the Savannah Water Works, received the commission to design Laurel Grove. Meant to combine the park and the garden, rural cemeteries directly influenced the public-park movement. Laurel Grove features an original cast-iron entrance gate for the north cemetery, with a two-story, stuccoed keeper's lodge to the right, a one-story porter's lodge to the left, and a one- story public receiving vault, all in the Italianate style by Sholl and Fay. Monuments and sculpture of varied styles and materials adorn individual and family plots laid out across an undulating landscape of moss- draped live oaks and crepe myrtles. Laurel Grove also reflects the particulars of nineteenth-century discrimination, with Catholics prohibited, Jews segregated, and blacks relegated to bottomland farther from the city. In the late 1960s, the 37th Street connector to I-16 severed the north and south halves of the cemetery.

11.10 Carver Village

1948, Cletus W. Bergen. Bounded by W. Gwinnett and Bowden sts., and Blun to Collat aves.

According to the 1940 census, 72 percent of African American households in Savannah lacked plumbing, while 75 percent had no running water, flush toilets, bathtubs, or showers, and 42 percent were severely overcrowded. Carver Village promised a remedy and was developed as one of the first black subdivisions in the United States. The City of Savannah purchased land, commissioned the Byck-Worrell Construction Company to develop the property, and in 1948 extended water and sewer lines to the development. Bergen, known for his work on public housing in Savannah, served as architect, with $2.5 million from the Federal Housing Authority (FHA). The FHA reversed its policy of segregated housing in December 1949, shortly after the project was completed. Carver Heights may thus ironically be one of the country's first black subdivisions as well as the last federally funded, racially restricted residential areas in the United States. Begun a decade later, Cloverdale, immediately west of Stiles Avenue and south of Blun Avenue (comprising two subdivisions now divided by I-16), was planned as a "new

Hand-Painted Commercial Signage

One of the defining characteristics of Savannah's built environment, particularly in its African American neighborhoods, is the use of hand-painted commercial signage, an ongoing tradition that has largely disappeared in other cities. Unlike conventional commercial signage, hand-painted signage has traditionally demonstrated a freedom of expression that often covers large portions of the store exterior, on both windows and walls. Such signs typically include illustrations depicting aspects or objects of the business inside, as well as stylized lettering, and are often used for barbershops, beauty salons, auto parts stores, churches, restaurants, and lounges. In both spirit and technique, they are analogous to folk art in representing an individual artist's vision and in reflecting the social values and priorities of a cultural group. Many extant examples are located on Montgomery and Bull streets north of Victory Drive. Three contemporary sign painters have authored most of the current signs visible in Savannah. Vietnam War veteran and former art teacher Jimmie Williams has painted signs since the 1970s, in a style combining illustrations (often with spray paint and three-dimensional materials) and text that draws on the sign-painting traditions of the early and mid-twentieth century, which he learned from his mentor, Savannah sign painter William Pleasant. The 1st Class Beauty and Barber shop at 2430 Bull Street is typical of his work with its muted color palette of black, brown, and white, as is

---

residential community for Savannah Negro families" and forms a notable midcentury suburban neighborhood.

11.11 Arbor Cottages

1920s. 3314 Ogeechee Rd.

Arbor Cottages is a cluster of individual and paired motel rooms, each set under its own gabled roof with adjacent spaces just large enough to park a Model T. Built when U.S. 17 was the primary north–south coastal highway, this motel's fortunes, like many along this route, have suffered with the advent of I-95.

Hand-painted signage, 1st Class Beauty and Barber shop

Bradley's Lock and Key on E. State Street, which is rare both for its downtown location and for being a white business. Leonard Miller, nicknamed the "Sandman" for the elaborate sandcastles he builds at Tybee Island, has painted since the mid-1980s and tailors his signs to suit the business, ranging from text to illustrated scenes with bold primary colors, as illustrated at Seafood Haven at 1915 Montgomery Street. A more recent sign painter, Marcus Polite, focuses on calligraphic designs, working in an iconic script of all capital letters with serifs. Given the ephemeral nature of hand-painted signage, many survive only as images, some of which can be viewed online at the Waddie Welcome Archive at Georgia Southern University (digitalcommons.georgiasouthern.edu/savannah-signs/).

11.12 Budget Inn (Howard Johnson's Motor Lodge)

1954, Carl Koch and Associates and Rufus Nims. 3702 Ogeechee Rd.

In 1925, Howard Johnson turned a small pharmacy in Quincy, Massachusetts, into such a popular soda stand that he franchised the idea, a radical innovation at the time. By 1954 he had licensed 400 restaurants in 22 states, a pioneering nationwide chain that was the largest in the world, employing 20,000 people, and decided to expand into motor lodges. The first of more than five hundred such motels built in North America by 1975, this pioneering example commands a 766-foot frontage on U.S. 17, with a two-story plantation house–styled office at the center of a massive court of 54 rooms surrounding an expansive lawn originally featuring a pool and play area. The restaurant, a Series 77 model designed to seat 80, sits just to the south of the court.

Thomas Square District

Savannah's Victorian suburbs, discussed at length in the downtown chapter, expanded as transportation systems provided access to available undeveloped land. With the city bound by the Savannah River to the north and by marshes to the east and west, the only easy expansion was to the south. A colonial-era mile marker that notes the one-mile distance from South Broad Street (now Oglethorpe Avenue), the city's southern boundary at the time, is located on the west side of Bull Street just south of Henry Street. The introduction of horse-drawn streetcars in 1867 and electric streetcars in 1888 allowed this southern area to be developed, and by 1883 Savannah extended its city limits south from Anderson Street to 42nd Street and Estill Avenue (now Victory Drive). Platted in 1884, Thomas Square was originally planned for an area stretching from Bull to Abercorn streets, but was only laid out along one block between 35th and 36th streets. Its name now applies to the surrounding neighborhood.

12.1 Sacred Heart of Jesus Catholic Church

1902–1905, Hyman W. Witcover. 1707 Bull St.

Established in Georgia in 1874 to help freed slaves, this community of the Benedictine Order first moved from the Isle of Hope to Skidaway Island and then to a block on Habersham Street between 31st and 32nd streets in 1880, where it built a church, an orphanage for African American children, and a school. Pressured by development in that neighborhood, the community's members moved again to establish the Sacred Heart Church and a high school for boys on a full block of Bull Street, set on land donated by Mother Mathilda Beasley, Georgia's first black nun, who lived out her last years in a cottage near this building. A late and subdued expression of High Victorian Gothic, the church was constructed of red pressed brick with white Georgia marble trim, and has twin spires and a red tile roof. The adjacent Notre Dame Academy was the first home of the Benedictine Military School (1904; 2001–2002 restoration, Gunn Meyerhoff Shay Architects), which moved to its remarkable modernist campus (**20.10**) in 1963. Attached to the rear of its earlier building is a Gothic Revival auditorium and armory (1924) by Levy, Clarke and Bergen, which is reminiscent of West Point in New York.

12.2 Gingerbread House (Cord Asendorf House)

1899. 1921 Bull St.

Built by the Hawley Construction Company at the peak of development occurring west of Bull Street, this two-story side-hall gabled house features a front and side double gallery. An example of Steamboat Gothic, it boasts Savannah's most elaborate wooden latticework and fretwork, as well as extended eaves and cornice brackets. A similar use of arched lattice frames in an overall simpler design can be found nearby at 1312–1314 Martin Luther King Jr. Boulevard, which dates before 1898, with its double gallery added in 1916.

12.3 Bull Street Public Library (Savannah Public Library)

1915–1916, Hyman W. Witcover; 1935 addition; 1995–2000 addition and restoration, Cogdell and Mendrala Architects. 2002 Bull St.

This library, the centerpiece of what was then the preeminent white neighborhood in Savannah, received $75,000 from the Carnegie Foundation, five times the amount that was previously given to the black Carnegie Library (**10.24**). The two-story masonry building includes a full-height entrance porch with Ionic columns, a wide frieze carved with the words "Savannah Public Library," a stepped parapet wall with an inspirational inscription quoting John Ruskin, and tripled windows with transoms. A sense of empowerment through knowledge is evoked by the inscription—"Make Books Thy Comrades"—carved into the lintel of the door. The WPA funds for the 1935 addition included a Robin Hood mural by local artists William and Martina Hoffman in the children's room (now an auditorium) inside the original building as well. One block of W. 36th Street was removed to make space for the library's expansion, which opened in 2000. The postmodernist addition evokes its predecessor in scale and its split-stone marble cladding, but sits back from the main building.

12.4 Dulany Industries Headquarters (Sexton Hall Mortuary Home; House)

1911; 2006 restoration, CLM Architects. 118 E. 35th St.

This Beaux-Arts classical house, which is now the office of Dulany Industries, commands its lot and features a modillioned cornice, quoined corners, and a central projecting pedimented frontispiece supported by paired colossal fluted Ionic pilasters. A wide entrance with a fanlight and sidelights is echoed by a similar entrance leading from the second story onto an ironwork balcony. This grandiose design well represents the Thomas Square neighborhood, the wealthiest residential suburb of its day. While much of the neighborhood is intact, many of its former houses have been adapted to commercial functions that similarly reflect the demographic shifts of the later twentieth century. In 1984, this building became Sexton Funeral Home, an African American–run business. Its restoration in 2006 was conducted by Bloomquist Construction. The equally grand Palladian-influenced Hull House (1906, Hyman W. Witcover) at 22 E. 34th Street, boasting one of the most impressive wraparound porches in the city, now accommodates the Brannen, Searcy, and Smith Law Offices.

12.5 The Collegiate Church of St. Paul the Apostle

1907, John Sutcliffe. 1802 Abercorn St.

Reminiscent of the mid-nineteenth-century Ecclesiological Society's emphasis on honesty of design, this revival of fourteenth-century English Gothic is set back on a large lawn, with massive gables descending nearly to the ground and red brick walls supported by stepped buttresses. The cavernous interior also features red brick walls supporting the lofty dark-stained timber roof framing, which sets off the German and English stained glass. All of the interior wood furnishings, including the rood screen, pulpit, and statues, were supplied by the Manitowoc Seating Company of Wisconsin, and crafted by workmen trained in Oberammergau, Germany.

12.6 The Georgia Infirmary

1838; 1872 reconstruction; 1942–1943 additions, Cletus W. Bergen; 2004 renovations and annex, Poticny, Deering and Felder Architects with Sladek Engineering and Rosser International. 1900 Abercorn St.

Chartered in 1832 by the Georgia General Assembly through a bequest of the Reverend Thomas Francis Williams, a Savannah Baptist minister, the Georgia Infirmary is the oldest-known African American hospital founded by whites in the United States. Initially located south of the city, the infirmary moved to this site in 1838, but its original brick two-story Greek Revival building was reconstructed after a fire in 1872, and it later received modern additions. Until 1896, this hospital remained the only place that provided hospital care for African American Savannahians until physicians Alice and Cornelius McKane established their hospital for women and children (**11.7**), which hosted an early nursing school for black students that opened in 1904 and continued until 1937. As integration provided health-care options at larger hospitals, the Georgia Infirmary was shuttered and reopened, first as a stroke rehabilitation day-center in 1974 and then as the nation's first Medicare-certified comprehensive outpatient rehabilitation facility in 1980. The high-rise Thomas Francis Williams Court Apartments nearby at 1900 Lincoln Street, completed in 1980, provides housing and services for low-income seniors.

12.7 Southern Pine Company (Star Laundry)

1929. 616 E. 35th St.

A notable example of adaptive reuse, this expansive single-story brick-faced light-industrial building is now a warehouse and mill that salvages and recycles historic lumber from demolished buildings. Large metal-sash windows and an exposed truss, sawtooth roof allow daylight into this former dry cleaner, which later became part of a complex that served as a beer garden. The nearby Daniel Flagg Villas (before 1916; 2004 restoration, Lominack Kolman Smith Architects) at E. 34th and East Broad streets, a colorful ensemble of historic railroad cottages, were rehabilitated as permanent housing for persons with HIV/AIDS and their families by the Union Mission's Phoenix Housing program, through a collaboration with city, state, and federal agencies.

12.8 Sisters Court (Little Sisters of the Poor)

1894–1915, Henry Urban; 1996–1998 renovation. 222 E. 37th St.

Following a mission "never to forget that the poor are Our Lord," the Roman Catholic Little Sisters of the Poor devoted themselves to the care of elderly women. Their H-shaped brick building's central section is faced by delicate iron galleries on all four stories, with the lower two framed by a brick arcade, save for a solid central bay crowned by a tall stepped gable. This site included a laundry (1912), a henhouse (1913), a carriage house (1916), and a brick and iron wall fronting the main building (all of which survive and now serve various commercial interests). After its decline, the property was renovated and opened in 1998 as an apartment complex for seniors.

12.9 City of Savannah Community Planning and Development (Abercorn Medical Center)

1968–1969. 2203 Abercorn St.

Massed as a series of squat pavilions, this modernist single-story white brick building by Brittain Construction demonstrates subtle decorative and spatial features. The offset pavilions energize the lot with their staggered arrangement, varying the distance from the sidewalk, an effect enhanced by perforated concrete-block screens framing the corners and the midpoint of the verandas. Above, a shallow-pitched roof turns into a low mansard roof. Decoratively, the long flat Roman split-face white brick is laid in running bond set off by slightly projecting pilasters of the same bricks, which provide rhythm and order.

12.10 The Cottage Shop (Drouillard-Maupaus House)
c. 1797; 1946 rear addition. 2422 Abercorn St.

As a refugee of the Haitian Revolution, Andre Drouillard arrived from Saint-Domingue in 1793. After purchasing 207 acres to grow cotton, he built this coastal Creole cottage, which is the most completely documented example in the city. The cottage's lack of alignment with the street (a rarity in Savannah) is due to the fact that it was built prior to the surrounding urban grid. Drouillard's one-and-a-half-story house on a raised basement of Savannah Grey brick has a two-story front gallery integral with the double-pitched roof and a central-hall double-pile plan.

12.11 Boyz II Men Barber Shop (The Bankers Health and Life Insurance Company)
1958. 2302 Bull St.

With its ground-hugging horizontality and modernist abstraction, this single-story rectangular building contrasts with its taller early-twentieth-century neighbors. The exterior walls of vertical cast-stone panels and continuous horizontal clerestory windows are shaded by the overhanging flat roof. An off-center porch projects to the front and features a gently bowed screen of polished brown granite vertical panels spaciously set within aluminum frames. Typical of African American businesses in Savannah, hand-painted signage spells out the shop's name on ribbons above and below a scene, drawn within an oval shape, that juxtaposes portrait busts with a stylized urban setting.

12.12 **Starland Design District (Starland Dairy)**
After 1916; 1998 renovation. Bound by Bull, W. 41st, and W. 42nd sts., and De Soto Ave.

Established in 1998, the Starland Design District is a neighborhood revitalization project centered on the former Starland Dairy, but encompassing as many as forty blocks of the surrounding commercial and residential area. The dairy is a white-stuccoed two-story building that processed milk and other products from surrounding farms. As production was centralized and Starland and other dairies were closed, this empty structure projected a forlorn atmosphere in the immediate neighborhood. The Starland Lofts mixed-use infill project (2006, Lominack Kolman Smith Architects, 2424 DeSoto Avenue) won LEED Gold status and gave Savannah its first taste of the clean contemporary look of precast concrete, brushed steel, stained wood, and glass in geometric modular units.

East Side Savannah

Drainage and transportation projects facilitated the development of Savannah's eastside neighborhoods. Recurrent yellow fever outbreaks compelled the City to dig the Bilbo Canal in 1874, which drained former marshlands and permitted building on the land. Jacob S. Collins established the Peoples Line electric streetcar along Gwinnett and Bolton streets, making these streets the spines for his speculative development, with Collinsville established in 1891 and the Meadows in 1900. Here, eclectic Italianate and Queen Anne houses feature broad front porches, complex massing and roofs, and towers, making the neighborhoods attractive to middle-class whites. As development continued, such common house forms as foursquares, cottages, bungalows, and 1950s ranch houses filled the area.

13.1 **Savannah Entrepreneurial Center (Fire Station No. 7)**
1908, Hyman W. Witcover. 801 E. Gwinnett St.

The Collinsville and Meadows neighborhoods received important city support with this two-story two-bay Romanesque

Revival firehouse designed by the architect of City Hall (**1.1**). As newer fire stations were built, this building became the Savannah Entrepreneurial Center, dedicated to increasing local business creation.

13.2 House

1893–1898. 1004 E. Park Ave.

Built for a lumber merchant, this house presents one of the neighborhood's more exuberant expressions of Victorian eclecticism, combining Queen Anne and Gothic Revival features, but organized in an unusually symmetrical manner with matching onion domes atop corner projecting bays. Pressed metal ceilings, wainscoting, an ornate staircase, and pocket doors are notable interior features.

13.3 Asbury Memorial Methodist Church

1921; 1956 education building. 1008 E. Henry St.

Although the congregation was organized in 1909, their church wasn't built until 1921. The design is a late example of Gothic Revival, but reflects the more abstract sensibilities emerging in the 1920s. A pair of boldly projecting arched stone turrets dominates the front facade and guides one toward the flanking entrances on the sides. The church's broad proportions make this a solid neighborhood anchor and, along with the Ramona Riley School (1907, Julien De Bruyn Kops; 1928 annex; 1108 E. Anderson Street), reinforced the once-dominant role of Waters Avenue as the main urban corridor in East Savannah. Faced with closure in the 1990s due to declining membership, the church revitalized its services through creative expression, which has attracted a strong revival.

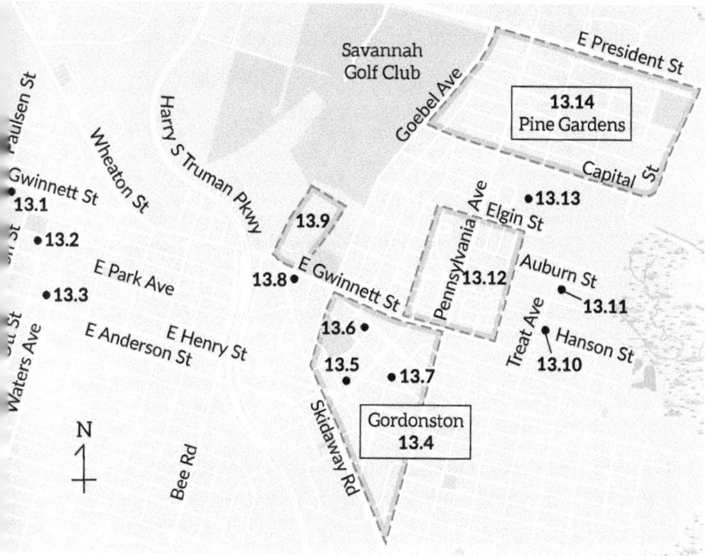

13.4 Gordonston

1917, J. G. Langdon, landscape architect and planner; 1927 park. Bounded approximately by E. Gwinnett St., Goebel and Pennsylvania aves., and Skidaway Rd.

An eighty-acre suburban development laid out in 1917 on family property by Juliette Gordon Low and her brothers and constructed through 1950, Gordonston is distinguished by its City Beautiful radial plan centered on Pierpont Circle. On a smaller scale, the layout resembles features of the District of Columbia's plan, where Langdon was in charge of the city's park system. Henry, Atkinson, and Kinzie avenues—also named after members the Gordon family—feature borders of live oaks and landscaped medians. Juliette Gordon Low Park is entered through gates flanked by panels designed by their namesake on Edgewood Road. The earliest houses were Craftsman bungalows set on the Thunderbolt streetcar line on Kinzie Avenue, with grander examples built just south on Gordonston Avenue. Large revival-styled houses followed in the 1930s, and more than fifty early ranch houses with carports or garages to accommodate automobiles were added between 1945 and 1950.

13.5 W. W. Gordon III House

1920, Olaf Otto. 2 Pierpont Cir.

Built for the developer and facing the neighborhood's central hub, this two-story brick Federal Revival house set a tone of grand Southern gentility. Tuscan columns frame a central portico that supports a prominent entablature with projecting cornice and a balustrade for a second-floor balcony. A single-story screened porch and sunroom extend to the side, and an original garage with an upstairs apartment is located to the rear.

13.6 House

1924. 101 Edgewood Ave.

This characteristic Gordonston bungalow features a large front-facing dormer and a full-width engaged porch. The Craftsman-style house is clad in wood shingles and includes casement windows, and its low-pitched roof is distinguished by exposed rafter tails and large brackets supporting the raking gable. Kinzie Avenue boasts several catalogue bungalows of this general design, while Gordonston Avenue features a few grander examples of this type.

13.7 House

1914, E. Lynn Drummond and Henrik Wallin. 411 Gordonston Ave.

One of many fine revival-style houses in Gordonston, this two-story Colonial Revival is set well back from the street and features weatherboard siding and a side-gabled roof with end chimneys. A single-story screened porch projects to one side

and a two-story side ell with an entrance arcade reaches in the direction of a detached garage.

13.8 Jack Stacy House

1958, Jack Stacy. 1711 E. Gwinnett St.

Architect Jack Stacy built the unassuming L-shaped brick and redwood-sided house as his home and office. A sixteen-foot-high main living space combines a living room and fireplace below with a dining room on a balcony space above. Parana pine–paneled walls, terrazzo floors, Philippe Stark fixtures, and Stacy-designed lighting all celebrate the diverse creativity of midcentury modernism. Just south at 1651 Skidaway Road is a more conventional midcentury ranch house design, with an unprecedented use of stucco to represent architectural features, as well as a dramatic diagonal-pier-supported carport.

13.9 Catholic Cemetery

1853. Wheaton and E. Gwinnett sts. at Skidaway Rd.

As Colonial Park Cemetery (**6.21**) closed and Laurel Grove excluded Catholics, Bishop Frances Xavier Gartland purchased eight acres of land, which was eventually enlarged to twenty-eight and laid out in a loosely gridded manner to provide burial for nearly 18,000. No Savannah monument is grander than that of Captain John Flannery, Civil War veteran, Savannah business leader, and benefactor of the Cathedral of St. John the Baptist (**8.19**) after the fire of 1898.

13.10 Jamie Baker and Cliff Bowers House

1956, Cliff Bowers. 2208 Hanson St.

This owner-built ranch house shows a refreshing mixture of propriety and innovation. The exterior largely follows expected lines with its single-story height, stretched Roman-tile bricks, rounded corner detail, and carport extension supported by decorative iron lattice, while the interior features a dramatic sunken living room with an even more dramatic convex ceiling hanging down toward the center of the room, covered with a thick layer of textured stucco.

13.11 First African Baptist Church of East Savannah

1897; 1950 rebuilt. 402 Treat Ave.

Strikingly traditional when it was rebuilt after a fire in 1950, this church closely resembles its namesake (**5.3**) on Franklin Square. A small portico marks the entrance to the tall stuccoed church, which has a two-stage tower, small belfry, and slender spire in the center of the facade. This institution anchored the 1872 neighborhood platted by prominent philanthropist Charles J. Hull (of Chicago's Hull House fame). Just as slaves had looked to the original First African Baptist Church as a beacon of salvation, this portion of East Savannah became a new and unusual land of opportunity—bounded by Gwinette Street to Jones Street (now Iowa) and from Long Avenue east to the marsh—a remarkably large expanse of freely usable land in an otherwise highly restrictive landscape of the Jim Crow South.

13.12 Savannah Gardens

2007–2013, Martin Riley Associates. Flanking Pennsylvania Ave. between E. Gwinnett St. and Elgin St.

Savannah Gardens continues the collaboration of Mercy Housing Southeast (see **11.7**), the City of Savannah, and the Community Housing Service Agency. Set on a forty-four-acre site previously occupied by temporary defense housing, this design retains that development's innovative sweeping arcs and adds some traditional City Beautiful–inspired design features, with a central park and formal axis more typical of late-twentieth-century New Urbanism and lined by historicist three-story apartment blocks in a variety of colors and materials. Outside the area defined by E. and W. Crescent drives, rows of single-family houses follow the lines of traditional bungalows.

13.13 Savannah High School

1998, Hussey Gay Bell. 400 Pennsylvania Ave.

Built on the northern edge of the former defense housing site, this 265,000-square-foot building can accommodate 1,750 students. Seeking to recall the former Savannah High School (now Savannah Arts Academy, **14.6**) on Washington Avenue, the architects used a "contemporary vernacular" (as they described it) of red brick and cast stone in a Classical Revival design. The entrance driveways frame a square reminiscent of those in a downtown ward. Inside, a two-story atrium with a grand staircase is lit by a sixty-foot-diameter skylight, and the building serves legal, business, and finance magnet programs.

13.14 Pine Gardens Neighborhood

1942–1943; 1950–1952 annex. Bounded by Goebel Ave., and Capital and Beech sts.

Pine Gardens provided up-to-date and affordable housing for defense workers at the Southeastern Shipbuilding Corporation (SSC) during World War II. President Franklin D. Roosevelt declared September 26, 1941, as Liberty Fleet Day, and noted that it was "a memorable day in the history of American shipbuilding—a memorable day in the emergency defense of the Nation." From early 1942 until late 1945, SSC operated as one of eighteen Liberty ship manufacturers in the nation, building and launching 106 vessels (including 88 Liberty ships)

Automobility in Savannah

A powerful force shaping Savannah's growth at the dawn of the twentieth century was the emergence of the automobile. Auto enthusiasts in Savannah early on promoted the city as a destination for this new technology. The T. A. Bryson Automobile Garage (**6.8**) of 1904 illustrates the quick embrace of cars, at least among the wealthy. In 1908, the Savannah Automobile Club, with the support of Savannah mayor George W. Tiedeman and Georgia governor Hoke Smith, promoted the hosting of a road race. Their success in organizing the first-ever stock-car race in America in March 1908 led to hosting the first American Grand Prix race in November 1908, Savannah having been selected by the Automobile Club of America (ACA) over other cities seeking to host this event, including Los Angeles, Philadelphia, and Atlanta. For the race, a nearly 20-mile course was laid out using convict labor that extended from Estill Avenue (now Victory Drive), where grandstands overlooked the start and finish line, southeastward from the city. The 402-mile race was the longest ever held in the United States to that point. The following year, Savannah failed to secure the Grand Prix races and demolished the grandstand. Ironically, Savannah secured the American Grand Prix races in 1910 and 1911 and the Vanderbilt Cup race

---

and employing a total of 46,766 workers—as many as 15,000 at a time. Pine Gardens was the premier working-class neighborhood of its time in Savannah, featuring spacious individual lots in a cohesive but varied pattern. As the president of Savannah Shipyards stated in 1941, "Our idea is to build a village that will not only be a model for Savannah, but for the entire country."

Five hundred relatively uniform single-family houses sit in the center of small rectangular lots with green lawns and mature shrubs and trees, with miscellaneous outbuildings in the rear. The four- or five-room layouts, originally serving unskilled and skilled laborers, represent styles commonly referred to as minimal traditional, American small house, war-era, or Victory Cottages. The leafy residential grid of streets and rear lanes also

Postcard view of the 1911 Vanderbilt Cup race

in 1911, for which a grandstand was erected along Waters Avenue inside the newly created Daffin Park. The only physical remains of the races are the wooden foundations of the Mercer Auto Camp on LaRoche Avenue and mile marker no. 8 (opposite 21 Bluff Drive on Isle of Hope). Among the city's leading automobility enthusiasts was Florida-native Harvey Granger, who moved to Savannah in 1889. He played a key role in hosting the "Great Savannah Races" and advocated for paved roads, chairing the Good Roads Committee of the Savannah Chamber of Commerce. Along with the Lattimore brothers (see **14.1**), he pioneered development of the city's first automobile suburbs (see **14.2**).

---

provide for a sympathetically designed single-story commercial center, the first of its kind as part of a planned community in the city, with ample parking as well as a fire station. Two churches and a neighborhood school were added in the 1950s.

Early-Twentieth-Century Suburbs: Ardsley Park, Chatham Crescent, and Parkside

By the late nineteenth century, development in Savannah extended as far south as Estill Avenue (present-day Victory Drive). In 1901, the City extended its southern limit to what is now 52nd Street, and by 1903 it proposed a conventional grid plan for the area. Just south of Estill Avenue and east of Bull Street, a small African American community named Sunnyside evidently prevented the plan's implementation. The community of roughly two hundred and fifty small wooden houses with streets and service structures had been erected in 1898 by the federal government for a planned hospital complex to serve anticipated casualties of the Spanish-American War, but the conflict ended before the complex was completed. Lying outside the city limits of the time, the hospital complex was purchased in 1900 by Horace Rivers (a real estate developer) and other investors, who sold the houses to low-income families, mostly African Americans. But this "negro settlement, known as Sunnyside" was deemed by Mayor George Tiedeman in his annual report of 1909 as having "long retarded the growth of the city in that section." In early 1910, the City granted brothers Harry Hays and William Lattimore permission to remove Sunnyside and develop the much larger and more affluent Ardsley Park neighborhood in its place. The early-twentieth-century creation of Ardsley Park, Chatham Crescent, and Parkside as the city's first consciously segregated white-only suburban neighborhoods (regulated by covenants to last twenty years) reflects the growing influence of Jim Crow segregationist values, but other forces were also at play in fostering these suburbs.

Progressive Era reformers sought to address social problems through improvements to the built environment, including access to recreation, parkland, and better-quality housing. These ideas had been promoted since the 1870s with the development of garden suburbs that aimed to separate residential neighborhoods from a city's industrial areas and increase the role of nature in an urban setting. By the early 1900s, however, these

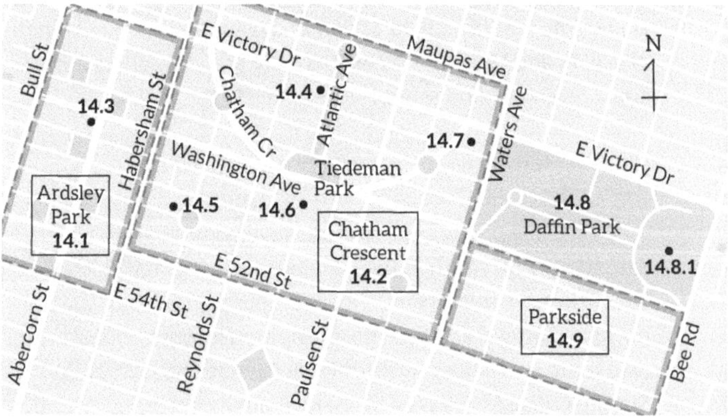

reformers also believed aesthetic improvements through civic grandeur were essential for enhancing the quality of life. These values strongly shaped the development of Ardsley Park and especially Chatham Crescent, as well as Gordonston (**13.4**), laid out in 1917. The first step was the 1907 creation of a major new municipal space, Daffin Park, as an anchor to the twentieth-century expansion of Savannah.

14.1 Ardsley Park

1910. Bounded by E. Victory Dr. and 54th, Bull, and Habersham sts.

Ardsley Park, developed by brothers and Savannah natives Harry Hays and William Lattimore, was an early automobile suburb, extending south from Estill Avenue (now Victory Drive). A generously wide Abercorn Street, distinguished by its central median, forms the spine of the grid-plan development. The area included five landscaped one-acre parks (designed by L. A. Berckmans of the P. J. Berckmans Company of Augusta, Georgia) inspired by the squares of downtown Savannah and set at regular intervals, but placed beside and not in line with Abercorn, to avoid interrupting traffic flow. Each had formal plantings that required intensive maintenance, which fell out of favor by the 1930s.

14.2 Chatham Crescent

1910, Georges Bignault, landscape architect. Bounded by Habersham and 51st sts., and Maupas and Waters aves.

The vision of Harvey Granger, president of the Chatham Land and Hotel Company that developed the neighborhood, Chatham Crescent was an early automobile suburb laid out at the same time and in coordination with Ardsley Park, but on a larger scale and with a more grandiose plan. The one-half-mile-square development is an example of the City Beautiful movement. Its grand symmetrical design features a broad pedestrian mall on Atlantic Avenue lined by palmetto trees as the central north–south axis leading to the prominent central building site, intended for a hotel but ultimately occupied by Savannah High School (**14.6**). A prominent crescent street with a median also leads to that site, its apex intersecting with Washington Avenue, a broad east–west street called 47th Street until 1932, also with a median, lined by three rows of majestic live oak trees. Each quadrant of the development centers on a circular park—effectively squares, but better suited to the movement of cars.

Chatham Crescent and Ardsley Park form a virtually seamless whole popularly known today as simply Ardsley Park. Their only visible distinction is the presence of tree lawns (grassy areas between sidewalks and streets) in Ardsley Park, whereas the sidewalks meet the curb in Chatham Crescent. Both developments include service lanes running east–west down the center of each block (continuing that feature from the Savannah plan) and extensive landscaping. The neighborhoods include numerous houses designed by prominent Savannah architects or by building contractor companies in all the fashionable styles of the early twentieth century, as well as many boldly individualistic variations on Craftsman houses and bungalows.

14.3 Harry Hays Lattimore House

1910, Percy Sugden. 39 Washington Ave., Ardsley Park

This house for Ardsley Park's codeveloper Harry Hays Lattimore was strategically located at the principal intersection of the development, and set the standard for the grandest houses in Ardsley Park and Chatham Crescent with its Beaux-Arts classical styling. A monumental portico with colossal Corinthian columns proudly proclaims the social status of its occupant. Other notable houses in this style include 2807 Abercorn Street (1913, Olaf Otto) and 920 E. Victory Drive (c. 1912).

14.4 Robert M. Hitch House

1910, Hyman W. Witcover. 2601 Atlantic Ave., Chatham Crescent

Among the most desirable building sites in the Chatham Crescent development were those fronting the spacious Atlantic Avenue mall, where the divided street flanks a generous green space and palmetto-lined walkway. Built for prominent Savannah lawyer (and later mayor) Hitch, the house stands back on its site, fronted by a landscaped and terraced front yard. The Mediterranean Revival house features stone-trimmed windows set against the stucco walls and crowned by a dramatically projecting and bracketed cornice, where small windows indicate a third floor. A porte-cochere on the north side strays slightly from the symmetrical composition. Witcover also designed the Spanish Colonial Revival house at 102 E. 44th Street.

14.5 House

1921–1922. 230 E. 50th St., Chatham Crescent

Situated on a sprawling corner lot overlooking McCauley Park, one of the four circles in Chatham Crescent, this house fulfills the suburban dream of being surrounded by green space. The Craftsman-style design boasts dramatically projecting eaves with angle brackets, and its deceptively compact mass is fronted by an extensive porch that extends westward to form a porte-cochere in a manner evoking Frank Lloyd Wright's Prairie Style houses. The porch piers are constructed of rounded field stones, giving the house a strongly vernacular character. The west side and rear parts of the property are densely landscaped in contrast to the open front yard.

14.6 Savannah Arts Academy (Savannah High School)

1935–1937, Levy and Clarke, supervising architects; Cletus W. Bergen, consulting architect; Henrik Wallin, Walter P. Marshall and Percy Sugden, associate architects. 500 E. Washington Ave., Chatham Crescent

As the focal point of the Chatham Crescent development, Harvey Granger planned the Georgia Hotel in an exuberant Spanish Colonial Revival style, designed by Wallin and Young. Construction began in 1912, but was abandoned in 1914. The incomplete ruins of the hotel remained until 1932, when they were used to solidify the shoreline of Bonaventure Cemetery (**17.1**). In 1935 the Board of Education acquired the site for Savannah High School. Designed to accommodate 2,000 students, it was the largest Public Works Administration (PWA) project in Georgia and the largest high school in the state. Its Georgian Revival style, popular for schools in the early twentieth century, was also used for the nearby 49th Street School (1929, Levy, Bergen and Wallin). In 1998, Savannah High moved to a new building (**13.13**), and a newly established public magnet high school, the Savannah Arts Academy, took up residence a year later.

14.7 Blessed Sacrament Catholic School

1958, Cletus W. Bergen and William P. Bergen Architects. E. 44th St. at Chatham Crescent, Chatham Crescent

Attached to the earlier Blessed Sacrament Catholic Church (1942, Henry D. Dagit and Sons), this modernist building confidently departs from traditional school architecture with its dynamic asymmetry and abstract planes. With the Cathedral Parochial School (**8.18**) downtown, the school showcases the Catholic diocese's commitment to a fresh image during the 1950s. Reinforced concrete fins and horizontal roof planes define the eight classrooms on the south facade and boldly project forward, shading the metal and glass window walls from the sun. Simple brick and glass walls mark the entrance, which is crowned by an arched concrete canopy.

14.8 Daffin Park

1906–1907, John Nolen; later modifications. Bounded by E. Victory Dr., Waters and Washington aves., and Bee Rd.

This eighty-acre rectangular park was the first significant addition of green space to the city since the designation of Forsyth Park (**10.1**) extension as a parade ground. It was named in honor of P. D. Daffin, the city's first park and tree commissioner. In 1906, the Park and Tree Commission hired Nolen to design the park, among the first in his illustrious career as a leading twentieth-century landscape architect and urban designer. His City Beautiful design, accepted by the City in 1907, is symmetrical in form and dominated by a central green mall, 210 feet wide and 1,440 feet long, planted with four rows of live oaks, and flanked by paved drives that terminated at each end in a circular drive from which diagonal drives led to the corners of the park. These drives were lined with live oaks from Ossabaw Island, a feature that still strongly defines the park. To the north and south of the mall the plan included a variety of athletic facilities, including tennis courts and playing fields, in keeping with the goal of it being an "Athletic Park." In keeping with the social ideals and prejudices of the Progressive Era, activities in the park were strictly programmed at first and open only to whites, except on certain occasions. The vast green field on the park's south side preserves Nolen's design, while evolving social needs led to various changes on the north side, most notably the 1920s addition of a public swimming pond in the shape of the continental United States. The lake was relandscaped and two sixty-foot-jet fountains installed in 1991–1998 as a legacy project of the 1996 Summer Olympics yachting events in Savannah. The most significant departure from Nolen's design (though not from the park's purpose) was the construction of a wooden municipal baseball stadium (**14.8.1**) in 1927 and to its east the 1938 planting of the Herty Memorial Pines (honoring Savannah native and leading American chemist Charles Herty), which dramatically altered the park's east end. Daffin Park welcomed the first airmail delivery in Georgia in 1911, served as a temporary airfield for mail service and private aviators from 1919 through the 1920s, and was the site of the annual arrival of Santa Claus (by plane) in the 1930s.

14.8.1 Grayson Stadium

1927; 1941 rebuilt; later modifications. 1401 E. Victory Dr.

The original Municipal Stadium was designed principally for baseball, but with parallel east and west concrete bleachers aligned for high school football games. After the main section of the stadium, constructed of wood, was heavily damaged by a 1940 hurricane, prominent Savannah civic, political, and social leader General William L. Grayson spearheaded the campaign to erect a new stadium and secured funding from the WPA. Constructed in 1941 by the Savannah Department of Engineering, but never fully completed due to World War II (it lacks the eastern half of a planned five-sided north end; a corresponding five-sided south end was never begun), the stadium was named in honor of Grayson, who died earlier that year. The polygonal brick exterior with its multiple arched entrances reflects the trademark features of major league ballparks of the early twentieth century, as does the wooden canopy over the seating supported on steel columns that partially block the spectators' view. The design incorporated the original west bleachers, which extend along the right-field line, while the original east bleachers remained detached but were demolished in 2007 after years of non-use. Grayson remains one of the oldest-functioning minor league baseball stadiums in the country.

14.9 Parkside

1913. Bounded by Waters Ave., Daffin Park, Bee Rd., and 51st Street Ln.

Initially called Parkside Place, this development was created by the Parkside Land Company. Reinforcing its connection to Daffin Park, the north–south streets are named after trees—Live Oak, Cedar, Ash, and Hickory. Less affluent than Ardsley Park and Chatham Crescent to its west, Parkside was a middle-class streetcar suburb. A few sizable Colonial Revival and American foursquare houses occupy the northwest corner of the development, but most of the houses are Craftsman bungalows (concentrated in the western half), Cape Cod cottages (found throughout), and ranch-style houses (set in the eastern half of the district).

Beyond Downtown and Its Immediate Suburbs

Savannah has always extended beyond what comprises the downtown area and its nineteenth- and early twentieth-century suburbs. Plantation lands; towns such as Thunderbolt, Montgomery, Beaulieu, and Parkersburg; African American communities such as Sandfly and Pin Point; and forts and islands occupied what remain peripheral parts of the county. What makes the city different from other American urban settings, beyond its unique riverfront and famous plan, is the manner in which the waterways between the Savannah and Ogeechee rivers shaped its growth from 1733 to the present. Small narrows, inlets, wetlands, and marshes made movement between the communities difficult before the arrival of railroads, streetcars, and automobiles. They also had a unique effect on development from the nineteenth century to the period of postwar sprawl. Yet despite the way water shaped Savannah, the outer communities were able to maintain a connection to the city while growing in a relatively autonomous and historically important way. This concluding chapter describes the architectural and urban significance of those areas beyond Savannah's celebrated downtown and earliest suburbs.

These more peripheral and in some cases rarely visited or studied places tell a more complete story of changes in the city's cultural fabric, lost architecture, and small communities, as well as the architectural history of its vital African American communities, which dealt with slavery and almost a century of segregation. The military structures, former plantation lands, suburbs, and the architecture of affluent and poor communities discussed in this chapter similarly highlight the costs and benefits of Savannah's rapid and often uneven growth, especially in the twentieth century.

Along the Savannah River: Savannah Forts, Oatland Island, and Tybee Light Station

The Savannah area boasts an especially rich variety of fortifications. Although none of these survive aboveground within the landmark historic district, archaeological excavations have revealed the remains of various Revolutionary War–era earthworks, including the Spring Hill Redoubt (see **7.1.6**). A sequence of fortification sites extending along a remarkably short stretch of the Savannah River, from downtown Savannah to Tybee Island, documents the development of American coastal fortifications from the colonial period to the early twentieth century. The last of these defenses is adjacent to the historic Tybee Lighthouse Station (**15.7**).

An area of roughly fourteen miles extends from the mainland to Tybee Island, one of coastal Georgia's barrier islands. In between lie extensive tidal marshes and islands (the largest being Whitemarsh, Wilmington, and Talahi) that remained largely undeveloped until the 1970s. The relative isolation of the sites in this area contributed to their preservation. The erection of the Order of Railway Conductors Home (**15.3**) on Oatland Island in 1927 represented an important step in the area's development as residential suburbs of Savannah.

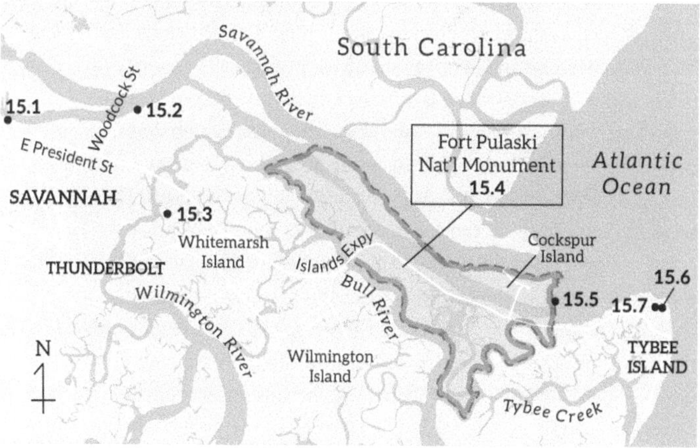

15.1 Fort Wayne Site (Fort Prevost)

1734, 1776; 1778 modification, 1808–1812 new fortification; 1871 retaining wall. Near intersection of E. Bay and E. River sts.

Yamacraw Bluff, commanding the eastern approach to Savannah, has been the site of several fortifications, beginning with a battery of twelve cannon roughly on the site of the Cotton Exchange (**1.4**), documented in the Gordon View print of 1734 (see page 6). By the time of the Revolution in 1776, American forces constructed a simple battery on the easternmost end of the bluff (incorporating part of the Trustees' Garden), which was captured by British forces in 1778 and rebuilt as a bastioned work named Fort Prevost. This was renamed Fort Wayne with the British surrender of the city. A new fort was built on the site beginning in 1808 as part of the Second System (a series of coastal forts authorized by the U.S. Congress in 1807). This fort consisted of a crescent-shaped earthen parapet, barracks and storage buildings, a magazine, and a shot furnace. The site was purchased in 1852 by the Savannah Gas Light Company. The present brick retaining wall overlooking the Savannah River, constructed by the City in 1871, roughly corresponds to the parapet of the Second System fort.

15.2 Old Fort Jackson (Fort Jackson)

1808–1812, 1845–1861, c. 1870. 1 Fort Jackson Rd.

Fort Jackson, at the confluence of the Savannah and the Back rivers, was the site of a Revolutionary-period earthwork. The present fort was constructed between 1808 and 1812 as a Second System work and is noteworthy as an early all-masonry fort built by the United States. It initially consisted of a polygonal casemated work for six cannon facing the river, which was left open to the rear. The magazine, landside defensive works, and sally port were added in 1845–1861 but never completed. The traverse magazine on the *terre plein* (upper level) was added c. 1870. Fort Jackson was the hub of Civil War defenses of the Savannah River, with several waterside batteries constructed in the vicinity and the ironclad CSS *Georgia* moored directly across the channel. (The submerged remains of the Confederate ship are being salvaged as part of the ongoing project to deepen the Savannah River channel.) The ruins of the largest of these batteries, Fort Lee, are visible on the shore at low tide adjacent to the pier immediately downriver. The fort was restored by the State of Georgia during the 1960s and briefly opened as a maritime museum before the Coastal Heritage Society assumed site operations in 1975. The fort's welcome center, the Tybee Depot (1888; 1990 moved and restored, Coastal Heritage Society), originally stood on President Street just east of downtown and served as the Savannah terminus of the railroad line connecting the city with Tybee Island from 1887 to 1933.

15.3 Oatland Island Wildlife Center of Savannah (Order of Railway Conductors Home)

1927, Wallin and Comer. 711 Sandtown Rd., access via Islands Expwy.

This sprawling two-story Georgian Revival building was commissioned by the National Order of Railway Conductors as a retirement home. It opened to fourteen members of the Order who arrived from Illinois to live here, and welcomed all members as well as their wives and widows. A burial plot dedicated to the Brotherhood of Railway Conductors exists at Bonaventure Cemetery (**17.1**). The home had a grand entrance, sixty-seven bedrooms, thirty-six baths, a dining room, modern kitchen, and lounge. It closed in 1940 for lack of residents. In 1941, the United States Public Health Service converted the building into a research hospital for women, children, and victims of such diseases as syphilis. In 1945, after the discovery of penicillin, the facility was offered to Malaria Control in War Areas (MCWA), an organization that responded to the threat of disease in World War II's Pacific theater—work that led to the formation in 1946 of the Centers for Disease Control in Atlanta. The Savannah Board of Education was granted the property in 1971 and converted it to the wildlife center, Georgia's first environmental education facility.

15.4 Fort Pulaski National Monument

1924. Cockspur Island

Fort Pulaski is located on Cockspur Island at the mouth of the Savannah River and includes elements of several fortification periods, as well as a monument (1951) sponsored by the Georgia Society, Colonial Dames of America, marking the site where John Wesley landed after crossing the Atlantic Ocean and held a thanksgiving service on February 6, 1736. The fort, the island, and surrounding marshland were designated a national monument in 1924, and comprises an area of 54,000 acres, all but 450 of which are tidal marshes and mud flats. The National Park Service acquired responsibility for the site in 1933.

15.4.1 Fort Pulaski Visitor Center

1962–1963, National Park Service Eastern Office of Design and Construction (EODC), Levy and Kiley, supervising architects; Donald S. Nutt, supervising engineer

Constructed as part of the National Park Service's Mission 66 program to expand visitor services leading up to their fiftieth anniversary in 1966, the Visitor Center stands outside the fort in order to preserve the site as a "period exhibit." The modernist design of this cylindrical brick building complements the simplicity of the historic fortifications and is positioned precisely so that its exit positions the visitor on axis with the center line of the fort. The architects drew inspiration from Eero Saarinen's design for the MIT Chapel (1955) for its circular plan, base arches, rusticated brick, and surrounding gravel moat. A functional sunscreen of aluminum panels positioned vertically on brackets is on the southwest side of the building.

15.4.2 Fort Pulaski

1829–1847, Joseph G. Totten, engineer

Robert E. Lee, as a newly commissioned West Point graduate, was assigned for two years to Cockspur Island, where he was involved in the early stages of draining and building up the site in preparation for constructing the fort. The fort itself is a Third System work (fortifications authorized by the U.S. Congress be-

ginning in 1818). The Third System differed from earlier coastal fortification programs in being conceived as an integrated system to deny enemies maritime access to American waterways rather than defending individual ports. Fort Pulaski adhered to the concept of vertical forts embraced by the U.S. Army Corps of Engineers; such fortifications provided concentrated firepower against ships via multiple levels of cannon housed in masonry casemates. Although masonry walls were vulnerable to sustained cannon fire, the relatively small naval cannon mounted on constantly rocking ships minimized this threat.

Like its sibling, Fort Sumter (begun 1828) in Charleston Harbor, Fort Pulaski was designed for two levels of casemates, but the unstable marshy ground resulted in a single level of casemates with a second level of cannon on the *terre plein* above. Beneath the foundation, the soft ground was stabilized with a network of timber pilings, while the weight of the fort was dispersed through reverse arches and battered walls in the foundation. Within the casemates, a clear distinction can be seen between the local Savannah Grey brick employed for the piers and the stronger imported brick employed for the complex groin vaulting. The fort displays a level of masterful craftsmanship in its brick masonry that is matched by few buildings in the Savannah area.

The fort was designed primarily by Joseph G. Totten, head of the army's Fortifications Board and later chief engineer of the corps. It features Totten casemates, designed together with special fore-pintle gun carriages to provide a wide arc of fire through unusually small embrasures, originally protected by self-opening iron shutters. The thirty-degree arc of fire from centerline resulted in the truncated hexagonal shape of the fort, since the cannon mounted in adjacent waterside faces could turn at maximum traverse to provide continuous coverage. Vents in the casemate vaults assisted with clearing smoke from the cannon. The back side or gorge of the fort includes an elaborate sally port with drawbridges over the moat. Demibastions in the gorge flanks are equipped with special flank howitzers to rake the gorge wall with canister shot in the event of attack.

The National Park Service interpretation of Fort Pulaski is focused on its Civil War history and the rapid reduction of the fort by land-based, rifled cannon on April 10, 1862 (the first significant use of rifled artillery in combat, which heralded the end of masonry vertical fortifications). The eastern faces of the fort retain the damage from the 1862 bombardment, with multiple projectiles still embedded in the walls.

15.4.3 Fort Pulaski Demilune

c. 1874, Quincy Adams Gillmore, civil engineer

The demilune (the triangular construction opposite the fort's sally port), incorporates an uncommon example of the "Plan of 1870," which was a response to the failure of masonry fortifications and other lessons learned during the Civil War. Ironically, Gillmore, the army engineer responsible for the demise of Fort Pulaski, was also responsible for this upgrade c. 1874. The Plan of 1870 called for earthwork fortifications with underground magazines and shelters (bombproofs). Passageways leading to the gun batteries include a dogleg to block incoming artillery. The batteries were limited to two guns each and feature high earthen traverses to prevent flanking fire from dismounting the guns. Despite developments in rifling, the guns employed at this type of fortification were large smoothbore cannon, although sometimes these were rifled by inserting a steel sleeve in the bore. The Plan of 1870 was only partially implemented before the U.S. Congress abandoned funding for the program in 1876 as rapid developments in artillery outpaced defensive engineering. No new fortifications would be constructed until the 1890s, under a completely different program.

15.4.4 Battery Hambright

1899

Built but never completed as part of the Endicott system (see **15.6, 15.6.4**) that superseded the Plan of 1870, Battery Hambright was designed for two three-inch rapid-fire guns that defended an electrically controlled minefield across the Savannah River. In this early Endicott design the gun mounts alternate between the magazines; in later designs, the gun mounts flank a pair of centrally placed magazines for greater spacing between guns to minimize the debilitating concussion of muzzle blast on adjacent artillery crews. The gun platforms were designed for "masking parapet" mounts that concealed the guns below the concrete parapet when not in use. The two recesses in the parapet mark where the gun muzzle and breech would rest when concealed.

15.5 Cockspur Lighthouse

1836–1839; c. 1848 modified; 1855 rebuilt, John S. Norris. Savannah River, off the southeast tip of Cockspur Island

Beginning its life as a day marker, then upgraded to a lighthouse in 1848, this structure was rebuilt after it was damaged in an 1854 hurricane. Constructed on a shallow oyster bed (submerged at high tide) to mark the entrance to the south channel of the Savannah River, Norris's design reused the unusual prow-like base of the earlier structure. The lighthouse was abandoned in 1909 when the south channel became unsuitable for shipping. South of the lighthouse, Lazaretto Creek, which defines the west boundary of Tybee Island, is named for the quarantine station once located near here. Stipulated as part of the 1750 legislation repealing Georgia's antislavery provision in its founding charter, the lazaretto was located here from 1767 until 1785 and included several hospital buildings. The north shore of Tybee Island just east of Lazaretto Creek was the waterfront location of eleven Union batteries that bombarded Fort Pulaski in 1862.

15.6 Fort Screven

1897–1944. North end of Tybee Island

Land on the north end of Tybee Island that would become Fort Screven was acquired in 1875 for a new Plan of 1870 fort that was never built. The tract adjoined an earlier Second System work—a Martello Tower built in 1814 (roughly four hundred feet north of Battery Brumby and now a sand-dune field)—and the Tybee Lighthouse Station (**15.7**). Construction of the Fort Screven fortifications began in 1897 as part of the new coastal defense system outlined by the Endicott Board on Fortifications in 1885 and updated by the Taft Board in 1905. The Endicott system employed isolated concrete batteries faced with earthen berms that mounted a variety of modern breechloading guns. The batteries are noteworthy for their early large-scale use of reinforced concrete. The berms were landscaped to obscure their location when viewed from the sea, and some batteries employed "disappearing carriages" to hide guns when they were not being fired. Living quarters were no longer placed within the fortifications but dispersed among other service buildings in the military compound. The fort was deactivated in 1944, sold a year later to the City of Savannah Beach, and auctioned to developers in 1946. Over time, some buildings were demolished, others moved, and still others added, obscuring the fort's original appearance. The various support buildings of Fort Screven are generally standardized designs employed throughout army installations, mostly constructed between 1900 and 1910.

15.6.1 Tybee Community Center (Guardhouse, Fort Screven)

1905; 2006–2007 restoration, Greenline Architecture. Van Horne St. at N. Campbell Ave.

The single-story, rectangular form of the former guardhouse with its hipped roof and full-width front porch is the most common type found at army posts of the period, with minor individual variations, such as the front gable dormer included here. Its location, at the site of the main gate and adjacent to the post's parade ground, is also typical. In addition to providing guardroom space for the duty section and office space for the duty officer, the building also housed the post's prison. The restored guardhouse now serves as the Tybee Community Center and the adjacent parade ground is Jaycee Park.

15.6.2 Houses (Officers Row, Fort Screven)

1899–1905. Cedarwood Dr. between Rosewood and Cedarwood aves.

This row of eight (originally nine) houses with wraparound porches situated atop a raised berm overlooking the ocean

would have been the most desirable officers' quarters on the post. The wide expanse extending to the beach is now developed, but period photographs of assembled troops document its use as a parade ground. The two-story clapboard houses are all standard U.S. Army Quartermaster Corps designs. Despite their restrained appearance, the northern four houses, built 1899–1901, exhibit such Queen Anne elements as elaborate chimney masonry, steeply pitched roofs, and half-timber porch gables. The remaining four, built in 1905, are more restrained in style with low-pitched, hipped roofs and wide wraparound porches spanning both stories. The first of these, Building 38, was the post commander's quarters, and during 1932–1933 housed Lieutenant Colonel George Marshall, later renowned for the Marshall Plan.

15.6.3 Tybee Post Theater (Post Theater, Fort Screven)

1932; 2000–2015 renovation and restoration, Tybee Island Historical Society. Van Horne Ave., west of 2nd Ave.

The long, front-gabled hall with a shorter front-gabled entrance pavilion was a widely employed design for army theaters, and this example is virtually identical to scores of others. Built with a capacity of 398, it was among the first motion picture theaters in the area equipped for sound movies. The brick exterior evokes the Colonial Revival style with straight-line gables, simple corner pilasters, cornice returns, and round-arched windows with prominent keystones. After the post closed, this building was reopened in 1946 as the Beach Theater and continued operation until c. 1962; it was acquired by the Tybee Island

Historical Society in 2001 and is now owned and maintained by the Friends of Tybee Theater. Historic 1940s seats salvaged from the SCAD Trustees Theater (**3.10**) were installed in 2015 as part of a multiyear renovation conducted by J. T. Turner Construction.

15.6.4 Fort Screven Batteries

1898–1900. From Gurlick St. to Pulaski and Van Horne sts.

These six batteries conform to the three-part defense system of the Endicott plan: large-caliber batteries (Garland, Fenwick, Brumby) directed fire against ships; a mortar battery (Habersham) provided plunging fire against ships; and small-caliber, rapid-fire batteries (Backus, Gantt) defended an electrically controlled minefield beneath the shipping channel from smaller vessels.

Battery Garland (1899), now the Tybee Island Museum, mounted a single 12-inch gun with a range of eight miles. The network of spaces within the museum once included separate magazines for powder charges and projectiles, serviced by a system of overhead tracks and hoists for raising and transferring ammunition to the gun platform above. The latter is accessible on the roof level, but the loading platform has been filled with concrete. A stairway provides access to the wide concrete blast apron, now used as a viewing platform, which prevented muzzle blast from excavating the earthen berm in front of the battery. Battery Fenwick (1899), a near duplicate of Battery Garland, is now a private residence and cannot be viewed from public grounds.

Battery Brumby (1898) mounted four 8-inch guns on disappearing carriages. It is partly restored and partly accessible to the public, although the left gun emplacement is now a private residence and the right is the Tybee Island Shrine Club. Magazines and service rooms on the lower level are open to the rear and were secured by heavy wooden doors during operations, with additional iron gates that allowed the doors to remain open for ventilation. The gun platform above includes several early innovations. The working platform, the circular pit where the gun was mounted, now has cast-in steps to the surrounding loading platform. The wider loading platform provides access to the magazine hoists on the left with an added concrete bridge on the right for emergency access to hoists of the adjacent gun. There are two magazine hoists: the earlier balanced platform hoist with two access doors employed a pair of elevators that shared a central pulley system, while the more refined Taylor-Raymond Hoist used a continuous chain drive system. The concrete splinter shield above the hoists was an additional improvement.

Battery Backus (1900) was unusual in being designed to mount a single American-made 6-inch gun and two British 4.7-inch Armstrong guns. The 6-inch-gun platform is visible on the right. This small caliber battery did not employ magazine hoists, as the fixed ammunition (projectile and gunpowder combined in a shell) was hand-carried from the lower magazine up to the gun platform. The gun platform on the left side has partly collapsed due to the removal of the earthen berm.

Battery Gantt (1900) is artfully preserved as the foundation level of the residence on piers above. This battery mounted two 3-inch rapid-fire guns and is nearly identical to Battery Hambright at Fort Pulaski (**15.4.4**). It also employed fixed ammunition with no magazine hoists.

Battery Habersham (1900), which is privately owned but can be effectively viewed from the outside, represents the final refinement of the Endicott mortar battery, a passing concept in the development of American coastal artillery. The mortar battery directed plunging fire from a high trajectory into the poorly protected decks of early armored warships. The inherent inaccuracy of this tactic resulted in mounting a group of mortars that fired simultaneous volleys in a gridlike pattern. Unlike earlier examples that consisted of four enclosed pits arranged in a square, each with four mortars, this battery is linear and open to the rear, with magazine access from the rear as well. Its design dispersed blast effect, greatly reducing damage from the concussion of mortar volleys. The number of mortar pits was reduced from four to two as the result of more effective firing practices.

15.7 **Tybee Lighthouse Station**
1773; 1865 rebuilt and expanded; 1998–2008 restoration.
30 Meddin Dr.

The Tybee Lighthouse Station, a National Historic Landmark, is among the oldest and most completely preserved light stations in the nation. The 5-acre site includes all the original service buildings and structures in meticulously restored condition. A lighthouse has been located on the north end of Tybee Island since 1736. The first two lights were destroyed due to close proximity to the shore; the present structure stands on a site more removed from the shoreline and incorporates 60 feet of the third 100-foot-tall lighthouse constructed of brick in 1773. The lighthouse was damaged by retreating Confederate troops in 1861 and rebuilt immediately after the war to its present 154-foot height with a first-order (9-foot) Fresnel lens.

The surrounding light station was active until 1987, when maintenance support was transferred to the Coast Guard station on Cockspur Island. Light station buildings here include the Headkeepers House (1881) and the First Assistant Keeper's House (1885), built to identical ground plans in Stick Style. The Second Assistant Keeper's House (1861) was originally built as Confederate barracks before Union forces occupied the island. The small brick Summer Kitchen (1812) served the entire complex until 1910, when individual kitchens were added behind the three keepers' houses. The Fuel Storage Building (1890), added when the light was lit by kerosene, was constructed with fireproof materials, including a concrete floor, brick walls, and tin roof. The automobile garage was added to the complex in the 1930s. The beacon was automated in 1972. In 1987 the Tybee Island Historical Society took over responsibility for maintenance of the facility and in 1998 embarked on a multiyear, four-phase restoration of the complex, spearheaded by its director, Cullen Chambers.

Tybee Island

The development of Tybee Island as a seaside resort began in 1873, when the Tybee Improvement Company acquired most of the island for subdivision. The first hotel, Ocean House, was completed in 1876 (destroyed 1893). Initially serviced by steamboat, Tybee Island was linked to Savannah by railroad in 1887, and consolidated with the Central of Georgia Railroad in 1890. The small depot building (1888) at the Savannah end of this line now stands at the entrance to Fort Jackson (**15.2**). By the close of the nineteenth century, the island was an established regional resort, boasting an upscale grand hotel, several smaller hostelries and social clubs, and a number of summer cottages. The automobile road to Tybee was completed in 1923 and soon eclipsed the railroad line, which closed in 1933. With automobile access and the termination of rail service the island gradually evolved from a seasonal resort destination to a local beach town, renamed Savannah Beach from the 1950s to the 1970s, with a growing year-round population.

Hurricanes, fires, and unfettered development have all but obliterated the late Victorian and early-twentieth-century commercial resort architecture that shaped the island's urban fabric, but vestiges of it remain. The core of the resort extended from Butler Avenue to the beach between 14th and 18th streets. The railroad traversed what is now Butler Avenue and its primary stop fronted Hotel Tybee, the island's grand hotel, whose grounds occupied the entire block between 14th and 15th streets. The hotel of 1891 burned in 1909 and was replaced by a larger Mediterranean Revival building in 1911. This in turn was demolished in 1961, save for the diagonally oriented north wing which was converted into one of the several nondescript motel buildings that now occupy the site. Smaller hotels, restaurants, pavilions, and bathhouses were located near Hotel Tybee, and a cluster of boarding houses was located between Tybrisa (16th) and 18th streets.

Summer cottages from the resort era were constructed on large building lots and concentrated in two areas (designated historic districts in 1999): the Strand Historic District from Butler Avenue to the beach, between 12th and 14th streets, and the Back River Historic District along Chatham Avenue fronting the river. Both locations were relatively close to the social resources of the resort core. Today, these cottages are not easily viewed from public land due to lot subdivision, building infill, and landscaping. Their forms generally follow regional traditions for coastal cottages based in part on the Creole architecture of the Gulf Coast: wood-framed buildings sheathed in clapboard, raised on piers, with recessed, wraparound porches, and usually employing high-pitched, hipped roofs that extend out over the porches and have exposed rafter tails.

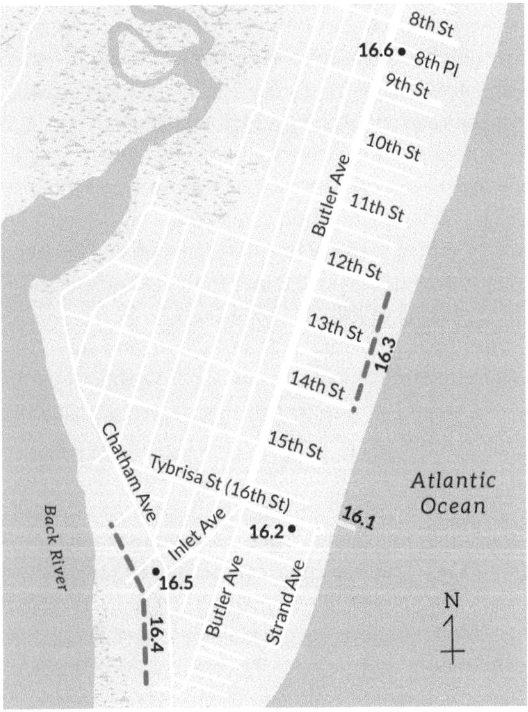

16.1 Tybee Pier and Pavilion

1996. Tybrisa St. (16th St.) at Strand Ave.

The resort's social life centered on the Tybrisa Pavilion, the largest of several seaside pavilions extending out from the shore that comprised food, dancing, and entertainment venues, as well as lounging verandas. Although the Tybrisa (built by the Central of Georgia c. 1900) was destroyed by fire in 1967, the current city pier and pavilion are built on its oceanfront site and evoke that tradition.

16.2 Carbo House

1932; c. 1990 dormers. 9 Tybrisa St. (16th St.)

The original Carbo House, constructed in 1914, was destroyed by fire in 1931. The present building, erected on a larger lot that incorporates the original lot to the south, is one of a few boarding houses remaining from the resort era and the only example that has not been significantly altered. The two-story frame building employs a low-pitched hipped roof with exposed rafter tails and wraparound porches across both stories. Exterior stairways are located within the porches along the sides of the building. Each story is divided into eight equal-sized rooms, four apiece on the long sides, accessed from the porches. Dormers were added to the roof in the 1990s when the attic level was converted into an apartment; otherwise the exterior remains unchanged.

16.3 Strand Cottages

c. 1895–1920. Beachfront from 12th to 14th sts. (view from 13th St. boardwalk)

The original strand cottage lots, which extended from Butler Avenue to the beach, have been largely subdivided, and the cottages are only effectively visible from the beach side. They are aligned in a row, separated from the beach by a spacious setback of sand dunes covered in native flora. Individual paths and boardwalks provide beach access, while a common walkway fronting all the cottages connected them with the Tybee Hotel grounds (a view down the walkway can be seen at 13th Street). The cottages vary in ground plan, but all employ a narrow rectangular footprint parallel to their slender lots and are raised a half story on piers, providing ground-level space for partially below-grade servants' quarters and changing rooms. Some were later raised a full story to accommodate automobiles. Living space on the single raised story is typically covered by a hipped or front-gabled roof with exposed rafter tails. All have ocean-facing porches that typically wrap the south side of the cottage and some include a polygonal gazebolike porch extension on the southeast corner.

16.4 Back River Cottages

c. 1890–1915. Chatham Ave., fronting the Back River

The Back River cottages are best viewed from the beach. Although they are more removed from the resort core, a common boardwalk fronting the beach originally connected them with the final train stop and railroad turnstile at Inlet Avenue. The wood-frame cottages are square in plan and slightly elevated on piers with two stories of living space above. They employ a pyramidal hipped roof with exposed rafter tails. Most of the cottages originally had full wraparound porches on both stories that are now often partially enclosed. The kitchen and dining and service rooms are located on the first story, with a living room and bedrooms on the second. Unlike the Strand cottages, servants' quarters and bathhouses were located in separate buildings to the rear.

16.5 House (Chatham Artillery Club)

1888. 1703 Inlet Ave.

Among the oldest surviving buildings on the island and one of the first erected on its south end, the Chatham Artillery Club was one of several private social clubs from the resort era that provided its members with hotel accommodations. Its typology is essentially the same as the Back River cottages, although the ground plan is different, with common rooms on the first story and bedrooms on the second story accessed by the exterior stairway on south side. Given its larger footprint, its pyramidal hipped roof rises taller than typical private cottages.

16.6 Mulherin-Righton Cottage

c. 1933–1935. 14 8th Pl.

This dwelling exemplifies the classic form of the Tybee Raised Cottage, a building type unique to the island which was developed in response to the much smaller building lots that were available beginning in the 1920s, as well as the need for off-street automobile parking due to the narrow lanes between lots. The cottage is square in plan, conforming to its small lot, and is raised a full story. The raised ground level, which is mostly open space to accommodate automobiles, is sheathed in vertical lattice, with garage doors facing the south side along 8th Place. The opposite (north) side includes a servant's room and bathing and laundry rooms, as well as the exterior stairway to the main floor, which comprises a central great room adjoining a recessed, wraparound porch spanning the south and most of the west side. Bedrooms, kitchen, and bathroom are concentrated on the north side. The single raised story is covered by a high-pitched, hipped roof with exposed rafter ends. These raised cottages were built from the early 1920s into the 1950s; later examples often deviate from the classic design but retain the raised main floor and full-story ground level. About a hundred can be identified throughout the island, although many are masked by later improvements.

Thunderbolt, Bonaventure Cemetery, and Savannah State University

Lying to the east of Savannah is a group of significant historic sites shaped by their proximity to the Wilmington River and the broad eastern tidal marshes. Native Americans first settled here roughly four thousand years ago, camped along Thunderbolt bluff in a small village which possibly was abandoned prior to the arrival of colonists. The name "Thunderbolt" (already appearing prominently on a regional map of 1740) is believed to derive from a native legend about a severe storm that emitted a smell of burnt embers, now attributed to the sulfur and iron in the area's springs. From the 1730s the division of land for plantations would shape the development of the area, particularly Bonaventure Cemetery (**17.1**) and Savannah State University (**17.5**). Thunderbolt itself boasted a rich and varied history, accommodating innovative agricultural, industrial, and leisure architecture that has now completely vanished, with little to suggest what the community looked like over its long history.

The area's location along the Wilmington River (also called Augustine Creek and Warsaw River), which drains directly into the Atlantic Ocean, made it a strategic defense point for successive groups occupying the area. Thunderbolt was one of several small "agrarian-military outposts" or "fortified farming villages" established by Oglethorpe in the early years of the colony. In the early 1730s, the Trustees granted Roger and James Lacey, Joseph Hetherington, and Philip Bishop county lots of five hundred acres each along Thunderbolt Bluff. From the American Revolution through the antebellum period, Thunderbolt comprised a network of large plantations, with only a few small farms. During the Civil War, Thunderbolt Battery was built to defend the Wilmington River from Union forces, using a palisaded earthwork armed by 1863 with fourteen cannon manned by the Phoenix riflemen volunteer militia. The earthwork and the town were abandoned in 1864 when Fort McAllister (fourteen miles south of the city) came under attack during Sherman's March to the Sea, and nothing remains of this significant Civil War site.

In 1856, Thunderbolt village was incorporated with the official name Warsaw (from Wassaw, which derived from the Creek word "wiso" for sassafras), but residents ignored this designation and continued to refer to the community as Thunderbolt. By the 1880s it had become a thriving resort community for city residents, who traveled here on suburban railways to escape the summer heat, flocking to hotels and boarding houses, as well as a casino, racetrack, golf course, and the Thunderbolt Yacht Club. The resort industry declined with the rise of the automobile and eventual destruction of Savannah's extensive streetcar and suburban railroad system after World War II, and

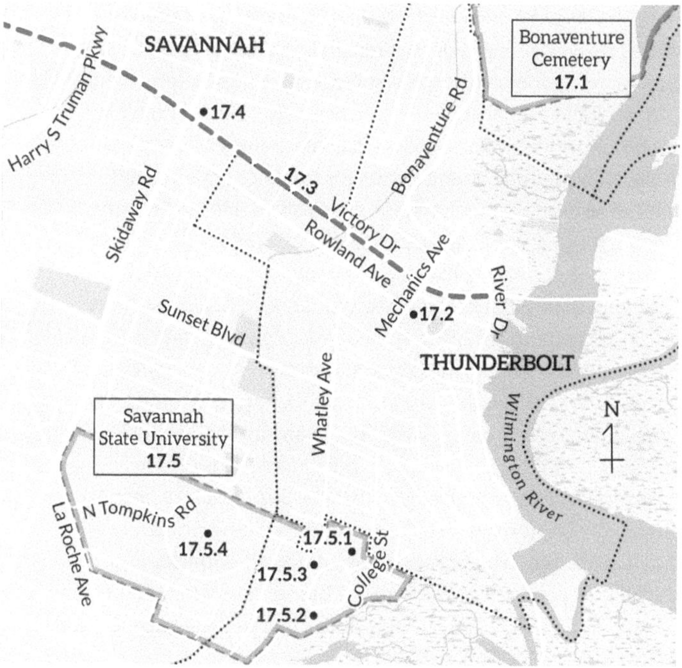

Thunderbolt became a prosperous fishing village during this period. Beset by ready supplies of imported shrimp and economic decline in recent decades, the once-thriving Savannah fishing industry based here retains just two facilities: one on River Drive and one across the river on Isle of Armstrong. In the twenty-first century, gentrification and condominium developments (such as Warsaw Bluff) have privatized what was once a publicly accessible and working waterfront.

17.1 Bonaventure Cemetery

1846. 330 Bonaventure Rd., Thunderbolt

Bonaventure (see page ii) traces its origins to the colonial era. British colonel John Mulryne, who owned more than nine thousand acres of land in Georgia including productive sawmills, settled his family in 1765 on a large six-hundred-acre plantation along the Wilmington River, naming it Bonaventure, from the French for "good fortune." In 1779 Mulryne's plantation was seized by French naval commander Charles D'Estaing, who arrived to drive the British out of Savannah. The Bonaventure plantation house was turned into a military hospital and Thunderbolt village became the locus of communication between the American land forces and the French fleet during the Siege of Savannah. Ownership of the plantation passed through several prominent Savannahians—John Habersham, Josiah Tattnall Jr., Commodore Josiah Tattnall III, and finally Peter Wiltberger in 1846, who set aside seventy acres for a public cemetery, but died soon after his purchase. His son William fulfilled his father's dream, forming the Evergreen Cemetery Company of Bonaventure in 1868 to sell and manage family plots in perpetuity.

Bonaventure typifies how Victorian-era cemeteries served as places to mourn while they emphasized the romanticism and ritual of death and provided space to escape the city for leisurely walks and picnics. In October 1867, naturalist John Muir stayed overnight for five days in Bonaventure and concluded, in *A Thousand-Mile Walk to the Gulf* (posthumously published in 1916), "If that burying-ground across the Sea of Galilee, mentioned in Scripture, was half as beautiful as Bonaventure, I do not wonder that a man should dwell among the tombs."

The City of Savannah purchased the cemetery for $30,000 in 1907 as a public burial ground, and acquired the adjacent

Greenwich Plantation in 1937. Significant gravesites in Bonaventure include those of local songwriter Johnny Mercer, poet Conrad Aiken, and Georgia's first governor, Edward Telfair. Yet the cemetery also reveals a broad and diverse history of the area, ranging from the small, often poignant graves that recall the staggering rates of child mortality in the nineteenth century to the large burial plot dedicated to the Brotherhood of Railroad Conductors, men who worked their entire lives for the Central of Georgia Railroad and retired to Savannah (see **15.3**).

17.2 H. R. Delany Ministries (St. Luke's Lutheran Church)

1962, Helfrich and Grantham. 2718 Mechanics Ave., Thunderbolt

Inspired by the boldly expressionistic designs of the Sarasota School of Architecture in Florida, Helfrich and Grantham here echo Victor Lundy's swooping concave gables (readily apparent at his St. Paul's Lutheran Church Fellowship Hall of 1959 in Sarasota). St. Luke's features an upturned ship's hull as a sculptural open-peaked nave roof rising to heaven. An equally distinctive horizontal base of red brick sweeps around the entire complex, which includes a single-story cloister containing offices and classrooms and a meditative garden entered through an artistic geometric screen. Notable details include use of vertical boarding with recessed joints inventively inverting traditional board-and-batten siding on the interior cloister walls, and floor-to-ceiling windows on the north-facing exterior walls. The original 1902 hipped-roof Gothic church sits next door and its parish hall is accessed through the rear of the court.

17.3 Victory Drive

Late 19th century–present. Victory Dr., from West Broad St. to River Dr.

Victory Drive (formerly known as Estill Avenue from West Broad Street to Waters Avenue and as Dale Avenue east from Waters to the town of Thunderbolt) served as Savannah's southern limit during the late nineteenth century. With the development of Chatham Crescent (**14.2**) in 1910, 460 palmetto trees were planted along Estill and Atlantic avenues, the central north–south spine of that development, with Georges Bignault consulting on its design. Victory Drive acquired its present name in 1923 to commemorate America's role in World War I, and during the early and mid-twentieth century it was a center of Savannah nightlife, with clubs, restaurants, and a drive-in theater (including Johnny Harris's Restaurant and Lounge, which opened in 1924 and still operates here). Some of the earliest strip malls in Savannah appeared at the intersection with Skidaway Road.

17.4 Starbucks (Our House Restaurant)

1959, Helfrich and Grantham; interior, Richard Ranowski of W. and J. Sloan; 2004 renovation. 2106 E. Victory Dr.

A popular eatery developed by restaurateurs Herb Traub and Jim Casey in 1945, the original Our House offered homey appeal styled as a Swiss chalet. The new incarnation of Our House, built following the establishment of the Crossroads Shopping Center (1955, Helfrich and Grantham), featured seating for forty in booths and twenty at a counter and was designed for both sit-down and drive-through service. Redwood beams complement Savannah Grey brick and stained glass in a dynamic diamond-shaped structure, arguably Savannah's best example of Googie architecture and possibly inspired by Frank Lloyd Wright's Auldbrass Plantation in Yemassee, South Carolina.

Closed soon after opening due in part to expenses associated with its construction (Morrison Construction Company was the developer), the building was then occupied by a Savannah Bank and Trust branch office, followed by a Starbucks coffeehouse in 2004. Fine examples of roadside architecture from the 1950s through 1970s exist along Skidaway Avenue both north and south of this building. The Krispy Kreme donut shop (2749 Skidaway Ave.) features the company's distinctive green-tile cross-gabled roof crowned by a rotating sign, a production wing where visitors can still view donuts being made, and a freestanding sign at the road.

17.5 Savannah State University

1891–present. 3219 College St.

Founded in 1890 as the Georgia State Industrial College for Colored Youth and briefly located in Athens, Georgia, this was the first black public university in Georgia and its history highlights the struggle for African American education and self-reliance in the face of segregation and racism. Lobbying by Savannah's African American religious community prompted the college's relocation in 1891 to a site south of Thunderbolt, comprising two donated parcels of land—ten acres from George Parsons, which included a three-story antebellum house, and sixty acres from Sara Postrell, out of what was once Placentia Plantation. Parsons's house, a barn, and Boggs Hall (a new five-bay, three-story building erected in 1891) constituted the entire campus at first, with the latter serving as a classroom building and then as a woman's dormitory for many years. Parson House and Boggs Hall were demolished in the 1950s, when the barn was relocated to its present site.

From the beginning, the president, faculty, and students had to make do with little funding and support, growing and selling their own produce, meat, and dairy products. Agriculture played a central role in the curriculum, and in 1893 the college began sponsoring fairs to spread knowledge about scientific farming techniques to African American farmers throughout the region. In 1916, the college partnered with the U.S. Department of Agriculture and the Central of Georgia Railway to sponsor an "agricultural school on wheels," which travelled across the state to demonstrate "the admirable collection of farm products produced by thrifty, energetic and intelligent black farmers."

In 1921, under the leadership of President C. G. Wiley, the college admitted its first female students, and in 1928 it became a four-year, degree-granting institution, abolishing its high school programs. The school was renamed three times: Georgia State Industrial College in 1932, Savannah State College in 1950, and finally Savannah State University in 1996, when it was fully integrated into the university system of Georgia.

Savannah State University has arguably the largest number of African American–designed and –constructed buildings in the South. By the 1950s the college spread over 136 acres with thirty buildings and was largest degree-granting institution for African Americans in the still-segregated state. After the 1950s, however, several of its original student-built structures were demolished and replaced with midcentury modern buildings. The Benjamin F. Hubert Technical Science Center (1958–1960, Larry Craig Dean of Logan and Williams Architects), the first $1 million architectural project for the college, represented an enormous investment in state-of-the-art equipment, allowing Savannah State College to offer an accredited four-year engineering degree, the first degree of its kind in the Southeast. Recently the university undertook a massive rebuilding program, creating new facilities and classrooms as well as living spaces for its now racially diverse student body. Felix Alexis Academic Circle is the classical campus core with the placement of the original buildings (demolished or relocated), reborn as a center for "Greek" student life.

17.5.1 Hill Hall

1900–1901, R. E. Cobb, Percy Ashley, and students of the college; 1999–2007 restoration, Gunn Meyerhoff Shay Architects

When the college first opened, math teacher R. E. Cobb and mechanical arts instructor Percy Ashley began to teach basic construction techniques, including surveying, which allowed the students to lay out the initial campus plan and build its first structures. Within a few years, woodworking, blacksmithing, carpentry, masonry, and mechanical drawing were added to what was known as the manual training program. In 1900, the students and faculty of the Industrial Department built a boy's dormitory known as Hill Hall in what was then considered the modern style. According to the *Savannah Tribune* (1902), this stunning masonry building on a raised white plinth, with its classical temple form and two-story Ionic facade, was "resplendent in its beauty and imposing in its proportions."

17.5.2 Hammond Hall

1909, faculty and students of the college; 1954 remodeled

Hammond Hall was initially used for women's domestic science programs before being converted to a shoemaking and tailoring building in 1931. Constructed of stone by the students of the Industrial Department, the one-story building has a heavy, articulated base with bands of brickwork to create a rusticated effect, a grand arched entrance, and a hipped roof. Red stucco was applied to the exterior walls to resemble the color of brick buildings in the vicinity. A pair of white stringcourses links the windows, with the upper band forming frames around their upper portion. The 1954 renovation added restrooms, a kitchen, dining room, and laboratory.

17.5.3 Adams Hall

1929–1932, Antonio Orsot

One of the most prominent and gifted architects to work on the campus was Antonio Orsot, a graduate of the Tuskegee School of Architecture in Alabama. He served as director of Trades and Industries at Georgia Industrial College from 1919 to 1952, teaching craft and design skills. With African American student builders, Orsot oversaw the design and construction of every building on campus from 1920 through 1947. Typical of his designs, Adams Hall reflects Orsot's meticulous use of brick masonry, classical symmetry, a delicate Ionic columned portico flanked by graceful wood-framed arched windows, and articulated corners. Other Orsot buildings include Powell Hall (1932), Morgan Hall (1936), Wilcox Gym (1936), Hodge Hall (1938), Herty Hall (1938), and Camilla Hubert Dormitory (1938).

17.5.4 Asa Gordon Library

1966, Cletus W. Bergen and William P. Bergen Architects

The Gordon Library was dedicated in 1966 and named for one of the college's most accomplished faculty members, Dr. Asa Gordon. Anchoring the Technical Sciences core of the university, this cylindrical building serves as a remarkable architectural statement of the college's transition from a largely segregated and self-sufficient school to a modern university, utilizing a postwar modernist vocabulary by mainstream white architects. This building's circular plan and minimalist yet rhythmic exterior of rough-textured concrete panels alternating with abstract piers and narrow vertical windows make the design among the boldest of the Bergens' work.

GREATER SAVANNAH TO THE SOUTHEAST

The Isle of Hope and Wormsloe

The Isle of Hope is one of the many islands that make up greater Savannah. The Spanish called the native people who lived here the Guale; after that group relocated to Skidaway Island in the seventeenth century, French Huguenots fleeing persecution settled here, on what they called "L'Isle

Desperance"—the Island of Hope. During the colonial era, the Isle of Hope helped guard the approach to British Savannah from Spanish Florida, and in the middle of the eighteenth century it was settled by James Oglethorpe's surveyor, Noble Jones (who took up residence at Wormsloe), as well as by Henry Parker and John Fallowfield. Jones was involved in laying out Savannah's famous plan, and held a variety of important positions in the colony. In 1737 and 1738 he took possession of approximately five hundred acres on the island, formalized as a King's grant from the Georgia Trustees in 1748, and over time amassed more than eight hundred acres. After the prohibition on slavery ended in 1751, he acquired up to fifty slaves. Parker, Georgia's colonial "president" in 1751–1752, officially received his plantation as a King's grant in 1753. In the eighteenth century the journey to the Isle of Hope necessitated either a ferry crossing at high tide or a slow ride over a rickety wooden causeway.

Wormsloe Plantation, an intact, colonial-era landscape, is one of the oldest and most complex historic sites in the coastal Georgia region. It uniquely spans the evolution of the Savannah area, highlighting a wealth of social, architectural, archaeological, and landscape features. It also provides a rare glimpse into the region's plantation culture, since most of the major plantations that fronted the Savannah River have been lost with the development of the port.

In contrast to Wormsloe, Parker's plantation was divided into five large lots by his family in the early nineteenth century, when the island was accessible via Shell Road from Savannah. During this period a small village known as Parkersburg appeared; the remnants of Parker's plantation were completely subdivided by the late nineteenth and early twentieth century. Now called Isle of Hope, the community's unusual planning derives from the curved shape of the subdivisions along the bend of Skidaway Narrows rather than the grid that dominates most coastal Georgia communities of this era.

In 1871 the railroad reached the Isle of Hope, ending at Barbee's Pavilion (now the site of the marina), where Savannah residents could escape the heat of downtown from the turn of the century through the 1920s to enjoy a zoo, bands, and other leisure activities. Thereafter, suburban neighborhoods filled in the open areas of the Isle of Hope throughout the remainder of

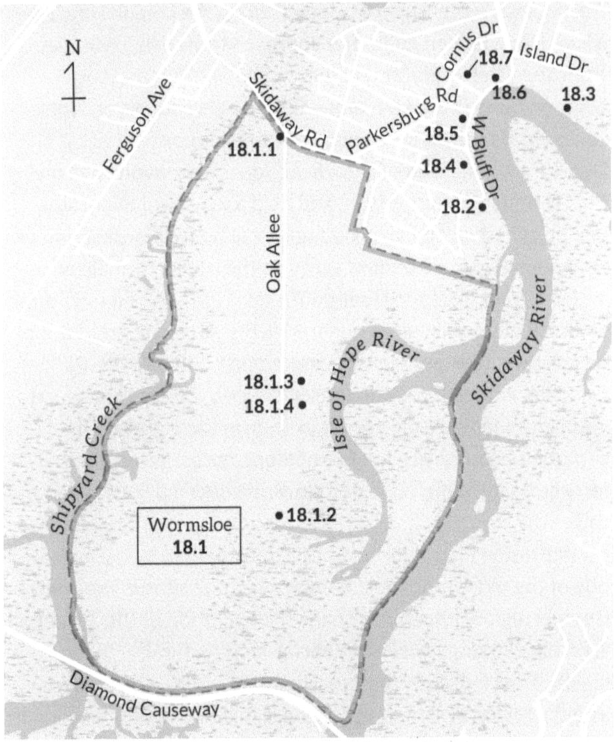

the twentieth century. The predominantly residential architecture on the island ranges from small homes to large mansions and displays a wide variety of styles and forms. Most of the dwellings are raised off the ground on brick foundations and include a porch, a typical adaptation for the local coastal climate.

18.1 Wormsloe (Wormslow)

1737–1917. 7601 Skidaway Rd.

The name Wormslow derives from Noble Jones's attempts to produce silk from silkworms that fed on the leaves of mulberry trees. During the mid-nineteenth century, George Jones (Noble Jones's great-grandson) pursued the role of a Southern gentleman farmer, acquired a cotton gin, and used much of the land, tended by slaves, to grow a small amount of cotton and some food provisions. Most of the remaining uncultivated land was used for grazing. The Jones family's wealth, however, came primarily from property investments in Savannah, as well as dividends from a wide variety of industrial ventures. During the Civil War, Wormslow was the site of a Confederate earthwork known as Fort Wimberly (still partially visible). After the fall of Savannah, Union troops vandalized the Jones house, and when the war ended the family fled to Europe, where George Jones was inspired to add Wymberley as his middle name and substitute De Renne for Jones. The De Renne family returned from Europe in 1870, received a federal pardon, purchased the Joseph S. Fay House (**8.2**) in the city, and used Wormsloe (the family's spelling of the name) as a summer retreat. The 65-acre Barrow Estate, with its 1826 house belonging to Jones's descendants, is now home to the Wormsloe Institute for Environmental History. The remaining 822 acres of Wormsloe were given to the State of Georgia in 1972.

18.1.1 Wormsloe Entrance Complex

1891 allée; 1913 gate and 1917 gatehouse, E. Lynn Drummond; 1998 gatehouse restoration

George Wymberley Jones De Renne returned from Europe in 1891 to revive the family's ancestral estate, and planted the signature 1.5-mile-long allée of more than 400 live oaks that same year. He took permanent possession of Wormsloe in 1893, and commissioned the arched entrance gate shortly before he died in 1916. The gatehouse was erected a year later. By 1998, when Sterling Builders and Restoration restored the building, termites had consumed half of its structural timbers, but left untouched its old-growth cypress cladding. The grounds opened to the public in the 1920s.

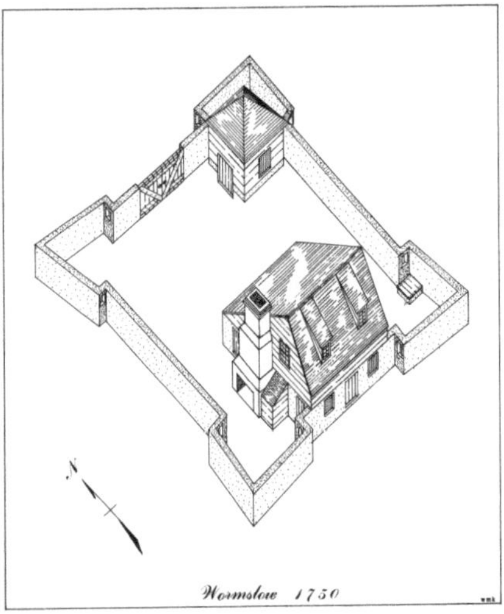

18.1.2 Noble Jones House

1739–1744

Around 1739, Jones began constructing a small wattle-and-daub house measuring 32 × 24 feet, which faced the river and was occupied until c. 1740. Given his responsibilities to defend the colony against the Spanish and other intruders, he then fortified his house with a rectangular tabby wall anchored by four corner bastions, finishing it in 1744. The careful design of the architecture demonstrates Jones's knowledge of both colonial construction techniques and military structures. The remains of the fortified house comprise one of Georgia's best surviving examples of tabby construction, using a mixture of lime, sand, water, and crushed oyster shells. Although debate surrounds the origins of the technique and even the term (which may be related to the Spanish word *tapia* derived from the Arabic *tabiyah*), by the seventeenth century the Spanish had introduced its use in North America, inspiring English colonists throughout the southern colonies to employ the method and materials for slave quarters, agricultural buildings, domestic buildings, sidewalks, and other urban improvements during the eighteenth and early nineteenth centuries. Brick buttresses were added to the tabby fort to stabilize the walls and a stone monument was placed there in 1875.

18.1.3 Wormsloe House

1828; 1850 additions; 1891 remodeling; c. 1920 restoration

George Frederick Tilghman Jones, Noble Jones's grandson, abandoned the tabby house site in 1828, building a modest two-story wood-framed house over a tabby basement on higher ground, with a long front that faced the river, where he lived until his death in 1838. His son, George Jones (later known as George Wymberley Jones De Renne), used Wormsloe as a country place during the winter, largely residing in Philadelphia and Newport, where the family built a large home now known as the Alexander Jackson Davis House. George Jones returned full-time to Wormsloe in 1850, renovating and expanding the house and turning it away from the water to face what is now Skidaway Road. The facade was lengthened to seventy feet, the plan altered to a double-pile with a central hall, a third story was added, and a gallery built on the back. George Wymberley Jones De Renne remodeled the house interior in an eclectic Victorian mode and transformed the exterior to resemble a Swiss chalet complete with Alpine towers and a Gothic Revival porte-cochere. In the twentieth century, his granddaughter, Elfrida Barrow, and her husband stripped off the then-derelict Victorian trappings to restore a version of the house's 1828 Classical Revival character. They also added a two-story veranda overlooking the river and a grand stairway to the front portico. South of the family cemetery are the remnants of ten pre–Civil War slave quarters aligned with the rear of the house. Of these, a two-family house survives in mixed condition.

18.1.4 Wormsloe Library (Wymberley Jones De Renne Library)

1907, Wallin and Young

A fireproof library of marble, concrete, and plaster was built to house the immense collection of books and papers on Georgia and their family history amassed by bibliophiles George Wymberley Jones De Renne and his three children, Wymberley Jones, Letitia, and Kentwyn De Renne. The eldest, Wymberley Jones, outlived his two siblings and commissioned this small, yet monumental, classical porticoed library building to protect the family legacy. The collection was acquired by the University of Georgia in 1938, forming an important part of Hargrett Rare Book and Manuscript Library. The building is now part of the Wormsloe Institute for Environmental History.

18.2 Deepwater Estate

1820s. 1 Noble Glenn Dr.

This remarkably intact raised coastal cottage, one of the earliest surviving houses built on the Isle of Hope, was formerly the residence of General Bernard E. Lee. The house is among the handful that had access to a deep-water channel, unlike those developed later along the Narrows. It has a low red roof, a covered porch raised up on brick piers, functioning gas exterior lights, and a lush riverfront landscape. The original house has been extended and its interior modernized, but special care was taken to ensure its historical integrity, particularly along the river-facing facade.

18.3 Whitehall

1850; 1920 interior modernized. Off Island Dr. on the Skidaway River (visible only by boat or from Bluff Dr. north of Noble Glenn Dr.)

Beginning in the 1840s, lots on what is now Bluff Drive, facing Skidaway Narrows, were sold to prominent families who built large houses along the water as summer retreats. An 1875 map reveals thirteen large lots along the bluff as well as smaller farms, with five larger lots on the eastern curve of the Narrows. Stately mansions now sit under enormous live oak trees facing across Bluff Drive to a river crowded with docks. This neoclassical house now occupies just over two acres of the plantation of colony founder Henry Parker. Whitehall was built in 1850 by his great-grandson, William Parker White, on the foundations of the original 1750 raised coastal cottage that burned just before the American Revolution. Two colossal Ionic columns frame a sweeping brick entrance staircase and two pairs of columns anchor the ends of the two-story porch. In 1874, Confederate major C. S. Hardee purchased the property, and Savannah mayor Wallace J. Pierpont bought the house in 1920 and renovated it. Successive owners have retained its neoclassical facade overlooking the Skidaway River, but repeatedly modernized and added to the house, which now encompasses more than ten thousand square feet.

18.4 House

1864; 1990 remodeled. 61 W. Bluff Dr.

This two-story house with outbuildings retains much of its initial form, with a one-room-wide second story, a wraparound veranda, and original glass in the windows. The nearby house at 75 W. Bluff Drive was also built in 1864, but its extensive wraparound side porch (the second story of which has recently been enclosed) is unusual for Savannah.

18.5 Cottages

1898–1901. 27–33 W. Bluff Dr.

This set of modest single-story vacation cottages was built as summer retreats along Bluff Drive over a four-year period: 1898 (number 27), 1900 (number 29), and 1901 (number 31). Each cottage features a central door between original double-hung windows that begin at floor level and four delicate Tuscan columns supporting a covered porch. Number 29 best retains the original form. A fourth cottage built in 1920 at 33 W. Bluff resembles the others, but its porch columns are larger.

18.6 House

1864. 7 W. Bluff Dr.

The neoclassical house at 7 Bluff Drive has a deep two-story porch framed by six slender double-height Roman Doric piers, with pocket sash windows providing porch access on both levels. It sits on a raised brick foundation and is crowned by a railing at the roofline reminiscent of colonial plantation houses. Enormous live oaks fill the front yard. A few houses to the east, a raised house at 3 W Bluff Drive, dating to 1848, is one of the original structures from the first Parker subdivision. With its wide front steps, shallow sloped roof, and long front porch, it may be unique to the area and has been recently expanded.

18.7 St. Thomas Church

1923. 2 St. Thomas Ave.

St. Thomas Episcopal Church is a traditional one-story, wood-framed, white-clapboard chapel, with a small steeple and windows shaped in a Gothic Revival style. The interior has magnificent original cross-braced wooden trusses. In 2013 the church was refurbished and repainted and, despite being in a historic district, the wooden steps were replaced by an oversized concrete stair and ramp.

Sandfly, Bethesda, Pin Point, and Skidaway Island

Although today the site of recent suburban residential, retail, and recreational developments, the transitional area where mainland meets the marshes and tidal creeks south of Savannah has a long and rich history catering to individuals and groups at the lower end of the economic ladder—free African Americans at Sandfly and Pin Point and orphans at Bethesda. Yet the area was also home to communities of summer houses for wealthy Savannahians, including Vernonburg, Montgomery, and Beaulieu.

The construction of the Diamond Causeway in 1971 connected the mainland to Skidaway Island, the largest island among the marshes east and south of Savannah, prompting the development of The Landings (**19.8**), the region's first gated community.

Sandfly was established in the 1870s, when families of former slaves purchased property south of the Isle of Hope along the suburban railway lines which connected Savannah to its surrounding areas and encouraged development in the years after the Civil War. The community grew between the 1870s and the 1890s, and by 1900 many of the more than 300 residents were employed as carpenters, masons, bricklayers, seamstresses, and cobblers, working on or in many downtown buildings. Only a handful of sites testify to the heritage of a community whose descendants and buildings stem from some of the oldest families in Savannah. Suburban development and gentrification has disrupted most of the once-larger and vibrant African American community, despite efforts by a coalition of families to form the Sandfly Community Betterment Association. Although economic decline and pressure from development forced many residents to sell their land, a number of houses and families remain along Central Avenue, north of Montgomery Cross Road to Skidaway Road and south of Norwood Avenue.

The community of Pin Point, located eight miles south of downtown Savannah, is best known as the place where U.S. Supreme Court associate justice Clarence Thomas lived until the age of six. The name Pin Point derives from the Chinquapin Point, a piece of land with a stand of chinquapin trees. The community was formerly a small part of the six-hundred-acre Beaulieu Plantation. The plantation's lands were sold to Henry McAlpin, who subdivided most of them for affluent residences but allowed freedmen, such as Benjamin and William Bond and Benjamin Dillwood (who fled here after an 1893 hurricane devastated Ossabaw Island), to purchase the remaining property. Other freedmen came from Burnside, Green, and Skidaway Islands after the Civil War.

Guale Indians inhabited Skidaway Island and the surrounding coastal region for thousands of years prior to the arrival of the Spanish. Pottery, tools, and other implements, some dating back four thousand years, can be seen at the Skidaway Island State Park Interpretive Center. The island was one of the first settled by Europeans after the arrival of Oglethorpe in 1733, although

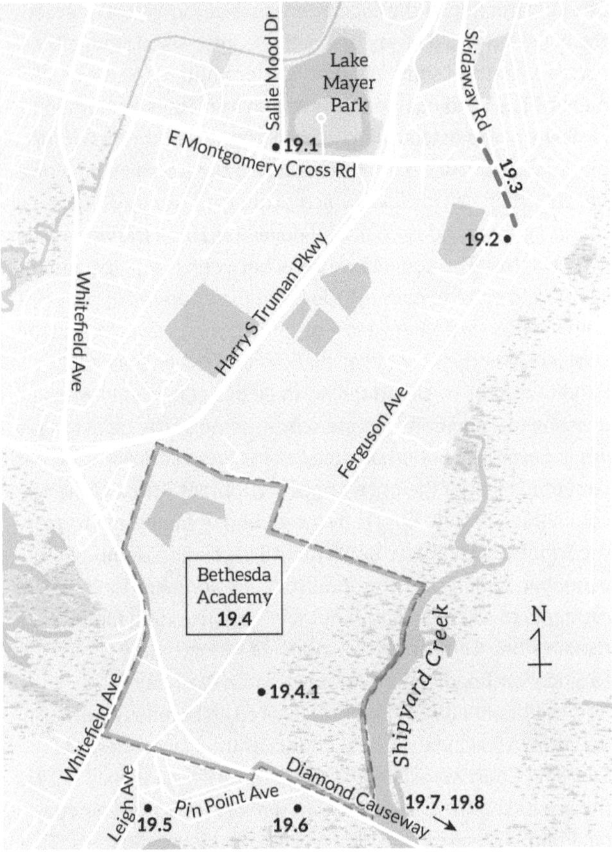

the saline soil and lack of supplies made living here difficult. Beginning with statewide prohibition in 1908, the island—which was only accessible by boat until a bridge was built for new developments in 1971—became a haven for moonshiners.

19.1 Eugenia Cemetery

c. 1828. E. Montgomery Cross Rd. at Sallie Mood Dr., Sandfly

This primarily African American cemetery has headstones dating back to 1828 when it was a burial ground for slaves and their descendants. The distance between Eugenia Cemetery and Old Church Cemetery off Skidaway Road reveals the full scope of what was once a continuous sequence of vibrant post–Civil War African American towns, which have since been fractured by new development, gentrification, and the Truman Parkway. Old Church Cemetery, along the east side of Skidaway Road just south of Ferguson Avenue, is another historic black cemetery. Built in 1863, and entered via its beautiful wrought-iron gate, this cemetery is named for a Catholic church that used to occupy this site.

19.2 Isle of Hope Union Baptist Church

c. 1870; c. 1930 moved; 1941 rebuilt. 8415 Ferguson Ave., Sandfly

In the Reconstruction era, free black communities built their own churches to express their individual sense of religious freedom. In and around Sandfly, these churches continue to be placed prominently at important crossroads. The Union Baptist Church was originally located in the heart of Sandfly, before it was moved to its current location. The chapel with its wood frame and white horizontal siding is a little worn, yet retains most of its original character, even after its midcentury reconstruction. The short tower sits in front of the facade over a small shed dormer and the main entrance.

19.3 Luten Hill Neighborhood

1887 to 1950s. Skidaway Rd. at E. Montgomery Cross Rd., Sandfly

This residential community is owned by the descendants of a former Worsmloe slave, Mathilda. Her son Ben married Chaney Ownes, the daughter of former slaves from South Carolina, and the couple acquired the land along the streetcar tracks by Skidaway Road in 1887, building homes for themselves and their seven children. The houses demonstrate the quality of early-twentieth-century African American craftsmanship in Sandfly and the coastal South. The modest wood-framed or concrete-block homes, seemingly built in a group without apparent order, are actually sited intentionally to facilitate family life. These nearly century-old Luten homes stand as a testament to the architectural and community legacy of a multigenerational family that helped build Sandfly. Representative houses are on Skidaway Road, including number 7337 (1910), numbers 7314 and 7321 (1920s), and number 7239 (1925). The houses at 7318 and 7345 Skidaway Road (1950s) reflect the continued vitality of the neighborhood following World War II.

19.4 Bethesda Academy (Bethesda Home for Boys)

1883. 9520 Ferguson Ave., Bethesda

Bethesda Orphan House and Academy was founded in 1740 by the Great Awakening preacher George Whitefield on a grant of five hundred acres between William Stephens's Beaulieu Plantation and Noble Jones's Wormsloe Plantation (**18.1**), southeast of Savannah on the banks of the Vernon River. Whitefield founded Bethesda in conjunction with James Habersham Sr. as a home for orphaned, abandoned, and needy children in keeping with the charitable spirit of the newly founded Georgia colony. It is the oldest extant charity in North America. Fire destroyed the original Orphan House designed by Whitefield in 1773, and the institution was reestablished as the Bethesda Home for Boys following the American Revolution. In 2011, the school rebranded itself as Bethesda Academy. The existing main building has two wings that date from the 1883. Bethesda Canopy Road with its allée of trees between Whitefield and Ferguson avenues was planted in the late eighteenth century and led straight to the entrance gate; the tree-lined road, while visible from Ferguson Avenue, is however no longer fully accessible and has been damaged by development and road widenings crossing its path.

19.4.1 Whitefield Chapel, Bethesda Academy

1916–1925, Simons and Lapham

Erected by the Georgia Society of Colonial Dames and commemorating Bethesda's founder, this modest yet elegant structure recalls the restrained classicism of the colonial chapels-of-ease that adorn the Carolina lowcountry. Noted Charleston architect Albert Simons paid careful attention to details in this regard, including the use of variously tinted bricks laid in Flemish bond; arched windows with 16-over-16, double-hung sashes; brick quoining and a bull's-eye window and floating entablature over paired entrance doors capped by an arched transom and surrounded by alternating brick voussoirs and quoins. The interior is likewise austere, with white plaster walls and wooden wainscoting, a shallow rear gallery, and simple wooden pews (built by A. S. Bacon and Sons of Savannah) resting on a brick floor laid in a herringbone pattern. The chancel arch frames a raised chancel terminated by a stained glass window centered above the altar commemorating James Habersham Sr., Bethesda's administrator during its first five years. Designed by Simons and made by the Willett Studios of Philadelphia, the clear amber glass window with an ornamental border depicts Christ blessing a pair of children below a medallion of a burning bush, the emblem of Bethesda.

19.5 Sweet Field of Eden Baptist Church and Cemetery

1897; 1961 rebuilt. 9630 Lehigh Ave., Pin Point

Sweet Field of Eden was built as the successor to Ossabaw Island's Hinder Me Not Church when the congregation migrated to Pin Point. Its triangular plot is one of the first that William Bond and Benjamin Dillwood acquired from Henry McAlpin in what is now Pin Point. They built the original church on land purchased for one dollar, and that building became the center of the community, also serving as a local school until 1926. This concrete-block structure, which is still a traditional single-room church with a small front steeple, replaced the original building. Over the door is a delicate block cross, with classical molding around the entrance and windows. Sweet Field of Eden remains a vital part of the Pin Point community.

19.6 Pin Point Heritage Museum (A. S. Varn and Sons Oyster and Crab Co.)

1926–1927; 2011 restoration, Lominack Kolman Smith Architects. 9924 Pin Point Ave., Pin Point

By the early twentieth century, Pin Point residents were actively engaged in the fishing industry, harvesting and processing crab, oysters, and shrimp from the local waters. In 1926, Algernon S. Varn, who ran the Varn and Platt Company on Bay Street, leased a lot in Pin Point for a crab-processing house and the following year built a sophisticated crab and oyster factory that became a center for the local economy. The design divided labor among men and women. Streamlining the shucking and packing processes, the concrete-block crab house was partitioned between picking and canning, with sloped fiberglass tables designed to drain off water and waste. Adjacent to the picking room was a cooling room where the oysters were boiled overnight before canning. The oyster house built alongside the original crab house is unique in the region, with innovative gravity-fed bins where oysters were dumped from the outside by the male fisherman, to be shucked and processed on the inside by women, standing in puddles of water leaked from the shells through a long and grueling workday. By 1966 the Varn Seafood Company was relatively prosperous, supplying seafood up and down the East Coast, but the rise of commercial fleets and factories along with a declining harvest in the 1970s led the owners to cease operations in 1985. In recent years, under the patronage of Pin Point–native Clarence Thomas, the oyster factory has been meticulously restored and is now the Pin Point Heritage Museum, which opened in 2012. Nearby Pin Point Hall, originally built in 1925 by Charlie Devoe, Samuel Wiggins, Robert Edgfield, and David McIver, served as a local grocery "confectionery" providing basic goods. The store was completely rebuilt with concrete block in 1961 and declined during the 1970s, but was subsequently remodeled to regain its importance to the community.

19.7 Skidaway Oceanographic Institute

1967. 10 Ocean Science Cir., Skidaway Island

The Modena Plantation on Skidaway Island (so named in the mid-eighteenth century by John Milledge) passed through many owners before becoming a vacation spot and Black Angus beef farm for Robert and Dorothy Roebling in 1934. Combining donations of seven hundred and ninety acres from Dorothy Roebling and six hundred and thirty-five acres from the Union Camp Corporation, the Georgia General Assembly created the Skidaway Oceanographic Institute in 1967 to advance marine science. In 1971, the institute was transferred to the University System of Georgia. The growing investment in oceanographic research had direct implications for the design of the institute. The complex was planned to achieve unity between its three original parts: an educational institution, research center, and industrial development complex. The LEED Gold–certified Instructional Center (2010, Lord Aeck Sargent), the most recent of the institute's forty buildings, combines plantation-era and modern architecture.

19.8 The Landings

1969. Entrance at Bartram Rd. and Landings Way, Skidaway Island

Inspired by the success of residential developments on nearby Hilton Head Island, the Union Camp Corporation, under the auspices of its newly acquired Chicago-based subsidiary, the Branigar Organization (led by Harvey W. Branigar Jr.), began to develop forestland it owned on Skidaway Island as a gated residential community in 1969. To facilitate this ambitious project the State was persuaded to construct a bridge to the island in 1971 (replaced by a larger one in 2013), which also served the newly established Skidaway Oceanographic Institute (**19.7**) and the adjacent Skidaway Island State Park (1975). At 4,500 acres, The Landings remains the largest gated community in Savannah, with six championship golf courses, thirty tennis courts, forty miles of walking trails, several clubhouses, two marinas and a residential population of about 8,500.

GREATER SAVANNAH TO THE SOUTH AND SOUTHWEST

Midtown Savannah

Driving south along Abercorn Street is something akin to a midcentury history lesson. Abercorn Park (1949) on 60th Street

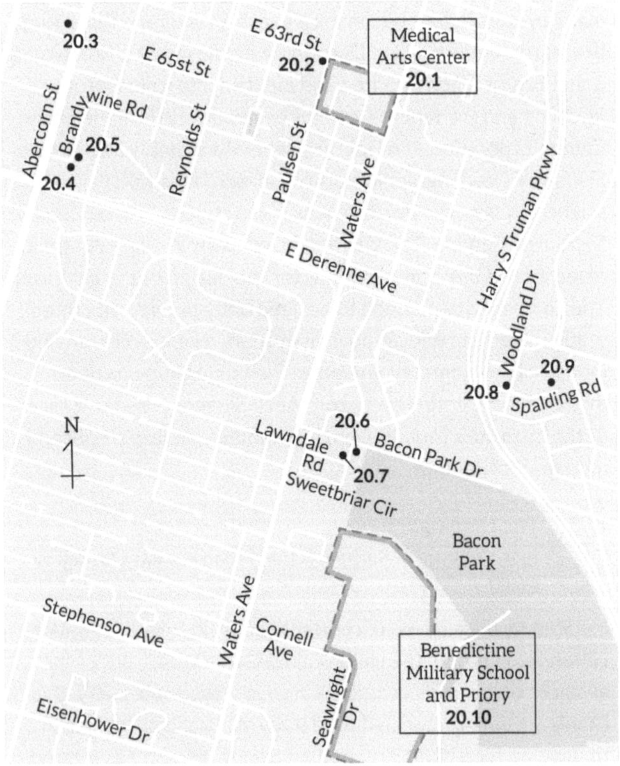

east of Abercorn features over thirty houses. Lamara Heights (1949) between Habersham and Reynolds extending from 60th to 65th streets established a trend of larger lot sizes with deeper setbacks and the absence of sidewalks, making ideal settings for the new sprawling ranch house. Abercorn Heights (1950), Brookwood (1950), and Manor Estates (1950) continued this pattern south to DeRenne Avenue, which became the official southern limit of Savannah in 1950. The plans for all of these subdivisions were designed and executed by the Savannah firm of Thomas and Hutton, Engineers.

South of DeRenne Avenue between Abercorn Street and Skidaway Road, four upscale subdivisions—Fairway Oaks (1950), Groveland (1950), Kensington Park (1951), and Magnolia Park (1953)—represent the most cohesive set of midcentury suburban ideals in Savannah. Unlike pockets of modern infill, this swath of development broke from traditional Savannah planning and followed the Federal Housing Administration (FHA) guidelines that prescribed curvilinear street plans, culs-de-sac, irregularly shaped lots, and isolation from major thoroughfares. House types include the American Small House, as well as split-level and ranch houses reflecting Colonial Revival and southwestern or California contemporary styles. In 2012, the Fairway Oaks–Greenview Historic District became the first mid-twentieth-century suburban residential district in Georgia to be added to the National Register of Historic Places.

20.1 Medical Arts Center

1957, Thomas, Driscoll, and Hutton; 1984 additions, Hansen Architects; 1991 additions, Thomas and Hutton Engineering and Forrest R. Lott; 1993 additions, Forrest R. Lott. Bounded by 63rd, 65th, and Paulson sts., and Waters Ave.

The Medical Arts Center is a ten-acre landscaped complex of doctors' offices built just west of Abreu and Robinson's 1955

Memorial Medical Center. Drawing heavily on California's Eichler Homes, the thirty modernist buildings feature low-pitched gable roofs with flared ends, wide overhanging eaves, and heavy exposed rafter beams. Details include textured pattern brick, board-and-batten siding, lattice screen brick walls, and open gable ends enclosed with glass. Many units share a covered entrance patio with built-in benches and plantings. Additional automobile-based professional and commercial services soon filled the area, including the immediately adjacent Medical Arts Shopping Center (1959) and the Professional Plaza Shopping Center (1962) at 5002 Paulsen Street.

20.2 63rd Street Fire Station (Fire Station No. 1)

1958, Cletus W. Bergen and William P. Bergen Architects. 535 E. 63rd St.

This is one of four modernist fire stations designed in the 1950s for the City of Savannah by the father-and-son team of Cletus W. and William P. Bergen. A dramatic flared gable projects over two fire-truck bays celebrating the prominence of the fire department and complements the suburban character of the neighborhood and the nearby Medical Arts Center (**20.1**).

20.3 Richard Lane House (Bob Kaminsky House)

1962, Carl E. Helfrich. 32 E. 65th St.

This house's generous lot allows for a dramatic carport drive on busy Abercorn Street, while a second entrance on 65th is set back at the rear of a Japanese-styled landscape. The modernist building is elevated off the ground with a low cantilevered main floor, which combined with wide eaves emphasizes dramatic horizontal breadth. Uniform tan glazed-brick walls set in running bond frame window walls featuring abstract geometric patterns. Numerous details enliven the design, from Asian-inspired dragon door hardware to inset cast-stone sculptural reliefs reminiscent of Aztec calendars to freestanding metal screens and a cantilevered entrance pergola at the rear. The interior boasts a central courtyard open via sliding glass doors to all the surrounding spaces.

20.4 House

1950, Helfrich, Grantham, Ritzert Associated Architects. 109 Brandywine Rd.

This midcentury home is Savannah's most horizontally stretched ranch house, with its powerful projecting eave over a subtly modulated facade with a slightly projecting stucco bay, set-back walls of vertical board-and-batten, and a massive Tennessee quartzite chimney stack marking the slightly recessed entrance. Varying lengths of clerestory ribbon windows slice along the upper edges of walls and alternate with a larger window wall serving the kitchen. A terraced treatment of floors defines interior spatial arrangements, while wall-to-wall, floor-to-ceiling sliding glass doors seem to embrace the large wooded lot and allow admiring views of the house's L-shaped plan.

20.5 House (Daniel L. Grantham House)

1956, Daniel L. Grantham. 111 Brandywine Rd.

The most modern corner in Savannah features Grantham's own residence, a seemingly modest flat-roofed midcentury ranch house with exposed brick walls, board-and-batten siding, a recessed glass-and-wood entrance bay, and a carport. Interest builds at the entrance where a pool passes from outside to inside, and excitement reigns on experiencing the bold open spaces of the interior and the rear patio and yard, courtesy of floor-to-ceiling sliding glass doors.

20.6 Weis House

1959, Mark Garrison Hampton. 5606 Sweetbriar Cir., Fairway Oaks

Designed for the owner of a local movie theater chain, Hampton brought the 1950s Sarasota School of Architecture, sometimes called "Florida Modern," to Savannah. The flat roof, metal-and-glass curtain walls, large sliding glass doors, wood sunshades, raised floors with floating staircases, verandahs, and concrete patios merited a 1959 *Architectural Review* prize for "outstanding design in steel construction."

20.7 Randolph Brooks House

1964, Juan Carlos Bertotto. 1234 Lawndale Rd., Fairway Oaks

Known more for his institutional projects, Bertotto designed this subtle house for a bank vice president. Standard midcentury features include a low-pitched roof with projecting gables, deep overhanging eaves, and exposed gable ends enclosed with glass. More unusual are the walls faced with rugged bricks and oozing mortar, long projecting vigalike beams reminiscent of houses in New Mexico's pueblos, and an interior trellised courtyard.

20.8 House

1955, John Ahern and Martin Smith, builder; 2010 restoration and addition, Celestino Piralla and Cornelia Stumpf. 5507 Woodland Dr.

Designed to say the most with the least, a single deep over-hanging and gently pitched front-facing gable is centered over the house's entrance and extends to cover a picture window, a chimney, a screened porch just visible beyond a privacy wall, and a carport. A recent renovation restored the 1950s modernist core of the house, as well as adding office and library space and a pool, earning a preservation award from the Historic Savannah Foundation in 2011.

20.9 John Ahern House

1956, John Ahern. 1526 Spalding Rd.

The neighborhood builder's personal residence, this midcentury ranch house, unassuming on the exterior, opens to a split-level plan featuring a curvilinear balcony running diagonally across the interior, separating the foyer and entrance-level bedrooms from the den, living room, dining room, and kitchen on the lower yard level. The entrance opens to a panoramic sweep of the entire interior and views of the yard. Features such as exposed roof beams and vertically fluted blonde oak paneling combine with reused Savannah Grey brick and interior plantings to add rich texture to the innovative spatial qualities.

20.10 Benedictine Military School and Priory

1962–1964, Juan Carlos Bertotto, with Thomas, Driscoll, and Hutton. 6502 Seawright Dr.

Continuing a tradition of Benedictine outreach in Savannah dating to 1874, this campus replaced the school's former location on Bull Street, where it had been since 1902 (see **12.1**). The complex is one of the most significant examples of modern architecture in Georgia, described by preservation consultant Robert A. Ciucevich as "a rare example of a complete modern campus

with intact buildings and landscapes." Georgia Tech graduate Bertotto worked with Thomas, Driscoll, and Hutton to celebrate Bauhaus-inspired modernism that also follows elements of the classical tradition, an essential hallmark of the then-popular New Formalist language. The harmonious yet distinct buildings are arranged around an open-sided quadrangle reminiscent of a medieval cloister, where a covered walk of concrete block posts and repeated "butterfly" prestressed concrete arches evoke the traditional arcade.

The central classroom and administration building establishes important stylistic and material themes that are repeated throughout the campus, including a slightly raised floor plane for the buildings (which are reached by a set of floating concrete treads), reliance on steel railings and columns complementing concrete block walls, the systematic variety in how the concrete blocks are laid, the use of striated brick veneer and such high-quality details as terrazzo flooring and features like aluminum grilles throughout. Inside, the central building features a sunken "well" at the crossing of the building's central axes, a powerful space where school assemblies and special guest events are held.

Anchoring the north end of the quadrangle, the gymnasium is the campus's tallest and most prominent building. A gently curving structure, it is characterized by a deeply cantilevered second story with a richly modeled surface alternating brick and smooth concrete, which houses a former locker room above, serving as a kind of portico and honoring the alumni who gave their lives in the two world wars. It is both muscular with huge steel braces and delicate with literal glasshouses at its base.

The gym behind is a proud functionalist box with exposed steel framing and a dramatic clear span on the interior.

The monastery and priory chapel, as requisite components of the Benedictine monastic order, occupy the south end of the quadrangle, connected by a covered walk but separated by an expanse of lawn from the other buildings, heightening their special status and distinction. While part of the overall composition, every detail of the cloister and chapel complex is distinct. The windows of the cloister's buildings and communal spaces are narrow round-arched projections. Inside, dark wood boards are used as vertically louvered screening to demarcate rooms from passages. The monastic cloister is privately sequestered and a bright open garden space. A bridgelike enclosure leads to the ten-sided central-plan brick and concrete chapel, which is surrounded by an expansive and meditative moat of water. Inside, a centrally positioned altar, notably predating liturgical changes inspired by the Second Vatican Council, is set in a lower central space, with finely crafted wood screens dividing it from a surrounding raised ambulatory level. Every detail is refined to be simple yet spiritually evocative. The blocks of concrete comprising the walls are subtly laid with repetitive patterns and regular projections. The furniture is steel, echoing the character of pieces used throughout the campus complex, but of a finer detail. Forceful concrete piers rise up to form a radial pattern overhead reminiscent of a Gothic ribbed vault.

Bertotto also designed the nearby U.S. Army National Guard Center (1961) and the Chatham County Health Department (1962), both located on Eisenhower Drive at numbers 1248 and 1395, respectively.

Southside along Abercorn, Hunter Army Air Base, and Armstrong State University

By the 1950s, when Derenne Avenue was the southern boundary of Savannah, the area to the south and east of Whitebluff Road (the extension of Bull Street south of Derenne) was mostly pastureland or small farms with more than sixty small dairies. Since 1953, this rural setting has been replaced by office parks, large malls, subdivisions, roadside architecture, big box stores, fast-food restaurants, parking lots, and car dealerships. Most of Chatham County's population lives, shops, and works in this large, formerly agricultural region and here, within the unique constraints of its multiple waterways and marshes, Savannah becomes much more typical of postwar American urban sprawl. Yet despite its typical and arguably banal suburban architectural character, this is also the region where the history of urban development reveals much of Savannah's hidden poverty and the city's economic diversity, ranging from pawnshops, payday-loan shops, gun stores, and gold buyers to grocery stores, ethnic restaurants, auto mechanics, and other vital small businesses and services. Southside is also a place where people can find affordable housing, since gentrification downtown and in the historic inner suburban neighborhoods has created a city that is unaffordable for many of its economically disadvantaged citizens. Indeed, while we may lament the loss of the rural character or its lack of formal historicism, Southside is not only an important part of Savannah's history of growth in the postwar era, but is also essential for the current residents of the city and county and functions as a vital part of a complete city.

21.1 World Globe Gas Tank

1956–1957; 1959 painted; 1999–2000 repainted. 14 E. 73rd St

This sixty-foot-diameter globe, built by the Savannah Gas Company as a storage tank, was located just south of the Derenne Avenue city limit to protect the residents from a gas explosion. Following the suggestion of R. E. Turner Jr. (media magnate Ted Turner's father), the company painted it to resemble a globe with traditional national boundaries. A to Z Coating and Sons purchased the globe in 1998 and repainted it in a more realistic manner that featured Hurricane Floyd, which threatened

Savannah in 1999. A three-foot-diameter moon at the curb on 73rd Street serves as its mailbox. The globe is now completely surrounded by the city, marking the beginning of the incredible scale and pace of development south of Derenne Avenue from the late 1950s to the present.

21.2 Hunter Army Airfield (Savannah Municipal Airport)

1929; many later expansions and modifications. White Bluff Rd. at Stephenson Ave.

Although the first airplane to land in Savannah touched down in Daffin Park (**14.8**), the city's first airport would evolve into one of the most significant military air bases in the country. Savannah purchased the 730-acre Belmont tract of rural land from J. C. Lewis in 1928 for a new airport at a cost of $30,000, and Savannah Municipal Airport opened in 1929. In 1940, the airport's name was changed to Hunter Field, after Savannah native and World War I flying ace Lieutenant Colonel Frank O'Driscoll Hunter. The U.S. Army Air Corps established the Savannah Army Air Base on the site in 1941 and promptly erected military structures. Throughout World War II the airfield was used to provide training for various bomber groups and was the site of activation for the famous Eighth Air Force. The airfield briefly returned to civilian use after the war, but in 1950 Hunter was offered to the U.S. government, along with 3,500 additional acres, in exchange for Chatham Army Airfield (which became Savannah–Hilton Head International Airport), so that the military would remain in the Savannah area. During the 1950s, Hunter served as a Strategic Air Command base due to its 11,375-foot runway, now the army's longest east of the Mississippi. In 1966, control of the airfield passed to the U.S. Army, and the site became Hunter Army Air Field. Covering an area of over 4,000 acres, the airfield played a decisive role in channeling the city's suburban expansion to sprawl southward along Abercorn Street.

21.3 Armstrong State University (Armstrong Atlantic State University, Armstrong Junior College)

1966 with later additions, Oscar M. Hansen. 11935 Abercorn St.

Armstrong State University began as a city junior college in 1935, accommodated in the former house (**8.43**) of shipping magnate George Ferguson Armstrong across from the northern

edge of Forsyth Park. The school evolved into a girls' school through the 1940s and, as it rapidly expanded, began to acquire and erect buildings near the house. In 1959 the white-only Armstrong College joined the University System of Georgia and in 1964 achieved four-year, degree-granting status. Its campus comprised six buildings clustered near Monterey Square, and local preservationists feared the impact of its continued expansion. To preserve the historical integrity of the Monterey Square area, Donald Livingston and the Mills B. Lane Foundation (of Mills B. Lane Jr.) donated 250 acres of land ten miles south of downtown to Armstrong for a new campus, which opened in 1966. Laid out around a symmetrical rectangular quadrangle, eight buildings using a simplified Georgian Revival style constituted the original campus designed by Hansen and built by the Whally-Strong Company. Over time, numerous buildings have been added, as well as a wide variety of plantings, turning the campus into an arboretum. The college was desegregated in 1979, and in 1996 it acquired university status and a new name—Armstrong Atlantic State University—which was simplified to Armstrong State University in 2014.

Bibliography

Savannah is a well-documented city. Archival and published sources from the colonial period to the present are vast and generally accessible, with many available on the Internet. Among these are the records of the Georgia Trustees, colonial council, and city council, along with numerous diaries, letters, sermons, pamphlets, newspapers, and travel literature. Harold Davis's "Bibliographical Essay" in *The Fledgling Province: Social and Cultural Life in Colonial Georgia, 1733–1776* (Chapel Hill: University of North Carolina Press, 1976) offers an excellent discussion of the documentation of the colonial period. The twenty-six-volume *Colonial Records of Georgia* (CRG) is an invaluable resource. Hundreds of historic nineteenth- and early-twentieth-century publications relating to Savannah can be viewed online through the Internet Archive (https://archive.org) and the Hathi Trust Digital Library (www.hathitrust.org).

Savannah is fortunate in possessing extensive archival records, housed in three principal repositories. The most extensive records, including documents, maps, architectural drawings, Sanborn Fire Insurance atlases (including unique amended versions), photographs, newspapers, clippings files, and rare publications can be found at the Georgia History Society (GHS; www.georgiahistory.com). A wealth of municipal records, including maps, architectural plans, council and departmental records, tax records, and building permits, are housed at the City of Savannah's Research Library and Municipal Archives (CSRLMA; www.savannahga.gov/index.aspx?nid=745). The Kaye Kole Genealogy and Local History Room at the Bull Street branch of the Live Oak Public Library (Chatham-Effingham-Liberty Regional Library; www.liveoakpl.org) has rare publications, extensive clippings files, and the remarkable Gamble Collection scrapbooks. Smaller collections of material are also held by the Historic Savannah Foundation (HSF; www.myhsf.org), the Armstrong Atlantic State University's Lane Library (http://library.armstrong.edu), and the Savannah College of Art and Design (SCAD) Archives and Special Collections at Savannah (Jen Library; http://library.scad.edu/screens/speccoll.html#savannah).

Significant historical material, including maps and photographs, can be accessed online through various institutions outside of Savannah. These include the Hargrett Rare Book and Manuscript

Library at the University of Georgia Libraries in Athens, Georgia (www.libs.uga.edu/hargrett), and the Georgia State Archives, Morrow, Georgia (www.georgiaarchives.org, with "Georgia's Virtual Vault" at http://cdm.georgiaarchives.org:2011/cdm). Mid-nineteenth-century Savannah is extremely well documented within the Dennis Collection of historic stereographic photographs at the New York Public Library (http://digitalcollections.nypl.org/search/index?utf8=%E2%9C%93&keywords=Dennis+Collection#/?scroll=0). Particularly useful for understanding the evolution of Savannah's built environment from the mid-nineteenth through early twentieth centuries are the full digital scans of Sanborn Fire Insurance maps (1884, 1888, 1898, and 1916) the Annual Mayoral Reports (1855–1923), historic newspapers (1809–1880), and numerous historic photographs, available through the Digital Library of Georgia (http://dlg.galileo.usg.edu). The Library of Congress (www.catalog.loc.gov) includes numerous photographs and maps of the city, as well as the extensive Historic American Building Survey (HABS) records of Savannah from the 1930s (http://www.loc.gov/pictures/collection/hh).

Published Primary Sources

Candler, Allen D., et al., eds. *The Colonial Records of the State of Georgia.* 39 vols. Atlanta: Franklin, 1904–1916; vols. 1–26 reprinted, New York: AMS Press, 1970; vols. 20, 27–39 reprinted, Athens: University of Georgia Press, 1977–89.

Chadbourne, Christopher, and Associates, with Clarion Associates. "A City of Streets and Squares: Savannah Design Guidelines for the Historic District." Published report, Savannah, 1992.

The Code of the City of Savannah of 1907: Containing the Charter of City of Savannah with General State Laws Affecting Municipal Corporations, Also Ordinances Adopted by the Mayor and Aldermen of the City of Savannah, Now of Force, with an Appendix. Savannah: Morning News Print, 1907.

Martyn, Benjamin. *Reasons for Establishing the Colony of Georgia, with Regard to the Trade of Great Britain, the Increase of Our People, and the Employment and Support It Will Afford to Great Numbers of Our Own Poor, as Well as Foreign Persecuted Protestants. With Some Account of the Country, and the Design of the Trustees.* London: Printed for W. Meadows, 1733. www.archive.org/details/reasonsforestab00mart.

Oglethorpe, James Edward. *Some Account of the Design of the*

Trustees for Establishing Colonys in America, ed. Rodney M. Baine and Phinizy Spalding. Athens and London: University of Georgia Press, 1990.

Nineteenth-Century Descriptions and Guidebooks

Buckingham, James Silk. *The Slave States of America*. Vol. 1 (esp. 116–250). London, 1842. Excerpts published in Mills B. Lane, *The Rambler in Georgia*, 137–78. Savannah: Beehive Press, 1973.

King, Edward. *The Great South; A Record of Journeys in Louisiana, Texas, the Indian Territory, Missouri, Arkansas, Mississippi, Alabama, Georgia, Florida, South Carolina, North Carolina, Kentucky, Tennessee, Virginia, West Virginia, and Maryland*. Hartford, Conn.: American Publishing Company, 1875 (esp. 358–70).

Mackay, Robert. *Letters to His Wife: Written from Ports in America and England, 1795–1816*, ed. Walter C. Hartridge. Athens: University of Georgia Press, 1949.

Savannah Illustrated, Indelible Photographs. New York: A. Wittemann, 1893. http://archive.org/details/savanahillustratoonewy.

Wilson, Adelaide. *Historic and Picturesque Savannah*. [Boston]: Published for the subscribers by the Boston Photogravure Company, 1889.

Savannah History

Baine, Rodney M. "James Oglethorpe and the Early Promotional Literature of Georgia." *William and Mary Quarterly*, 3rd ser., 45 (1988): 100–106.

Baine, Rodney M., and Louis De Vorsey Jr. "The Provenance and Historical Accuracy of 'A View of Savannah as It Stood the 29th of March, 1734.'" *Georgia Historical Quarterly* 73, no. 4 (Winter 1989): 784–813.

Bell, Preston, and Barbara Hines. *Savannah: A History of Her People since 1733*. Savannah: Frederic C. Beil, 1992.

Debolt, Margaret Wayt. *Savannah: A Historical Portrait*. 3rd ed. rev. Gloucester Point, Va.: Hallmark Publishing, 2001.

Ettinger, Amos Aschbach. *James Edward Oglethorpe, Imperial Idealist*. Oxford: Clarendon Press, 1936.

Fancher, Betsy. *Savannah: A Renaissance of the Heart*. Garden City, N.Y.: Doubleday, 1976.

Federal Writers' Project in Georgia, Works Progress Administration. *Savannah*. American Guide Series. Savannah: Review Printing Co., 1937. http://hdl.handle.net/2027/mdp.39015038921634.

Fraser, Walter J., Jr. *Savannah in the Old South.* Athens: University of Georgia Press, 2003.

Gamble, Thomas. *A History of the City Government of Savannah, Ga., from 1790 to 1901.* Savannah: s.n., 1901.

Gregory, G. A. *Savannah and Its Surroundings.* Savannah: Press of the Morning News, 1890. https://archive.org/details/savannahits surr00greg.

Harden, William. *A History of Savannah and South Georgia.* 2 vols. Chicago and New York: The Lewis Publishing Company, 1913.

Jackson, Harvey H., ed. *Forty Years of Diversity: Essays on Colonial Georgia.* Athens: University of Georgia Press, 1984.

Johnson, Whittington B. *Black Savannah, 1788–1864.* Fayetteville: University of Arkansas Press, 1999.

Jones, Charles Colcock, O. F. Vedder, Frank Weldon, and D. Mason. *History of Savannah, Ga., from Its Settlement to the Close of the Eighteenth Century.* Syracuse, N.Y.: D. Mason & Co., 1890. http://archive.org/details/historyofsavanna02jone.

Kane, Sharyn, and Richard Keaton. *In Those Days: African-American Life Near the Savannah River.* Atlanta: National Park Service–Southeast Region, 1994.

Lannen, Andrew C. *Liberty and Authority in Colonial Georgia, 1717–1776.* Baton Rouge, La.: Louisiana State University, 2002. http://etd.lsu.edu/docs/available/etd-1023102-173923 /unrestricted/Lannen_dis.pdf.

Mackall, Leonard L. "The Source of Force's Tract 'A Brief Account of the Establishment of the Colony of Georgia, Under Gen. James Oglethorpe, February 1, 1733.'" *American Historical Review* 30, no. 2 (Jan. 1, 1925): 304–8.

McDonough, Gary W. *Black and Catholic in Savannah, Georgia.* Knoxville: University of Tennessee Press, 1993.

Nichols, Joel A. "Religious Liberty in the Thirteenth Colony: Church-State Relations in Colonial and Early National Georgia." *New York University Law Review* 80, no. 6 (December 2005): 1693–1770. http://papers.ssrn.com/sol3/papers.cfm?abstract_id=702644.

Olmstead, Charles. "Savannah in the '40s." *Georgia Historical Quarterly* 1 (Sept. 1917): 243–53.

Perdue, Robert E. *The Negro in Savannah, 1865–1900.* New York: Exposition Press, 1973.

Quattlebaum, Julian K. *The Great Savannah Races.* Athens: University of Georgia Press, 1983.

Ready, Milton L. "The Georgia Concept: An Eighteenth Century Experiment in Colonization." *Georgia Historical Quarterly* 55 (Summer 1971): 157–72.

——. "Land Tenure in Trusteeship Georgia." *Agricultural History* 48, no. 3 (July 1974): 353–68.

Rivers, Lou. *Remembering Crawford Square: Savannah, Ga.* Bloomington, Ind.: AuthorHouse, 2005.

Rubin, Saul Jacob. *Third to None: The Saga of Savannah Jewry, 1733–1983.* Savannah: Congregation Mickve Israel, 1983.

Russell, Preston, and Barbara Hines. *Savannah: A History of Her People since 1733.* Savannah: Frederic C. Beil, 1992.

Sieg, Edward Chan. *Eden on the Marsh: An Illustrated History of Savannah.* Northridge, Calif.: Windsor Publications, 1985.

Sieg, Edward Chan. *The Squares: An Introduction to Savannah.* Norfolk, Va.: The Donning Company, 1984; exp. ed., 1996.

Smith, Julia Floyd. *Slavery and Rice Culture in Low Country Georgia, 1750–1860.* Knoxville: University of Tennessee Press, 1985.

Stewart, Mart A. *"What Nature Suffers to Groe": Life, Labor, and Landscape on the Georgia Coast, 1680–1920.* Athens: University of Georgia Press, 1996.

Troxler, Carole Watterson. "William Stephens and the Georgia 'Malcontents': Conciliation, Conflict, and Capitulation." *Georgia Historical Quarterly* 67 (Spring 1983): 3–34.

Vorsey, Louis de. "Maps in Colonial Promotion: James Edward Oglethorpe's Use of Maps in 'Selling' the Georgia Scheme." *Imago Mundi* 38 (Jan. 1, 1986): 35–45.

Wade, Richard C. *Slavery in the Cities: The South, 1820–1860.* New York: Oxford University Press, 1964.

Waring, Joseph Frederick. *Cerveau's Savannah.* Savannah: Georgia Historical Society, 1973.

Weeks, Carl Solana. *Savannah in the Time of Peter Tondee: The Road to Revolution in Colonial Georgia.* Columbia, S.C.: Summerhouse Press, 1997.

Savannah and Lowcountry Architecture, Urban Planning, and General Built Environment

Anderson, Stanford. "Savannah and the Issue of Precedent: City Plan as Resource." In *Settlements in the Americas: Cross-Cultural Perspectives,* ed. Ralph Bennett, 110–44. Newark: University of Delaware Press, 1993.

Anderson, Stanford. "The Plan of Savannah and Changes of Occupancy during Its Early Years: City Plan as Resource." *Harvard Architecture Review* 2 (Spring 1981): 60–67.

Bacon, Edmund N. *Design of Cities*. Rev. ed Cambridge, Mass.: MIT Press, 1965 (esp. 216–21).

Bailey, Tanya A. *The First American Grand Prix: The Savannah Auto Races, 1908–1911*. Jefferson, N.C.: McFarland, 2014.

Bannister, Turpin C. "Oglethorpe's Sources for the Savannah Plan." *Journal of the Society of Architectural Historians* 20, no. 2 (1961): 47–62.

Bell, Laura Palmer. "A New Theory on the Plan of Savannah." *Georgia Historical Quarterly* 43 (March 1964): 147–65.

Bonner, James C. *A History of Georgia's Architecture*. Athens: University of Georgia Press, 1964.

"Central of Georgia Railway: Savannah Repair Shops and Terminal Facilities." Historic American Engineering Record, HAER No. GA-1. Washington, D.C.: Department of the Interior, 1975. Including Beth Lattimore, "Architectural History," 4–35; Donald A. Grinde Jr. "The Central of Georgia Shop Complex," 36–87; and Donald A. Grinde Jr. "William M. Wadley and the Development of the Central Railroad of Georgia," 88–108.

Ciucevich, Robert A. "Benedictine Military School & Priory: A Modernist Landmark on Savannah's Suburban Southside." *Recent Past Preservation Network (RPPN) Bulletin* 2, no. 2 (Spring 2011): 41–50.

——. *Tybee Island: The Long Branch of the South*. Charleston, S.C.: Arcadia Publishing, 2005.

Crane, Edward A., and E. E. Soderholtz. *Examples of Colonial Architecture in South Carolina and Georgia*. New York: Hessling and Spielmeyer, 1895.

Cox, James A. D. *Savannah Tour of Homes and Gardens*. Savannah: Historic Savannah Foundation, 1996.

D'Alonzo, Mary Beth. *Streetcars of Chatham County: Photographs from the Collection of the Georgia Historical Society*. Charleston, S.C.: Arcadia, 1999.

Dick, Susan E., and Mandi D. Johnson. "The Smell of Money: The Pulp and Paper-Making Industry in Savannah, 1931–1947." *Georgia Historical Quarterly* 84 (2000): 308–23.

Edwards, Jay D. "Architectural Creolization: The Importance of Colonial Architecture." In *Architectural Anthropology*, ed. Mari-Jose Amerlinck, 83–120. Westport, Conn: Bergin and Garvey, 2001.

Edwards, Jay D. "The Complex Origins of the American Domestic Piazza-Veranda-Gallery." _*Material Culture: Journal of the Pioneer America Society* 21, no. 2 (1989): 3–58.

Gaines, William C. "Fort Screven: The Modern System of Defense at Savannah, 1886–1946." *Coast Defense Journal* 11, no. 3 (1997): 30–60.

———. "Second-System Fortifications at Savannah, Georgia: 1807–1825." *Coast Defense Journal* 17, no. 4 (2003): 4–23.

Gobel, David. "Interweaving Country and City in the Urban Design of Savannah, Georgia." *Global Environment: A Journal of History and Natural and Social Sciences* 9 (2016): 108–48.

Green, Venus. "A Preliminary Investigation of Black Construction Artisans in Savannah from 1820 to 1860." Master's thesis, Columbia University, 1982.

Hall, Clyde W. *One Hundred Years of Educating at Savannah State College, 1890–1990*. East Peoria, Ill.: Versa Press, 1991.

Hanchett, Thomas W. "John Nolen and the Planning of Savannah's Daffin Park, 1906–1909." *Georgia Historical Quarterly* 78, no. 4 (Winter 1994): 810–27.

Hodder, Robert S. *Savannah's Changing Past: A Generation of Historic Preservation Planning in a Southern City, 1955–1985*. Ithaca, N.Y.: Cornell University Press, 1993.

Jones, Carmie M., ed. *Historic Savannah: A Survey of Significant Buildings in the Historic Districts of Savannah, Georgia*. 3rd ed. Savannah: Historic Savannah Foundation, 2005.

Lane, Mills B. *Architecture of the Old South: Georgia*. Savannah: Beehive Press, 1986.

———. *Savannah Revisited: History and Architecture*. 4th ed. Savannah: Beehive Press, 1994.

Lerski, Hanna Hryniewiecka. *William Jay, Itinerant English Architect, 1792–1837*. Lanham, Md.: University Press of America, 1983.

Linley, John. *The Georgia Catalog, Historic American Buildings Survey: A Guide to the Architecture of the State*. Athens: University of Georgia Press, 1982.

Longstreth, Richard. "The Continuous Transformation of Savannah's Broughton Street." In *Looking beyond the Icons: Midcentury Architecture, Landscape, and Urbanism*, chapter 13, 170–94. Charlottesville: University of Virginia Press, 2015.

Lounsbury, Carl R. "Christ Church, Savannah: Loopholes in Metropolitan Design on the Frontier." In *Essays in Early American Architectural History: A View from the Chesapeake*, 143–53. Charlottesville: University of Virginia Press, 2011.

Martin, Van Jones. *Classic Savannah: History, Homes, and Gardens.* Savannah: Golden Coast Publishing Company, 1987.

Morrison, Mary Lane, ed. *Historic Savannah.* 2nd ed. Savannah: Historic Savannah Foundation and the Junior League of Savannah, 1979.

——. *John S. Norris, Architect in Savannah, 1846–1860.* Savannah: Beehive Press, 1980.

Osman, Mary E. "Savannah's Victorian District: Attempting Restoration without Wholesale Dislocation." *American Institute of Architects Journal* 67, no. 2 (Feb. 1978): 50–55.

Pinkerton, Connie Capozzola, Maureen Burke, and the Historic Preservation Department of the Savannah College of Art and Design. *The Savannah College of Art and Design: Restoration of an Architectural Heritage.* Charleston, S.C.: Arcadia, 2004.

Porter, Marc, and Kristen O'Connell. "Savannah & Ogeechee Barge Canal, Historic American Engineering Record, HAER No. GA-139." Washington, D.C.: Department of the Interior, n.d.

Reinberger, Mark. "Oglethorpe's Plan of Savannah: Urban Design, Speculative Freemasonry, and Enlightenment Charity." *Georgia Historical Quarterly* 81 (Winter 1997): 839–62.

Reiter, Beth Lattimore. *Victorian District Building Survey and Evaluation.* Savannah: City of Savannah, 1980.

Reps, John. "$C^2 + L^2 = S^2$? Another Look at the Origins of Savannah's Town Plan." In *Forty Years of Diversity: Essays on Colonial Georgia,* ed. Harvey H. Jackson and Phinizy Spalding, 101–51. Athens: University of Georgia Press, 1984.

——. "Town Planning in Colonial Georgia." *Town Planning Review* 30, no. 4 (Jan. 1960): 273–85.

Rossell, E. G. Daves, and Marisa C. Gomez, eds. *Savannah and the Lowcountry.* Field Guide for the 28th Annual Meeting, Vernacular Architecture Forum, Savannah, Georgia, March 28–31, 2007. Savannah: Savannah College of Art and Design, 2007.

Sickels-Taves, Lauren B., and Michael S. Sheehan. *The Lost Art of Tabby Redefined: Preserving Oglethorpe's Architectural Legacy.* Southfield, Mich.: Architectural Conservation Press, 1999.

Simo, Laura Beth. "Constructing Savannah's Cityscape, 1837–1854." Master's thesis, University of Delaware, 2008.

Spector, Tom. *The Guide to the Architecture of Georgia.* Photography by Susan Owings-Spector. Columbia: University of South Carolina Press, 1993.

Sprracher, Luciana. *A History of Thunderbolt*. Thunderbolt, Ga.: Thunderbolt Museum Society, 2003.

Stephenson, R. Bruce. *John Nolen, Landscape Architect and City Planner*. Amherst: University of Massachusetts Press, 2015.

Stevenson, Frederic R. "Charleston and Savannah." *Journal of the Society of Architectural Historians* 10, no. 4 (Dec. 1951): 3–9.

U.S. Army Corps of Engineers (Seattle District). *Context Study of the United States Quartermaster General Standardized Plans, 1866–1942* (November 1997).

Walker, Nathaniel Robert. "To Gather in War and Peace: The City Squares of Savannah, Georgia." In *Ordnance: War ± Architecture & Space*, ed. Denis Linehan and Gary Boyd, 9–31. Farnham: Ashgate Publishing, 2013.

——. "Savannah's Lost Squares." *Journal of the Society of Architectural Historians* 70, no. 4 (Dec. 2011): 512–31.

Weaver, John R., II. *A Legacy in Brick and Stone: American Coastal Defense Forts of the Third System, 1816–1867.* McLean, Va.: Redoubt Press, 2001.

Williams, Robin. "The Challenge of Preserving Public Memory: Commemorating Tomochichi in Savannah." *Preservation, Education, and Research* 5 (2012): 1–17.

——. "'A Well-Paved City': Variety, Locality, and Modernity in Paving Savannah's Streets." *ARRIS: Journal of the Southeast Chapter of the Society of Architectural Historians* 24 (2013): 20–39.

Williford, Glen M. "The Transitional Coast Defense Generation, American Seacoast Defenses of the 1870s." *Coast Defense Journal* 21, no. 2 (2007): 51–84.

Wilson, Thomas D. *The Oglethorpe Plan: Enlightenment Design in Savannah and Beyond.* Charlottesville: University of Virginia Press, 2012.

Winslow, Col. Eben Eveleth. *Notes on Seacoast Fortification Construction.* Number 61, Occasional Papers, Engineer School, United States Army. Washington, D.C.: Government Printing Office, 1920. https://archive.org/stream/cu31924030766046#page/n5/mode/2up.

Illustration Credits

CMH-LC	Carol M. Highsmith Archive, Prints and Photographs Division, Library of Congress
DR	Daves Rossell
HABS	Historic American Buildings Survey, Prints and Photographs Division, Library of Congress
HAER	Historic American Engineering Record, Prints and Photographs Division, Library of Congress
PH	Patrick Haughey
RBW	Robin B. Williams

Maps by Nat Case, Cartographer (incorporating information from the Savannah Area Geographic Information System, and provided by the South Carolina Department of Natural Resources, with further information available by contacting the Spatial Data Manager, Technology Development Program).

Front Matter and Introduction

Page ii, PH; page 6, courtesy of V. & J. Duncan Antique Maps & Prints; page 7, HABS; page 8, courtesy of Kaye Kole Genealogy and Local History Room, Bull Street Library, Live Oak Public Libraries; page 10, drawing by Jessica Archer; page 14, courtesy of Georgia Historical Society, Savannah, Georgia; page 16, Detroit Publishing Company Collection, Prints and Photographs Division, Library of Congress; page 17, courtesy of V. & J. Duncan Antique Maps & Prints

Downtown

1.1, 1.4, 1.7 RBW; page 29, PH; 1.12 RBW; 1.13 PH; 2.2, 2.4, 2.6 RBW; 2.7 courtesy of City of Savannah, Research Library & Municipal Archives on behalf of V. & J. Duncan Antique Maps & Prints; 2.9 RBW; 2.12 photograph by Myrtle Jones (c. 1970), Savannah College of Art and Design Archives and Special Collections at Savannah (Jen Library); 2.13 photograph by L. D. Andrew (1936), HABS; 2.16, 2.18 RBW; page 47, photograph by Jack E. Boucher (1958), HABS; 2.19 CMH-LC (c. 1980); 2.21, 2.23, 2.24, 2.25, 2.28, 2.31 RBW; 2.32 from Charles E. Jones, *Art Work of Augusta and Savannah* (Chicago,

1902), courtesy of V. & J. Duncan Antique Maps & Prints; 2.36 RBW; 2.37 photograph by Brian Jolley (2003), Virtual Historic Savannah Project, SCAD; 2.38 c. 1910 photograph, Detroit Publishing Company Collection, Prints and Photographs Division, Library of Congress; 2.39 photograph by Adam Kuehl, courtesy of Sottile and Sottile; 2.42, 2.43, 3.3, 3.5, 3.6 RBW; 3.7 photograph by RBW (2003), Virtual Historic Savannah Project, SCAD; 3.9 RBW; 4.2 from Charles H. Olmsted, *Art Work of Savannah* (Chicago, 1893); 4.4, 4.5, 4.8 RBW; 4.11, 4.12 CMH-LC (c. 1980); 4.14 photograph by Jeffrey E. Klee (2006); 4.16, RBW; 4.17 DR; 5.3 RBW; 5.4 c. 1940 photograph, courtesy of Housing Authority of Savannah; 5.6 photograph by Branan Sanders (1934), HABS; 5.7 DR; 5.8, 5.9, 5.11, 5.14, 6.2 RBW; 6.3 photograph by Louis I. Schwartz (1966), HABS; 6.7 RBW; 6.8 DR; 6.10, 6.11, 6.13, 6.14, 6.17 RBW; page 115, Rotch Library, Massachusetts Institute of Technology; 6.19, 6.20 RBW; 7.1 c. 1940 photograph, courtesy of Central of Georgia Railway Historical Society; 7.1.1, 7.1.2 photograph by Jack Boucher (1976), HAER; 7.1.3, 7.1.4 RBW; page 127, Prints and Photographs Division, Library of Congress; 7.1.8, 7.1.10 DR; 7.3, 7.5.1 RBW; 7.8 from Pleasant A. Stovall, *Fruits of Industry* (1895); 8.1, 8.3 RBW; 8.4 photograph by Frances Benjamin Johnston (c. 1939), Prints and Photographs Division, Library of Congress; 8.5, 8.8, 8.11 RBW; 8.12, 8.15 DR; 8.19, 8.21 RBW; 8.25 photograph by Bill Cornelia (c. 1974), courtesy of Jerry Lominack; 8.26, 8.31, 8.32, 8.33, 8.36, 8.39, 8.41, 8.43 RBW; 8.47 c. 1910 postcard, Savannah College of Art and Design Archives and Special Collections at Savannah (Jen Library); 9.1, 9.6, 9.7, 9.8, 9.10 DR; 10.1.1, 10.2, 10.4, 10.5 RBW; 10.7 DR; 10.10, 10.12 RBW; 10.13 c. 1940 photograph, courtesy of Georgia Historical Society, Savannah, Georgia; 10.18, 10.19, 10.20, 10.22 RBW; 10.24 DR

Historic Suburbs and Near Downtown

11.1, 11.3, 11.5, 11.6, 11.8 DR; page 205, RBW; 12.2, DR; 12.3 RBW; 12.7 DR; 12.8 c. 1915 postcard, courtesy of City of Savannah, Research Library & Municipal Archives on behalf of V. & J. Duncan Antique Maps & Prints; 12.9, 12.10, 13.2, 13.5, 13.7, 13.12, 13.13 DR; page 221, Tanya A. Bailey, Great Savannah Races Museum; 14.2, 14.3, 14.5, 14.7, 14.8.1 RBW

Beyond Downtown and Its Immediate Suburbs

15.3, 15.4.2, 15.6.2, 15.6.4, 15.7, 16.2, 16.4, 16.6, 17.2, 17.4, 17.5.1, 17.5.3, 17.5.4, 18.1.1 DR; 18.1.2 drawing by William M. Kelso, courtesy of the University of Georgia Press; 18.1.3, 18.5, 18.6, 19.3, 19.4.1, 19.5, 19.6, 20.1, 20.3, 20.5, 20.7, 20.9, 20.10, 21.1, 21.3 DR

Index

Note: Properties named for individuals or families with a given surname are indexed in the form *surname (first name)*. Page numbers in **boldface** refer to illustrations.

BUILDINGS OF THE UNITED STATES is a series of books on American architecture compiled and written on a state-by-state basis, with separate guides for specific cities. The primary objective of the series is to identify and celebrate the rich cultural, economic, and geographical diversity of the United States as it is reflected in the architecture of each state. The series has been commissioned by the Society of Architectural Historians, an organization dedicated to the study, interpretation, and preservation of the built environment throughout the world. To date, twenty volumes have been published, covering Alaska, Colorado, Delaware, the District of Columbia, Hawaii, Iowa, Louisiana, Massachusetts (Metropolitan Boston), Michigan, Nevada, North Dakota, Pennsylvania, Rhode Island, Texas (Central, South, and Gulf Coast), Vermont, Virginia, and West Virginia.

SAH/BUS City Guide

Buildings of Savannah, Robin B. Williams, with David Gobel, Patrick Haughey, Daves Rossell, and Karl Schuler (2016)

Robin B. Williams is Chair of the Department of Architectural History at the Savannah College of Art and Design, where his coauthors—Professors David Gobel, Patrick Haughey, Daves Rossell, and Karl Schuler—are members of the faculty.